APPRECIATING
D R E A M S

APPRECIATING DREAMS

a group approach

MONTAGUE ULLMAN, M. D.

SAGE Publications
International Educational and Professional Publisher
Thousand Oaks   London   New Delhi

For information address:

SAGE Publications, Inc.
2455 Teller Road
Thousand Oaks, California 91320
E-mail: order@sagepub.com

SAGE Publications Ltd.
6 Bonhill Street
London EC2A 4PU
United Kingdom

SAGE Publications India Pvt. Ltd.
M-32 Market
Greater Kailash I
New Delhi 110 048 India

Printed in the United States of America

Library of Congress Cataloging-in-Publication Data

Ullman, Montague.
    Appreciating dreams: A group approach / by Montague Ullman.
      p. cm.
    Includes bibliographical references and index.
    ISBN 0-7619-0127-2 (acid-free paper). — ISBN 0-7619-0128-0 (pbk.:
acid-free paper)
    1. Dreams.   2. Psychoanalysis. 3. Dreams—Therapeutic use.
4. Dream interpretation. 5. Group psychotheraphy.   I. Title.
BF175.5.D74U45   1996
154.6'3—dc20   95-50167

This book is printed on acid-free paper.

96 97 98 99 10 9 8 7 6 5 4 3 2 1

Project Editor: *Christina M. Hill*
Sage Copy Editor: *Linda Gray*

To Janet
Whose love and laughter have
filled my days

Contents

Foreword

I first came on Monte Ullman's experiential dream group method many years ago when he asked me to discuss a paper he was presenting at a meeting of the American Academy of Psychoanalysis. It was one of his first presentations of the method to a body of psychoanalysts. His paper received a mixed reception. Many questions arose from the lively discussion, including apprehensions about the fact that the dream group method deviated materially from the conventional approach to dreams by most psychoanalysts. I shared some of these doubts because I had been oriented throughout my training and career and long years of practice to formal investigation of dreams with patients in the clinical setting.

In my own experience, within the time limitation of the analytic hour, the analyst and patient worked on a dream, sharing interpretative exchanges in a process that was held together by the analyst's knowledge of the mechanisms of dreaming, the anatomy of the dream, its symbolisms, metaphor, and imagery. The process was always decisively affected by the leadership of the analyst. So one of my concerns with Monte's experiential dream group method was whether it was really possible to analyze dreams without that expertise and, if so, whether the analyst as group leader would contaminate freedom of interpretation by the other group members who would naturally turn to the leader as the expert on the dream's meaning. My discussion of his paper suggested these doubts while at the same time respecting the new approach and the author's preeminence as an esteemed psychoanalyst and investigator.

Thus began my interest in Monte's experiential dream group work. I was especially fascinated by his work after I read the first book on the dream group, *Working With Dreams* (1979) coauthored with Nan Zimmerman. The book described in detail how the process worked in its practical application: the structure of the small group, the stages of development of the process in working with the dream sharer's production, and the healing component of working on the dream in a social setting. This book was followed by *The Variety of Dream Experience* (1988) with Claire Limmer, coeditor.

Eventually, I attended one of Monte's dream group leadership workshops and saw the process in operation firsthand. My reservations about the method dissolved in the realization of how fertile dream groups are in opening up dreams. The limitations of working on the dream either by oneself (as Freud did) or with a psychotherapist in the dyadic conversation becomes apparent when the group begins to work together sharing insights into the dream's material. In a dream group, more attention is paid to the dream than is possible within the confines of the analytic hour. The group method can reach further into the metaphor of the dream, the imagery, and all of the associative material of the manifest content. The socializing process of exploring makes the dream more "useful" in waking reality. Realizing this amounted to a metamorphosis in the way I thought about dreams based on my work with patients over many years.

I have encouraged a number of my patients to participate in the experiential dream group while in therapy and even after finishing their work with me. I have found no conflict in combining individual therapy and working within the dream group. In fact, there is almost always a marked enhancement of the therapy and a greater exposure of the unconscious material as a result of the group dream work.

The main thrust of *Appreciating Dreams* is to make the dream into a more psychically useful vehicle for the reality of waking consciousness. The book deals exclusively and in detail with the process Monte Ullman has developed carefully over the period of two decades to accomplish that usefulness. This process can be learned and perfected by anyone with a serious curiosity about dreams and dreaming.

In the past four decades of dream research and interest in dreams by a host of disciplines, writing has emerged on nearly every aspect of the dream and dreaming: psychoanalytic, neurophysiological, phenomenological, and phylogenic to name but a few. This volume is special and unique because it represents the distillate of experiences of a dream researcher who has had careers as a psychoanalyst, neurologist, and community psychiatrist in addition to the experimental work he has done in parapsychology. His unbounded enthusiasm to seek and remain curious about the inner experience of the exciting and mysterious phenomena of dreams has been evident throughout his professional career.

Ullman's work with dream groups was stimulated in the 1970s when he was asked to teach in Sweden. There was an enthusiastic reception of his work, resulting in the establishment of a network of dream groups in educational institutions, training centers, and other organizations. It was there that he developed the experiential group approach to dreams described in this book. It is a compendium, a guidebook, a resource manual, and an overall description of dream life and its potential for extending our dreams in community and national life. One might speculate about the efficacy of sharing the dreams of our national (and international) leaders. Their dreams affect not only their own personal lives but their decision making as well.

In a personal communication, Ullman touched on the honesty with which dreams reflect both personal tensions and the way that unresolved social issues play into these tensions. He noted that the degree of freedom we have in our lives "is contingent on the clarity with which we allow our dreams to confront us with both the personal constraints we have internalized unique to our individual life history and the constraints we have internalized that are more broadly social in origin."

He believes that our dream imagery comes from an incorruptible core of our being that seeks to overcome the fragmentation of the human species and preserve our connectedness to others in a way that will enable us to survive. He posits the notion that the dream exposes the social through the personal and that sharing dreams would result in beneficial behavioral change. That change is the direct result of the exposure of whatever personal and social constraints have been hampering "the dreamer's freedom to be all he or she can be. . . . Both personal and social honesty have to evolve together if there is to be any genuine growth."

Theoretical systems of dream interpretation that focus on the latent content have a way of stifling the flow of fresh insights and natural originality. At certain times, education and theoretical expertise can be an inhibiting force making people less open. It can be a destroyer of truth and creative imagination. Ullman's approach offers a technique that lifts us out of previously held theoretical blind spots in thinking about dream imagery. Whatever takes place in the dream is unique to the dreamer. It is his or her own mental production, creative in character, a personal and valued message with its own unmistakable stamp of originality, couched in its own metaphor. It is the dreamer's own unconscious speaking clearly the inner truth about himself or herself.

This is the healing component of dream work. Personal honesty is allowed to flourish in a social context in a way that enhances the dreamer's and other dream group members' waking reality. Allowing others to stimulate, encourage, and help us free our creative imagination is one of the most exciting elements in the dream group experience. We all have much to learn about ourselves, and in ordinary intercourse, we often ignore the truths that others see. Through Ullman's method, a newly experienced, more honest self emerges in the accepting presence of others, in a safe environment of discovery. Trust in the dreamer's capacity to "know" the dream's meaning with help from the socializing dynamic of the group is the healing factor in this kind of process. The group activity brings out the element of surprise at the intuitive skills we all possess. This surprise factor fosters trust in our inner reactions and sets the stage for more confidently intuitive behavior in our waking lives.

This book as a manual is an excellent reference as one gains experience with the dream group process. For those interested in leading dream groups, there are specialized chapters. It offers an exhilarating journey toward a new appreciation of the magic world of our unconscious mental life and is a practicum for real dream work for the dreamers we all are.

JOHN P. BRIGGS, M.D.
Amherst, Massachusetts

Introduction

Our dreams speak to us in a language all of us can learn. This book is written in the belief that we can all do better with our dreams than we are now doing and that working in small groups can be an enormously effective way of realizing this goal. It will be useful to anyone interested in helping others with their dreams. The small-group process to be described has been bidirectional in its evolution. Originally developed as a way of teaching psychotherapists about dreams, it proved to be an equally useful way of introducing anyone to the significance of dreams and what benefit they have to offer. The book is therefore addressed to both a professional and a lay audience.

Although the emphasis is on dream sharing in a small-group arrangement, the strategies and skills described in this book will also be found useful for those preferring to work with dreams on their own. The principles and rationale shaping the group approach can, with some modifications, provide reliable guidelines within which to pursue dream work in any context.

For the clinician, my interest is to show how the group approach can be a powerful educational tool by providing a structure that, with but slight modifications, can be equally applicable in the working through of dreams in the course of therapy. Certain basic strategies make for effective dream work regardless of the theoretical predisposition of the therapist.

Adopting a group approach to dream work, although a not-unexpected outgrowth of the way I have always thought about dreams, did represent a major change for me. For most of my professional life, I have worked with dreams in the privacy of the consulting room. Although not as public an arrangement as a group, this setting does bring the dream out into the open in the special social context known as therapy. Throughout my years of psychoanalytic practice, I have felt drawn to the dreams of my patients, and to a greater and greater degree, dream work became the central focus of our work together. The classical Freudian view I was taught never felt quite right to me. It seemed to me that in their dreams patients were creating very expressive metaphorical images that revealed rather than concealed the workings of their inner lives. It also didn't make sense that something as natural as dreaming could be decoded only in the framework of psychoanalytic theory. That this view of the dream still largely prevails in professional circles is a consequence arising out of Freud's early concern with the psychopathology of hysteria. The scientific psychology of dreaming he sought to build developed in a way that paralleled the theoretical lines shaping his thoughts about the unconscious origins of the hysterical symptom. As a colleague of mine once remarked, "Might our current view of the dream be different if the nature of dreaming had been first set forth and developed by a poet?"[1]

In a sense, we have learned how not to relate to our dreams. We have been taught to look at the world outside ourselves in a disciplined and objective way. There has been no analogous learning oriented to developing our potential for inner vision. It will be no easy task to root dream work securely, effectively, and safely in the community. The beginnings are there. Groups are forming in ever-increasing numbers. The orientation to dream work and the skills necessary to carry it out can be made available to the public. A greater degree of cooperation between those trained in the various healing professions and the layman would facilitate the process.

In an earlier book, *Working With Dreams,* coauthor Nan Zimmerman and I made a statement to the general public that serious dream work could be pursued without a background in psychiatry or psychology if the interest and motivation were there. Based on the conviction that dreaming, a universal human experience, can and should be made universally accessible, we presented a group approach that provided a context in which a dream could be heard as it was meant to be heard, without anything impinging on its integrity as a personally crafted communication. It was the function of the group to be helpful without being intrusive, respecting the dreamer's privacy yet engaging actively with the dreamer in the exploration of the dream.

To accomplish this, the group has to be trained in the art of oneiric[2] midwifery. Just as most babies are born to physically healthy mothers, so most dreams occur under circumstances in which the dreamer is ready to be confronted by the information in that dream. The group members, functioning as midwives to the dreamer, ease into view the meanings and feelings embedded in the imagery. To continue the analogy, midwives have nothing to do with the conception of the child nor do they have anything to do with its upbringing. Their task is to assist in the natural function of birth. They are guided in this by what they know about the birth process of the mother and the care needed for the safe passage of the fetus through the birth canal. The midwife is maximally helpful and minimally intrusive. The analogy to dream work is apt. The dream is a newborn creation taking shape in the hidden depths of its bearer's psyche. The group facilitates its transformation into a healing social event. This is not to be construed as usurping the role of the therapist. When complications are apt to arise in childbirth, it is good to have at hand an obstetrician and all that modern medical care can offer. In the case of certain dreamers, more than what a dream group has to offer will be needed. In both instances, we are dealing with natural processes despite the fact that, occasionally, specialized professional help is needed.

Over the years, a number of groups have gotten started based on the procedures outlined in *Working With Dreams*. Although the general results have been positive, it was obvious that there were stages in the process where problems arose. For example, although we offered guidelines for putting questions to the dreamer in the dialogue (Stage 3B in the process), there was neither a rationale nor a structure for ordering the questions so that they would focus the dreamer's associations in the most productive way. Questions were put to the dreamer in too random and anarchic a way and, on occasion, the questioning would get out of hand in the group's eagerness to solve the mystery of the dream.

I also found a need for greater clarity about how this approach to dream work differs from the way one works with dreams in a formal therapeutic setting. This is of particular importance to those who come to the work as experienced therapists. We dispense with the role of the therapist in a dream appreciation[3] group. The leader is a coequal participant, sharing dreams as do the others. His or her special role is to ensure the safety of the dreamer through the mastery of the process and to guide the group through the process. The reader will find an extended discussion of the differences between the approach to the dreamer in one of my groups and what takes place in the interaction between a patient and a therapist working together on a dream in the therapeutic hour. Although some of the principles remain the same, the responsibilities of the therapist are different as are the theoretical underpinnings and the techniques invoked to deal with the resistances of the patient. In therapy, there is a therapist in control of the proceedings in contrast to the way we ensure the dreamer's control in the dream group—for example, the right of the dreamer not to share a dream or, if he does, to still maintain any level of privacy he chooses. The therapist is inevitably working within a hierarchical arrangement. In the dream group, we attempt to do away with that by shifting the control to the dreamer and including the leader as one who also shares a dream.

It is the purpose of the present volume to present a comprehensive description of the process as it has evolved along with an analysis of the issues that arise at each stage. Readers familiar with *Working With Dreams* will encounter the same basic view of the dream. The group process has, however, been refined and enriched by the experience I have had since the publication of that book, in teaching the process and in training and supervising dream group leaders. The reader will find a clearer conceptualization of the skills involved in group dream work, a much more carefully structured dialogue, and greater attention paid to the technique of helping the dreamer arrive at a sense of closure through what I have referred to as *orchestration*. The response to this new structure by those well versed in the old has been very positive. The principles of dream work have remained the same. This book addresses the difficulties that groups have had in putting these principles into practice. The rationale for the changes is easy to grasp and more productive when applied.

This book has a more specific focus in regard to the role of the leader. I have felt that a handbook was needed that would address all aspects of the leadership role. This would include the range of responsibility, a knowledge of the problems that arise, and guidelines as to their management. Although leadership training is the best preparation for leading groups, it is not likely to be available on the scale needed until there are many more experienced leaders than now exist who can undertake such training. It is my hope that this volume can serve as a practical manual for all who wish to use this approach and, in particular, for those who lack the opportunity for firsthand training. I have attempted to provide a sound grounding in the rationale for each stage of the process and a detailed presentation of the kinds of problems I have encountered as my experience with the process and with the teaching of the process grew. In contrast to *Working With Dreams,* which presented the process in the context of a more general discussion of dreams, the current volume deals exclusively with the process.

I favor dream sharing in a group as the natural facilitating agency for dream work. For a group process to be successful, the participants must be clear about what a dreamer needs from others and must learn and practice the skills necessary to be of help to the dreamer. Each step of the process to be described has been carefully thought out to provide a group a structure within which those needs can be met. These helping strategies have proven successful in maintaining the safety of the dreamer and in bringing to light the information needed by the dreamer to work toward a felt sense of connection between dream imagery and waking reality. The main thrust of this book is that the transformation of the dream into something meaningful in the waking state is best viewed as a social happening, one taking place in a properly prepared social milieu.

The emphasis on the group approach should not deter the individual dreamer from doing dream work on her own. My interest is not to disparage the individual's attempt to work out her own dream but to place the problem of dream work into its proper perspective. That perspective takes into account the reality that each of us can benefit from outside help when it comes to probing the unconscious domain. To explore certain emotional residues from our past, as we do in dreams, often requires help in lowering defenses associated with those residues. Problematic aspects of our lives, unlike physical wounds that the body can attend to by itself, tend to be barred from view by defensive mechanisms, such as denial or rationalization. It requires the help of others to bring them out in the open. To the extent that this is done, healing can take place. The group provides a natural environment for this to occur. My goal is to describe what has to take place in that environment and suggest how to surmount the many obstacles that can be encountered.

As my experience with the process has grown, so has my awareness of the nuances and subtleties of dream work, the nature of the skills involved, and how to help others, therapist or layman, acquire these skills. The approach I use to dream work follows the natural contours of the dream and is devoid of theoretical biases. The process can be mastered by anyone. Some of my readers may simply want to learn how to make their ongoing group work more effective. Others may wish to perfect their leadership skills with the intent of initiating new groups. For therapists in practice, I believe it will supplement their theoretical knowledge by grounding that knowledge in a "hands-on" approach geared to the very specific needs of the dreamer. I see it as a legitimate extension of their concern with the issue of emotional healing and growth.

Ultimately, dream work will extend beyond the confines of the consulting room. Those in the mental health profession can play a role in bringing this about. The skills they have developed in the course of working with the dreams of their patients, their knowledge of personality development, and their mastery of group process all prepare them for a leadership role in this endeavor. Aside from grounding them in the basics of practical dream work, it is my hope that their exposure to the group approach would stimulate their interest in applying it to various target groups in the population that may be at risk psychiatrically—for example, the older population; teenagers; special patient groups, such as those in a hospice setting; patients with AIDS; and so on. Small beginnings have been made along these lines, but there is much more that could be done. The fact is that our dreams are a very underused personal and social resource. For this reason, the book is addressed to the profession as well as to the laity. It is time that we all became more familiar with what Erich Fromm called our "forgotten language."

Over the two decades during which I have worked this way with dreams, I have witnessed with much gratification the development of dream groups under competent leadership, both lay and professional, here and abroad, and am convinced of the soundness of this approach. Culturally, we are a dream-deprived society. We have not paid sufficient attention to the natural curiosity we all have about dreams, to what we stand to gain were we to reown our dreams, and to the help we need to appreciate the remarkable creative energies at work in selecting, shaping, and giving meaning to the very personal images that make up the content of dreaming consciousness. What you will find between the covers of this book is simply where I have come to in my effort to master the art of dream work and helping others master that art. It is not intended as a final statement. If the principles set forth are fully grasped and the basic skills are mastered, the structure and format can evolve into an approach more in line with your own interests and goals.

I hope this volume will be of help to confirmed oneirophiles[4] and will open new vistas for those seeking to join their ranks.

How to Make
the Best Use of This Book

I have used two approaches to consolidate the reader's grasp of the process. After an initial orientation in Chapter 1, the succeeding chapters,

2 through 7, provide a detailed description of the rationale and techniques employed in each stage and substage. Chapters 8 through 12 focus on the roles of the leader, the dreamer, and the members of the group at each stage of the process. This arrangement lends itself, at the risk of some repetition, to ready reference as problems arise in the development of a group. A number of specialized chapters (13-18) deal with some of the ramifications of the group experience.

I have included a section on theory as an appendix. This requires some explanation in that I refer to the work I do as an atheoretic approach to dreams. It is atheoretic in the sense that it is not rooted in the metapsychological theories of either Freud or Jung. Their basic contributions, as distinguished from their metapsychological systems, have contributed to our understanding of the essential features of dreaming consciousness. These are considered briefly in Chapter 1 and are further elaborated in the appendix. Here, I evoke theoretical considerations in an attempt to link the psychological significance of dreaming consciousness to its physiological correlates and phylogenetic origins.

Notes

1. Richard Jones.
2. Pertaining to dreams.
3. Dr. Marianne H. Eckhardt, a colleague of mine, in seeking to emphasize the creative and aesthetic aspects of the dream, suggested that *dream appreciation* is a more felicitous term than *dream interpretation.* I agree.
4. Lovers of dreams.

Acknowledgments

I do all my writing in longhand, which has been known to pose a problem when being transcribed. Few people have mastered my script, and I am most grateful to those who have. My wife, Janet, labored through a first draft, drained it of redundancy, repetition, and verbosity (to illustrate what I mean). Anne Leon, who worked with me so faithfully as my secretary at an earlier time, offered considerable help with the typing, as did Violet Greenstein. I am indebted to my son Bill whose mastery of the computer helped enormously and to Lauren Schnitzer who did a fine job in preparing the final copy. To Edward Storm, Steven Rosen, and Nan Zimmerman, who reviewed the manuscript in part or in whole, go my thanks for the many helpful suggestions they offered. To Eleanor Friede, who was so instrumental in the publication of earlier works of mine, I am again most grateful for the on-target changes she suggested and for the guidance she offered at each step in the progress of the book. I also want to thank her colleague Barbara Bowen for being so helpful in the final stages of the preparation of the manuscript. I owe a special debt of gratitude to Claire Limmer for the care and skill with which she helped me with the revision necessary to make the manuscript more organized and readable. I want to thank Linda Gray and Christina Hill of Sage Publications for the skillful and helpful way in which they prepared the manuscript. My final debt goes to the dreamers who were kind enough to allow me to share their dreams with you.

A Note on Gender

To avoid awkward constructions in references to gender, I have resorted freely to the use of both male and female pronouns.

A Dream[1]

Before awakening on a Tuesday morning, I had the following dream:

I was in a large room. It was somewhat like a classroom setting where a test of some kind was being administered. I was aware of others there who, like me, were being given the test, although I didn't see anyone clearly. The person in charge was a woman who had prepared a special kind of testing situation. She had an air of authority and competence, a being-in-charge kind of person. The testing apparatus consisted of two pieces of legal-sized paper, each one folded in half with one edge inserted in a wooden base. The idea was to breathe gently into the space between the folded sheets so as to have them bend over. When my turn came, I discovered I had only one piece of folded paper in the base and, although I could make it bend over, I felt quite inadequate about not having the two pieces and being able to do it right. I expected a negative reaction from the person in charge. Instead, I was surprised when she singled me out to have a meal together. I was puzzled but pleased about her invitation because I had expected her to be critical of me.

I usually sense where the imagery of my dream is coming from, but this time I drew a blank. Although in my dreams I am not infrequently in a testing situation of one sort or another, I could not make any connection to the strange nature of the test nor did I have any associations to the woman in charge.

A weekly dream group of mine meets on Tuesday evening. When I issued my usual call for a dream, I also indicated I had a dream I wished to share. No one else volunteered, so I shared the dream.

As the group made the dream their own and began to talk about their feelings and then about the meaning of the imagery, relevant associations began to occur to me. It was not easy to stay with my own thoughts while taking notes of what was coming from the group. What follows are some of the group's productions at the point in the process where the others work with the dream as their own. The other column notes the associations that began to occur to me, associations that I later shared with the group.

Group Projections	*My Associations*
I felt someone was judging me. Authority figures can be unfair.	It suddenly occurred to me that the woman in the dream was my agent, Eleanor Friede. She had had parts of the manuscript for this book for several months, and I had been anxiously waiting word of her reaction. The Saturday before the dream, I had received a letter from her. Her response was very enthusiastic, but in her typically straightforward way, she made a number of suggestions for changes. She was critical of one dream I had selected.
It brings me back to my own child-hood insecurity. I felt somewhat intimidated.	I can still feel insecure in any situation in which I or my work is being judged. It is easy for me to feel intimidated in the presence of authority. Although Eleanor is not someone who uses her authority in any intimidating way, she is direct and confronting, and that can set things off in me.
I feel lonely.	It is hard for me to judge my own work. I do need validation. Eleanor has handled many successful books by prominent authors. I did feel uncertain and anxious about her reaction to a book she might consider too specialized

and too much like a handbook for popular consumption.

I was intrigued by the test but felt at a disadvantage from the others.	It dawned on me that the folded papers in the dream referred to the fact that the original draft for this book was written in longhand on yellow legal-sized pads. The fact that my test was limited to one paper may express a sense of being at a disadvantage when compared to her other clients.
There was some kind of transformation going on, almost like the metamorphosis of a butterfly. The test involved gently blowing the breath of life into something. I passed the test.	The mention of something flying like a butterfly immediately brought to mind an image I saw at a family gathering several nights before the dream. It was that of a beautifully designed bird made of wood, with wings that moved in a graceful flying motion when a string was pulled. I still felt puzzled by the appearance of this image in the dream. I certainly felt this way after getting Eleanor's letter. I called her just prior to the dream to discuss her comments.
The meal represents the "nourishment" I got from her.	She said she would be in New York soon and set a date for us to meet in a restaurant.

Final (Orchestrating) Comments of the Group

You can fly with only one wing. Despite the handicap, you were able to wing it. You felt nourished by the validation despite the fact that your first effort was not 100% OK. You were comparing yourself to some of her best-selling authors.	These comments all felt right, but the session ended without the kind of excited sense of closure one gets when a single flash of insight brings the whole thing together.

When the group met the following week, I acknowledged the help I had gotten and had nothing new to report. There was still something about the paper image that eluded me.

About 10 days after the dream, I did meet Eleanor at a restaurant where she was having lunch with a colleague of hers. They were quite excited about the impending sale of movie rights to a Hollywood producer for a book published in 1976 that had been rediscovered by Eleanor and that was now reissued and gaining in popularity. In the presence of her friend, she again expressed her enthusiasm for my manuscript. In a lighthearted manner she chided me for sending her a chapter that was over 100 pages long when it could easily have been broken down into four chapters. She spoke enthusiastically about the movie project, and on returning to her office, gave me a copy of the book.

That night, as I thought back to the meeting with Eleanor, the sought-after flash of insight came. Eleanor's excitement at the rediscovery of a book that was only now attracting attention reminded me of a similar situation a number of years ago when Eleanor, guided by her own intuition, picked up a book that had been turned down by several publishers and then succeeded in having it published. It was *Jonathan Livingston Seagull,* and it set a phenomenal sales record. In retrospect, the wooden bird I had seen was in the shape of a seagull. Its metaphorical transformation into the winglike pages of a book expressed the hope that when life was breathed into it, it would take off like Jonathan Seagull did. In the dream, I realized this was not to be. What I did produce was a book-bird that could not take off on one wing into the rarefied atmosphere of six or seven digit returns but that would nevertheless be accepted for what it was. The group had given me a push in the right direction. A life circumstance brought me the rest of the way.

Note

1. Inasmuch as everyone in the group is free to share a dream, I thought it appropriate to start with one of my own. Subsequent dreams will reflect the unfolding of the process in greater detail.

1

■

The Dreamer and the Dream

An Overview

Let us begin by considering the predicament of the dreamer who, on awakening, has had a dream that leaves him curious about the imagery he has created. Dreams tend to be confusing because of the seemingly illogical and implausible way they tell their story. Part of the confusion lies in the form of the communication and how radically different it is from the way we ordinarily communicate with each other. Awake, we enjoy a mutually reciprocal means of communication. At whatever point language developed, it served our need as social creatures. It became, in effect, the matrix of social life by means of which we could speak to each other about the world we lived in and about our orientation in time and space. For it to be effective as a social tool, it had to have an underlying structure that was the same for everyone. It had to be built on a common syntactical, grammatical, and semantic structure.

Turning to the form that dreaming consciousness takes, we notice immediately the sharp difference from ordinary language. It is primarily a concrete sensory language with visual imagery playing a prominent but not exclusive role. The question of how this came into being and what purpose it serves the sleeping organism has not yet been clarified. There are probably vestiges of a more primitive imaging capacity in animals lower on the evolutionary scale than humans. Somewhere along the path of becoming social creatures and evolving a cultural tradition, we learned to use dream imaging in a most interesting way. As we began to move away from using it as a literal or photographic reproduction of real events, we began to use it symbolically to represent particular tensions arising in our lives at the moment. In effect, we created a language that was not a communication to the outer world but an internal communication of some kind that monitored, registered, and coped with internal subjective events.

Looked at from the point of view of the waking state, the images of our dream turn out to be metaphorically crafted references to feelings and concerns that surface while we are asleep. If their metaphorical message could be unraveled, their connection to life experience present and past would become apparent. Asleep and dreaming, we are, in effect, manufacturing potential visual metaphors of a very personal and interesting kind.

Because the concept of the visual metaphor is so basic to dream work, let me offer a few illustrative examples. Suppose I have a dream in which I find myself in my car, driving down a steep hill when suddenly my brakes fail. If taken not literally (there's nothing wrong with my car) but metaphorically, what might the meaning be? The answer, of course, is obvious. The reference is apt to be to a life situation that is potentially dangerous and is rapidly getting out of control. The visual metaphor, arising in some way from our experience and in that sense being our own creation, presents itself as quite independent of, and often quite surprising to, our waking sense of self. The images are not static but in motion, and a story is told as they unfold. They arrive unbidden and are shaped and reshaped in some truly mysterious way leading to what may be seen as a form of self-confrontation. In the preceding example, my dreaming psyche puts me in the car, places the car on a steep hill, takes the brakes away, and I am left with no choice but to feel the fear that would arise in a situation like that.

The following examples are taken from actual dreams: A middle-aged woman facing increasing difficulty in walking because of increasing weakness in her legs had a dream in which the following fragment occurred:

A girl comes into a natural pool of water. She squats like a frog or a squatting Balinese dancer getting her lower body wet. Then she does three very long jumps across a field of great elms, and she lands like a frog a football field away.

The dream occurred at the end of a very inspiring weekend workshop devoted to various techniques of visualization. The people she met and the work that was done left her inspired with renewed self-confidence. She described it as "extraordinary . . . powerful . . . I felt so grounded. . . . It took me to a real high, almost spacey." She went on to say she felt more in her element there than she does in the surroundings of her home.

Although the metaphorical potential of a frog image could go in many different directions, for her the emphasis was on an animal with legs so powerful it could make incredible leaps. She is more easily mobile in water. She expected to find herself at a great disadvantage over the weekend because of her legs. Instead, the experience proved to be unexpectedly positive. She came up with an image that expressed the transformation of an impaired sense of self-esteem related to her physical handicap into one expressing the powerful uplifting effect of the weekend.

In another example, a woman receives an invitation to attend a wedding at a very elegant beach resort some distance from her home. She felt drawn to the romantic possibilities the place offered. A recent widow, she felt resistant to going alone and also was reluctant to set aside time from a new work project. The dream depicted a beach scene but one toward which she felt unable to move. She felt as if she were trying to walk through quicksand. The quicksand image alluded to deeper anxieties about her life that were triggered by the ambivalent feelings she had in response to the wedding invitation, a response in which she was certainly dragging her feet.

A third example is of a suburban housewife who has a dream, one scene of which takes place in a post office. At the time the dream was presented, no metaphorical meaning was developed around that image. In the follow-up session a week later, the meaning of the image became clear to her. It had to do with recent discussions at home around her husband's retirement. What would he be doing following (post) his retirement (from the office)?

Not infrequently, an image conveys metaphorical meaning by means of a pun. The dreamer whose illness began to impair her ability to walk to the point where she had to resort to using a cane dreamed of taking a walk with the English actor Michael Caine (my cane).

In a workshop I conducted in Sweden, a woman dreamed of someone she knew named Margareta. The person herself was not important in the dream, but the name was. In the course of her associations, she described a scene in which while having dinner with a male friend, she complimented him on being so observant. He thought she was teasing him. This led her to her own vulnerability to being teased, a theme that came up in the dream. "I get confused when people tease me. I try to avoid being in a situation where I might be teased. I have difficulty taking it. My dream tells me I'm moving away from that problem." These associations followed her sudden awareness of the Swedish pun in the name Margareta: Mare = sea, reta = teasing. For most of her life, these were dangerous waters for her.

If we stop to think of the power of the image to encapsulate in metaphorical form information that so specifically speaks to our subjective state at the moment, I think it is not unreasonable to assume that some creative energy is at work in its manufacture. We usually don't characterize something as creative unless its creative components are socially visible. In the dream, which is a very private communication, there is nothing to immediately call attention to a creative impulse at work. That impulse becomes visible and palpable only when the dream is socialized and the information it contains comes to light. ("Socialization of the dream" refers to the act of making the meanings expressed in the dream part of the context of waking life.) Then the unique crafting and information-conveying power come together as a creative event.

Three Aspects of Dream Content

Although described separately, three aspects of dream content form an essential unity: (a) the relevance of the dream to our immediate situation, (b) bringing together pertinent information from the past, and (c) the reliability of that information. Taken together, they account for the special quality of dreaming consciousness and the potential healing power of the dream. The dream starts with the residual tensions we take to bed with us on the night of the dream. Some aspect of our daytime activity stirs up feelings that are not resolved at the time and remain at the fringe of our consciousness. Such events play an important role in shaping the imagery of the dream and influencing its course. They have the power to do so because the tensions they set up resonate with older, unresolved tensions from the past. Such tensions are reawakened along with the events that surrounded their occurrence and gain expression in the imagery. The net effect is to bring together information from the past in its connection to the present, more information than is immediately available to the dreamer while awake. These references to the past bridge space and time to establish an emotional continuity between present and past. This provides us with an unusual perspective on our life, one taken from a historical or longitudinal point of view. The working out of this continuity is a special feature of dream work. By bringing aspects of our individual historical past into the picture, we provide ourselves with a more in-depth view of the ramifications and implications of the issue being explored.

The fact that there is more information is not enough. What is of even greater importance is the quality of that information. It derives from the actuality of our life experiences and not from that actuality as edited and altered to suit our particular social facade. In short, our dreaming consciousness is concerned with reflecting back to us the actual subjective impact of particular events in our life, past and present. We are being honest with ourselves asleep and dreaming to a far greater extent than we generally are while awake. As we play out our lives as social creatures and as actors on the social scene, we have all learned how to maintain a social facade at the expense, at times, of emotional authenticity. We are all clever at keeping at a distance aspects of the truth about ourselves that we do not wish to face. We do this by invoking one or another of what have come to be known as mechanisms of defense. Among the most prominent of these are denial, repression, and rationalization. The dream, on the other hand, will have none of that. While dreaming, our feelings speak to us in their own true voice, regardless of whether we wish to hear the message or not. It is as if nature were trying to ensure our contact with the truth about our personality and our behavior, inexorably and repetitively, on a nightly basis.

These three features of dreaming consciousness (relevance to the immediate situation, pertinent information from the past, and reliability of information from the past), taken together, warrant the view of the dream as a potential healing instrument. Emotional healing rests on the ability to bring forth a new and more authentic view of ourselves by seeing connections between past and present that, in scope and honesty, go beyond what we have seen before. This is what dream work is all about.

My experience has led me to the conviction that for the dream to be transformed into its *fullest* potential as a healing instrument, it has to be shared with another or with others. This is not to say that with experience in dream work one cannot make connections on one's own between dream and waking reality but that optimal healing involves more than one can manage alone. It means that emotional healing, through dream work or otherwise, involves coming to a more deeply felt understanding of oneself in and through a social support system. Dream work is risk taking, and support is necessary. Whatever secrets the dream holds, they are best dissolved in the act of sharing them with other people. My intention is to show that with regard to dreams, this can also be arranged outside of formal therapy through dream appreciation groups. Let us now turn to the rationale for such groups.

Why Work in Dream Groups?

The dreamer who wishes to get into better contact with her dream faces a dilemma. On the basis of her general experience with her own dreams, she has some awareness that dreams come from some very private part of her psyche. Paradoxically, to get at that private area, she has to go public with the dream. As already noted, the reason for this is that, while awake, it is not as easy for her to be quite as honest with herself. Awake, she is once again an actor on the social scene and capable of invoking one or another way of not allowing herself to see what the dream might be saying. She needs help and support to get back to that kind of honesty.

The public exploration of private matters in the course of dream work shapes the two basic needs the dreamer has that have to be met by the helping agency. The first need is to feel safe. Regardless of the extent to which we may or may not be able to make sense of our dreams, there is an awareness that our dreams touch on very personal and intimate concerns. Although an occasional dream seems to invite being shared with others, many of them resist public display. To coax them out into the open, the dreamer has to be assured that it is safe to do so. This means that the dreamer must be able to monitor the level of self-revelation and that whatever comes to light does so in a supportive and nonjudgmental atmosphere. A dreamer who shares a dream is diving into water the depth of which is not known in advance. Thus, there are two reasons why safety (hereafter referred to as the *safety factor*) is so important. First, the content often touches on deeply personal matters that in the ordinary course of events we would prefer to keep private. Second, it is necessary to minimize the risk involved in that there is no way of knowing in advance where the initial disclosure might lead. In a later section, attention will be called to the way in which this safety factor is built into each stage. In a general way it rests on three important guidelines:

1. The dreamer always has the option of sharing or not sharing the dream. That decision is his and his alone. No outside pressure from any source or for any reason should try to influence that decision. When a decision is made on this basis to share the dream, it signifies that for the dreamer the risk of self-exposure is less than the desire to discover what the dream has to say.

2. The dreamer controls the level of self-exposure. There is no pressure by anyone at any time on the dreamer to go any further in sharing his personal life than he feels comfortable with. It is the dreamer's responsibility to set his own limits and to monitor them accordingly.

3. The process is subject to the dreamer's control and can be stopped by the dreamer at any point, with or without any explanation to the group. The group is there as a helping agency only to the extent that the dreamer wants that help. The dreamer is not there to satisfy the curiosity of the members of the group or to meet their concern about their skills at dream work. Caution is essential in dream work, and that caution must be exercised by all concerned—the dreamer, the leader, and the group.

Although safety is a paramount factor, it is not the only one. Safety is the necessary precondition for meeting a second need of the dreamer—namely, to be stimulated by the group to make discoveries about the dream that are difficult to make by oneself (the *discovery factor*). This need derives from the difficulty the dreamer has in unraveling the dream by himself. It is up to the group to offer the kind of help needed to do the unraveling. This involves the group in a number of strategies, all designed to help the dreamer move more deeply into the connections between dream and waking reality. When carried out properly, these strategies are designed to respect the limits being set by the dreamer and, most important, the dreamer's authority over his own dream.

Before outlining the process, the following should be noted.

The Rationale. The reason for each step of the process should be clearly understood by everyone. This is one of the important ways in which the process differs from formal therapy. No one plays the role of a therapist in possession of a body of theoretical knowledge and therapeutic techniques not privy to the dreamer. In the process to be described, the rationale for each step is clearly set forth in the beginning. There is no hidden agenda.

The Roles. Everyone should have a clear idea of his or her role at each stage of the process. The dreamer is helped to understand that it is both her right and her responsibility to maintain control over the process. The group members have to understand how to use the various strategies without ever taking the control out of the hands of the dreamer. As the process evolves, it is important to remember that none of the strategies is obligatory. Each one succeeds the other only at the behest of the dreamer. The leader has a dual role. She has the special role of leading the group through the process while maintaining its integrity. In her role as a member of the group, she participates in the same ways as the others. These various roles are considered in subsequent chapters (Chapters 8, 9, and 10).

An Overview of the Process

The process unfolds in four stages as shown in Figure 1.1:

Stage 1. The presentation of the dream (Stage 1A) and the opportunity to ask clarifying questions (Stage 1B).

Stage 2. The dreamer listens while the members of the group work with the dream as their own and generate as their projections whatever feelings the imagery evokes (Stage 2A) and whatever metaphorical meaning they can give to the imagery (Stage 2B).

Stage 3. The dreamer then responds with her own associations and to whatever help came from the group (Stage 3A). A number of other stages follow at the dreamer's request. These involve a dialogue in which an effort is made (a) to help the dreamer recapture the recent thoughts and feelings that triggered the dream (Stage 3B.1), (b) to further enrich the associative matrix by reading the dream back to the dreamer (Stage 3B.2), and finally, (c) to deepen the dreamer's grasp of the dream by the group by offering what I refer to as *orchestrating projections,* a way of calling attention to possible connection of image and reality that the dreamer has not yet seen (Stage 3B.3).

Stage 4. At a subsequent session, the dreamer has the opportunity to share any further thoughts with the group.

To acquaint you with the way this structure is implemented, the following session is presented along with commentary interjected at various times that reflect my silent thoughts as the process unfolded.

Joya's Dream

Joya is a woman in her 40s who has been in the group for several years. She is a writer and suffers from a disabling illness that makes walking difficult without the use of a cane. There are references to her dreams on pages 2 and 8 (this page). Joya is a gifted poet and works well with her dreams. She pursues them with fervor and sensitivity. Her illness has spurred her search for creative and emotional fulfillment.

Stage 1: Sharing a Dream

The following dream occurred the night before the group met:

> *I am walking on a city street carrying my cat Vishnu. There is another woman there. I consider asking to join her and we would travel some-place together, perhaps downtown. Then I decide not to because I feel*

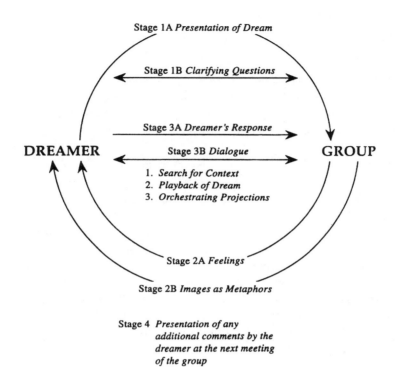

Stage 1A *Presentation of Dream*

Stage 1B *Clarifying Questions*

Stage 3A *Dreamer's Response*

DREAMER Stage 3B *Dialogue* **GROUP**

1. *Search for Context*
2. *Playback of Dream*
3. *Orchestrating Projections*

Stage 2A *Feelings*

Stage 2B *Images as Metaphors*

Stage 4 *Presentation of any additional comments by the dreamer at the next meeting of the group*

Figure 1.1. The Four Stages of the Dream Work Process

being solo gives me greater freedom to move at my own pace and do the things I want to do. I cross the street intending to go home. I leave a sweater, and maybe something else that is valuable, behind and unattended, deciding to sacrifice them.

I see a man and a woman walking on the street where I am standing. They are walking down a hill and walking toward me. We are all going into the same building. They have a dog on a tight leash. It is a black chow chow. I tell them I had a black chow who could run freely without a leash and that it was not dangerous. They tell me their dog is mean. The dog looks uptight.

They invite me to their apartment. The woman introduces herself as Rippling Water. The man is a leader of a workshop with psychic and spiritual content. He paces the floor muttering something about women with blond hair and Aryans joining his group. This makes me suspicious of his motivation.

I am looking for a comfortable place to rest. I consider sitting on the carpet in the far corner but then reject it as it is too near the bustle of life and activity around the bathroom. I go to explore the terrace, but it is closed as a protection against the wind and the salt air. I look at the kitchen. It has been emptied of furniture. I consider if I want to put my body and sleeping bag there and think I do not. It's a wooden floor.

The clarifying questions of the group elicited the following information: Joya does have a cat. At one time she did have a chow. In mentioning the dog, she added, "Chow chows have long hair, purple tongues, and a bad reputation." Describing the apartment in the dream, she said it was set up for a video showing. People were coming and going. The workshop leader was a man of about 45. The rug in the room was Persian. In the dream, she felt she wanted to be apart from the video crowd.

Comment: This is a good-sized dream. My concern as the leader is with the question of how far we can get in developing all the images contained in the time available. To leave sufficient time for the dreamer, I may have to limit the time in Stage 2.

Stage 2A: Feelings

Here are some of the feelings the group came up with as they made the dream their own:

"I feel independent. In each of the scenes, I go my own way."

"Having my cat with me gives me a secure and happy feeling. My cat is my best companion."

"I feel a kind of freedom I haven't felt since my college years. I'm not letting myself get tied down."

"My dream has a religious and spiritual quality to it."

"Letting my chow run free, even though unconventional, leaves me with a wonderful feeling."

Stage 2B: Imagery as Metaphor

The group then turned to the possible meaning of the imagery:

"Our animal nature, represented by the dog, is something others, in contrast to myself, feel should be restrained."

"The reference to blonds and Aryans is scary. It conjures up the whole Nazi scene."

"I'm looking for a place to rest but can't find a place where I feel comfortable. I don't know what I want, but I know what I don't want."

"Vishnu is the god of creativity. It's a male god."

"The kitchen, a place where there should be the life and spirit of a family, is empty of furniture."

"I'm upset by the way these people keep the dog on a tight leash. I would like to show them that I trust my dog and that's why I'm not afraid to let it be free."

"A leash to me is a powerful image of restraint and control."

"In the first scene, I'm in a dialogue with myself about going downtown, perhaps referring to getting deeper into my unconscious."

"In my dream, I'm trying to face the prospect of my own death, and want to make the most of my life. I want to settle on my true priorities."

"The bathroom is a very private place where people go to relieve themselves."

At this point, Joya interrupted to make the point that the bathroom didn't seem important in the dream. It was more that she was reacting to the hustle and bustle of the people going in and out. The group members continued with their projections:

"In that apartment, I had the same feeling I had as a child in school, not wanting to sit in the first row."

"I very strongly feel the need for greater freedom."

"The video and the leader may be references to the dream work and perhaps pulling back from the dream group."

Comment: Both feelings and metaphorical projections are invited in this second half of the second stage and are often interspersed as they were in this instance. What is characteristic is that responses vary from staying with the concrete qualities and aspects of an image—for example, working with the image of a dog as a dog to working at a more abstract metaphorical level of the dog as symbolic of the need of our animal nature not to be under such tight restraint. Also to be noted is the fact that Joya intervened appropriately when she felt the group had not quite grasped an aspect of the dream.

Stage 3A: Joya's Response

"I was reading a catalog just before falling asleep. It was from a growth center where I had been taking courses for many years. There were so many good things being offered, but at the same time, I wasn't sure where my next efforts at self-exploration would be. I couldn't decide among writing, spiritual development, and healing in thinking about this coming summer. I never had that problem before. Maybe my dream was telling me I didn't want any of those workshops. I say that because there was something about the guy with the dog that was like a workshop at this center."

Comment: This connection was not quite clear at the time she made it. Later on she spontaneously went back to it:

"I felt conflicted about saying good-bye to all this New Age stuff after it had been so much a part of my life for 20 years.

"Walking with the cat, as someone said, I had a very whole and good feeling.

"When I first moved up to the suburbs, I assumed it was OK for animals to go about freely. I always felt safe with my dog (Little Bear), and I could also walk anywhere with him.

"The part about the Aryans and blond hair reminds me of a TV program I saw last night about the rise of skinheads and neo-Nazis in Germany and their hatred of foreigners. I felt deeply troubled and upset at how difficult it is for us all to live together. I don't have an answer, but it bothered me very much last night. I even had an insight into our economic plight, but I lost it. I work in a library and found myself wondering recently, Would there be books that could teach me how to deal with the problems and economic issues we face now? I'm aware I need something different from the workshops I went to every summer, something more worldly than spiritual. It reminds me of a quote of Vaclav Havel: 'What is important is to be a citizen of the world.'

"The dog looked so neurotic, having its animal nature so harnessed.

"I've also been looking in another direction for this summer. I was looking into programs offered by the Theosophical Society based on the work of Mme. Blavatsky. Years ago, her book was my first connection to the idea of spirit. I was solo at the time. I would like to reconnect with those feelings. Last night, my husband was sick, so I slept alone in the den, my own private place. It was cozy and comfortable, and I was aware of very much enjoying it. Maybe I don't have to go away to recapture that feeling."

Comment: In her response, Joya has revealed her mixed feelings as she read through the catalog just prior to falling asleep. Courses at the center she referred to had been so much a part of her life that she still felt drawn to it. On the other hand, she was experiencing for the first time feelings of resistance to continuing on that path and an awareness of the need to engage in more "worldly" issues. Sleeping alone the night of the dream, she was also again relishing the once felt joys of a "solo" existence. She seems to be at a transitional point, wondering how to become a "citizen of the world."

Joya invited the dialogue.

The Dialogue: Stage 3B.1—The Search for Context

Question Is there anything more you can say with regard to your feelings and thoughts just before falling asleep?

Response I had found a poet, Melissa Green, who I thought was fantastic. After reading her work, it kind of put a freeze on me. I fantasized writing her a letter asking how could I learn to write poetry like her. Compared to her, I felt the thickness and clumsiness of my imagination.

Question Can you say more about the reference you made to economics?

Response Capitalism is like animals that have gotten too big to survive—like the dinosaurs and giant turtles. In America, our standard of living has become too high for us to compete.

Question Anything else about last night?

Response I was thinking of taking a course in proprioceptive writing this summer. I was happy I wouldn't have to drive my husband to work in the morning and so I wouldn't have to wake up early. I went to sleep feeling very relaxed. I was concerned about having to make a trip to the bank in the morning to avoid being overdrawn. My daughter called yesterday. She was in a bad mood and feeling depressed.

Question Any other feelings about that or anything else?

Response None, other than it felt so good to be alone.

Comment: In her spontaneous response and then further in the initial dialogue, Joya said a good deal about the feelings she took to bed with her the night of the dream. Her aspirations and her good feelings about being alone were further amplified.

Dialogue: Stage 3B.2: The Dream Is Read Back to the Dreamer

The first scene was read aloud to the end of the first paragraph. Joya was asked if any further associations occurred to her:

Response There was a special quality to the energy I felt carrying Vishnu around with me. It was as if together we formed one soul. In so many ways in the past, I had lost that sense of identity.

Question One image not yet developed is the reference to leaving a sweater and some unknown object behind as a sacrifice.

Response If I don't have money, I would have to sacrifice going to workshops, but I wouldn't lose my 'beingness,' my way of continuing to blossom.

The next paragraph was then read back:

Response The last time I was at this center I recall feeling there was so much you had to do there. I felt everything was so scheduled. You had to be on time for the workshop. You had to be on time to get in line for the meals. I felt it was too much like being regimented.

Comment: Here, Joya has further developed the connection between the documentary concerning the neo-Nazi movement, the feeling of regimentation she felt on the last occasion she was at the center, and the imagery. At the point where she spoke of having to be on time for meals, one group member couldn't refrain herself from exclaiming, "a chow line," thereby suggesting an interesting possibility for the image of the dog. This was inappropriate in terms of the structure (it would have been more appropriate as an orchestrating projection later on) but harmless and possibly helpful.

The next scene was read back, ending where Joya was suspicious of the man's motivation:

Response One of my criticisms of those higher-consciousness group activities is the feeling they are trying to make a superior race of people. I certainly got that feeling from reading the catalogue. It had something in common with the Germans and their xenophobia. I have no insight into the root causes of these problems. I feel the need for more education. I need to be reawakened. I need a rebirth.

Comment: One image that should have been explored and wasn't was the unusual name of the woman accompanying the man—Rippling Water.

The remainder of the dream was read back:

Response I think I'm definitely saying I don't want to go back to that center. I'm someone else now. It's like being married to someone for a long time, and then they are not there for you. The dream is saying I'm shopping for where to put my sleeping bag this summer. I'm in search of my Mecca. I also seem to be saying it's still in my house. I have always been bothered by the fact that in my bedroom there is no window where I can look out and see the stars. In my den, there is a skylight, and I can see the stars. I get relief from that connection with nature.

Question Anything more about the kitchen having no furniture and a wooden floor?

Response It's definitely my kitchen, and I have a wooden floor. In the dream, there is no table, nothing that would make it cozy. I know there is something in me that would like to get away from work in the kitchen. In my dream, I'm rejecting that as the place to settle down and rest.

Several other questions were asked pertaining to the earlier scenes:

Question Anything more about the reference to the video?

Response It was showing a movie on the screen. People were going to sit and watch it.

Question Anything more about the bathroom?

Response No. It was just that I was distracted by the commotion of the people going in and out.

Question Can you say anything about the reference to the terrace?

Response I was looking for a place where I could enjoy myself. Something in me would like to get near the sea this summer. The terrace was set close to the sea.

Comment: By this time, Joya seemed to have developed the connection of many of the images in the dream to deeply felt concerns stirred up by the recent events she had touched on. The fortuitous circumstances of her having seen the TV program that evening about neo-Nazis and reading the catalog and becoming aware for the first time that she was no longer drawn to that way of life all made her aware of the transformation taking place within her. She was aware there was still no resolution in the dream.

Always eager to hear from others in the group, Joya invited the orchestration.

Dialogue: Stage 3B.3: Orchestrating Projections Offered by the Group

When it comes to this stage of the process, we are all trying to pull together our thoughts after listening to Joya to see if we have anything to add that might be helpful. Immersed in my own thoughts, it is never easy to capture others' ideas in the group. What follows is only a condensed version of what occurred:

"The good feeling you had sleeping alone in your den is like going back to the safety and security of being a child. You are free of any responsibility. There are others, elsewhere in the house, who are responsible."
"The woman named Rippling Water is you. You ripple with energy and imagination."

Joya responded positively to that.

"I think you were at a feeling level between your life at home with your husband and the people around you and the feelings you were beginning to have about the center. You needed a greater degree of freedom, and sleeping in the den, you were blossoming."

My own effort at orchestrating was more in the way of summing up:

In the first scene, I think that both images are you and that they refer to you separating from the earlier self-image so deeply committed to the New Age pursuits. In doing so, you leave something behind. You can't separate from something that has been so much a part of your life for so long without sacrificing something. The sweater, something so close to you, was suitable. I also felt Rippling Water was a self-image, that part of you attached to the leaders of the courses you were interested in. Seeing all that now in a more negative light, you begin the process of separating yourself from what that man stood for, and in your struggle to get at a deeper understanding of the ills of the world you, at the same time, separate yourself from the Rippling Water image. In the process of transformation, you are aware of what you don't want and are struggling to discover what it is you do want.

Joya was invited to make any concluding remarks:

"I knew what this dream was about when I came in here, but now I see it with more richness and much greater clarity. It's as if periodically I hold up to myself a metaphorical mirror to see where I'm at. Thank you."

On behalf of the group I thanked Joya for sharing the dream and for the work she did with it.

Comment: Joya is a veteran dream worker. Note in her response how systematically she explores the recent context of her life and tries to address as many images as she can. The TV documentary she saw the night before served as a template to bring into focus aspects of elitism and regimentation that she became aware of for the first time in connection to a growth center that had played an important part in her life. Struggling against the physical constraints of her illness, she is, at the same time, trying to free herself of the social and psychological constraints she has encountered in her New Age pursuits and that she continues to encounter in her home life.

In the time available, we could not do justice to all the images that appeared in the dream. Our hope was that what we did succeed in bringing out would be of help to the dreamer in her private pursuit of the dream. When the group met the week following the dream, she shared further thoughts that had occurred to her.

Stage IV: Follow-up by the Dreamer the Following Week

"Little Bear is freedom, beauty, strength, courage. When I say that my chow ran free, I am affirming a belief in animal nature: that it is good and needs to be encouraged. The people in my dream see animal nature as something mean that needs to be controlled. Where in my life am I holding my animal nature on a short leash? In my marriage, am I expressing love and real affection? If not, isn't this harming me? What in my life am I controlling, keeping on a short leash? The part in me that ran freely now feels too tight. I think the dream is posing the questions, 'What kind of people, sorts of attitudes, and goals would harmonize with my nature instead of controlling it, or has the time come to find harmony in solitude?[1] Can I trust myself, give myself the same freedom I gave my dog, to feel comfortable, to feel at ease, to run freely?' If I am Rippling Water, there is no control over Rippling Water. If I am Rippling Water, what part of my life is like a glass window shut to the salt air and fresh breeze? Multiple sclerosis [her illness]?

"A sleeping bag is a symbol of freedom's lifestyle. There is nothing in the apartment that supports it.

"I do not want to be a passive watcher of a screen where the action is happening. I seek another space. I would like to be close to the sea and salt air.

"I must be responsible for Vishnu and not leave him. It would be like forgetting my soul.

"Regarding keeping the chow on a short leash and the tension it causes, that chow is me and I remember when my chow ran free; that uptight face is me."

When Joya reviewed the dream work in connection with its inclusion in the book she added the following comments:

"Little Bear gave me the freedom to walk anywhere and feel safe. This is gone in my life now. I can't run wild with Little Bear today, but I can prowl with my Vishnu, moving slowly with feline grace.

"When an owner projects his fears of his instinctual life onto a beast, a tension is created in the animal. Control distorts a free spirit. I find this very disturbing.

"I think I sacrifice some freedom when I cross the street to go into the apartment building.

"The kitchen is also not going to be a place for me to set up camp, to rest alone in comfort in my sleeping bag.

"The bathroom with the activity around it could be the discomfort I felt at the center when we were in the big circular room and I had to urinate all the time. Nothing in the dream is giving me sustenance.

"The dream involves the issue of freedom to move. The dog has lost his because of the master with the tight leash. I am walking on the street, carrying my cat Vishnu (a familiar attendant spirit in animal form). I feel happy and in charge of my life. I do not want to give away my freedom by having to choreograph my movement with even one other person. To move at my own pace and do the things I want to do, this is what my dog used to do. Others considered him dangerous. In their minds, he was, though not in fact. Am I thinking, 'Is it dangerous to move at my own pace and do the things I want to do?' "

Comment: This dream is offered as an example of how the group helped the dreamer bring forth much of the relevant associative data and how the dreamer, working on her own, developed the associative context further and came to a more deeply felt sense of what the dream was saying about her life. The orchestrations that had been offered were helpful in part but didn't quite open up the depth and intensity of her struggle around personal, spiritual, and physical freedom. Because no satisfying answer is yet on the horizon, the dream could not offer one. All it could do is mark where the dreamer is in her inner journey.

Note

1. In reviewing the dream prior to publication Joya added the following: "This dichotomy is too severe. I am looking for a way to bring spirit into the world."

2
■

Stage 1

A Dream Is Shared

Stage 1A:
Dream Selection

The leader begins by asking if anyone has a dream he or she wishes to share with the group. The question is asked in a way that emphasizes that the sharing of a dream is a voluntary decision made by the dreamer without any special pressure of any kind. This sounds quite simple, but it isn't. Let us assume for the moment, however, that any difficulties have been surmounted and someone volunteers to share a dream. It is important to make clear to the dreamer that in telling the dream he is to limit himself only to the dream as remembered. His task is to reproduce the dream as accurately and in as detailed a way as possible. He is not to include any associations or ideas about what the dream means.[1] He is to include any feelings he was aware of while dreaming and details such as his age in the dream, the presence of color, and background features, such as whether it was day or night. A number of issues have to be considered in the selection of the dream to be shared.

Recency of the Dream

To understand the relevancy of this issue, one must appreciate what the role of recent experience is in shaping the content of a dream. Every moment of our waking lives, we are all moving into our own futures. Regardless of how secure we may feel, there is always an element of the unknown. At any moment, tensions within us may arise that endure and ultimately influence the direction taken by our dreaming consciousness. These tensions arise from an interplay of internal processes and external events. Feelings that are ready to surface are given an added push by some seemingly trivial or incidental event that generally occurs shortly before the night of the dream. The actual event is not important in its own right. It assumes importance because of its connection to emotional concerns that have come close enough to consciousness to make their presence felt while dreaming. All of us are continually reworking unfinished emotional business from the past. Our dreams seem to be way stations along which these concerns pass, creating the possibility for recognition and exploration.

Although there is always an interplay between inner and outer processes, there are times when the external events play a more intrusive role in that, by their very intensity, they evoke feelings so strong that they remain with us during the night and are reexperienced when we are dreaming. Perhaps the most extreme examples of this are the nightmare dreams of combat soldiers. Feelings are evoked that are so all consuming they continue to reverberate, day and night, for months and even for years. In the same vein, but at a much lesser intensity, any incident may be capable of evoking sudden overwhelming feelings or triggering memory of such feelings in the past.

If no mention is made of when the dream occurred, the leader should inquire about the timing of the dream prior to its telling. When the time is known, the group members can begin to think of possible contexts for the dream as they listen to it. If, for example, in a new group the dream being presented occurred the night before the group met, the feelings about coming into the group may have acted as an anticipatory day residue. That is, it may have been on the dreamer's mind along with any anxieties or other feelings she may have had about doing dream work in a group setting. When an older dream is presented, it is also important to pin the date down as closely as possible. When that date is known, it may still be possible for the group to begin to generate ideas about a possible context of the dream. A dream reported soon after its occurrence during a Thanksgiving weekend may very well generate thoughts such as vacation time, feasts, family gatherings, and so on. More important, knowing when the dream occurred provides a focus for the dreamer later on in the search for the specific context that generated the dream.

When asked about the time of occurrence of an older dream, a dreamer may respond initially with some approximate range of time—for example, 2 or 3 weeks ago. Careful questioning may help the dreamer narrow it down and even get to a specific date: "Did it occur over a weekend or during the week? Anything else going on in your life that can help you date the dream (without telling us what that something was)? Any important media events going on at the time that can give a clue?" Even with a dream that may have occurred years ago, some approximate dating may be possible if the dreamer is encouraged to think back on what may have been going on in her life at the time (again, without revealing it to the group).

Sometimes in reporting a recent dream, a dreamer may note that she awoke in the middle of the night without a dream, went back to sleep, and then had the dream being reported. This is important because the context to be explored later can now include the thoughts the dreamer had before falling asleep again.

Frequently, an initial vagueness about the time of occurrence of the dream is subsequently sharpened as the process unfolds. More and more of what was going on in the dreamer's life at the time of the dream will be recalled.

Because it is a recent happening that gives rise to the tension that, in turn, channels the direction that dreaming consciousness will take, it becomes a matter of some importance to be able to help a dreamer identify that event and recapture the feelings associated with it. This isn't to say that the dream is concerned only with this event but, rather, that it marks the starting point of a journey the dreamer will take into her own past. The references to the past may be explicit, such as an image of a childhood home, or it may emerge in the associations of the dreamer. This journey is not random but is precisely programmed to link seemingly scattered residues from the past in their emotional relevance to the issue being focused on in the dream. In other words, although a dream starts in the present, it doesn't end there. There are, of course, times when the connections to the past are not obvious, particularly if not enough of the dream has been remembered.

It follows that the more recent the dream, the greater opportunity there is for the group to be of help to the dreamer in identifying the stimulus for the dream. This is done most easily with a dream presented the day after it was dreamed and generally becomes more difficult when a long time elapses after the dream. Having said that, certain qualifying comments are necessary. The only time it is essential to work with a very recent dream is in the initial stages when the leader is introducing the process to a new group. This provides an opportunity for the leader to demonstrate how one goes about framing questions designed to amplify the recent emotional context of the dreamer's life and, in so doing, identify the residual feelings she took to bed with her the night of the dream.

The following dream illustrates the importance of exposing the current context and how this in turn leads to the recall of earlier experience. The dreamer is a psychologist in his 50s. The dream occurred the night before he was to give a lecture on sex education to a group of 80 teenage girls. This was the first time he had ever been called on to do this:

> *I'm lying in bed in a room located somewhat at the periphery of a flat. I had the thought that being so far away from the center of the flat, I would be safe, because anyone who would want to hurt me would not be able to find me. I'm aware that it is dark. An old lady enters the room. I can see her clearly in spite of the darkness. I'm rather frightened at seeing her. She is carrying some books. It occurs to me that as long as she is carrying the books she won't hurt me. But I'm wrong. She grabs my hand and more or less crushes my fingers.*

He readily identified the old lady as his mother. The emphasis on the safety he thought he would feel because his room was at the periphery of the flat and so far from the center proved to be an interesting metaphorical use of space to represent time. The day was spent hard at work at his typewriter in preparation for the lecture. He felt uneasy about whether he would carry it off successfully. He felt himself back in his own adolescence as he tried to identify with this age group. This in turn stirred up thoughts of his mother's very controlling attitude toward him, severely restricting his activities outside the home because of her emphasis on study and homework. He felt used by his mother and victimized by her own fear of sex: "She was very insistent that I put all my energy into books and homework and seemed frightened at any desire on my part to go out and play. In fact she immobilized my hands. Everything I really wanted to do was stopped in one way or another." At this point, he picked up on a projection offered in the second stage that space could metaphorically represent time. Now, being older, he felt himself far distant from the time his mother was the center of his life. He went to bed the night of the dream with no thought of her but only of the sexual subject matter that had occupied him that day. The anxieties he had about doing a good job evoked the role his mother played in the frightening and crushing aspects of his own adolescence. His feelings in preparation for a lecture on sex resulted in the replay of his earlier experience metaphorically.

Once the group members are aware of the importance of identifying the emotional climate that preceded the dream, they will generally try to work with recent dreams. There are times, however, when there is the urge to present a dream that is days, weeks, months, or even years old. The dreamer, aware that with an older dream the group will not be able to do as much in uncovering the immediate precipitating context, has to take this into account in deciding whether or not to share an older dream. Two things should be noted in making this decision. First, if a dream is still remembered after a time lapse, it is probably of some importance to the dreamer. Second, although the group may not be able to help the dreamer zero in on the immediate context as precisely as she might wish, the chances are that much of the general context of the dreamer's life around the time of the dream is apt to be remembered. Once there is familiarity with the process, a dreamer should feel free to share any dream she wishes. Even though a group is more limited in working with an older dream compared to a more recent one, my experience has been that it can be of some help and often to a very satisfying degree. This has included dreams that have been 15 or 20 years old and even some that go back to childhood. More and more of the context often comes back as the various stages of the process unfold.

In the following dream, the circumstances surrounding the dream are remembered because of their connection to a highly traumatic event. A young woman reported a dream she had had 6 years earlier, about a month following a mastectomy. In the dream, she is with her mother in her apartment. She is only partially dressed, and as she looks down, she notices an emptiness where her breast had been. Then she notices that there is a slight mound there and as she looks at it, a drop of water comes out of the nipple and rolls down her body. The dreamer was new to the group, and this was the first dream she presented. What poured out as the group worked with her were all the feelings she had felt at the time about the surgery but had never openly expressed. She felt bullied into being "brave" about it all by her mother and her friends. She had never let herself mourn openly for the loss of her breast or expressed the fear and sadness she felt. It was as if she had been holding it all back until she found the safe and empathic environment of the dream group. Only then could the anger and grief be acknowledged openly.

Length of the Dream

There can be a problem with the length of the dream. A dream can be too long only because the process unfolds slowly, and it may not be possible to do as thorough a job as one would like in the time available. A dreamer tells a dream slowly so that those who want to write it down have the time to do so. A long dream might take 15 to 20 minutes to tell.

It is more often the case that someone refrains from volunteering a dream or volunteers apologetically because "it's only a fragment." A dream cannot be too short for the group to work on. This includes dreams that may consist of a single image. Even when only a small bit of a longer dream is recalled, it can have a holographic quality and touch on many aspects of the dreamer's life. This was the case in the following dream.

A middle-aged woman presented a dream consisting of a single image, a photograph of a group of people from the 1950s. Her mother, who was a dentist, is in the picture. In the dream, the dreamer is looking at the picture to see if her father and brother are there. They, too, are dentists. The work that was done with the dream illustrates the activity of a single image to highlight many important features of the dreamer's life. These included the tensions of her own adolescence (she would have been an adolescent at the time of the picture), particularly in relation to her mother; her feelings in relation to her adolescent daughter whom she had visited the night before the dream; and her anxieties in relation to her own career. She had applied for a new position she very much wanted but feared it would be given to a younger woman, even though she was the more experienced of the two. "That wouldn't happen if I were a man." At the end, the dreamer had this to say:

> It's amazing how much can be hidden in what I thought was just a photograph. I feel connected to the dream and the rivalry I felt to this younger woman about the job. I always felt my mother in competition with me. She was the good one and I was the bad one. She had praise only for my brother. Her attitude stopped me from showing what I could do. Now I feel free to believe in and display my own competence. I have difficulty with men like my brother who get what they want whether by fair means or not. Maybe I need some of my brother's "take-over" ability and not to worry so much about the feelings of others.

Accommodations can be made for both long and short dreams. A dreamer who has a long dream and wants to present it should not hesitate to do so, providing that he knows in advance that it will probably mean condensing some phases of the process.

How Interesting Must a Dream Be?

Just as looks can be deceiving, so can one's first impression of a dream. Any prejudgment of how interesting or uninteresting a dream may be before it's worked through is not only irrelevant but apt to be fallacious. It is a judgment rendered from the point of view of the waking state. If a dream doesn't contain interesting or exciting imagery, it might be cast aside as banal or dull. Only when a dream is worked through its connections to the underlying motivational streams that enter into it, can its value be assessed. Its importance is seen to lie not in its appearance but in the channel it opens to the larger dimension of our being, seeking to make its presence felt.

Writing the Dream

If one recalls a dream, it's a good idea to write it down as close to awakening as possible. Dreams are very elusive. It is as if they are aware that they don't belong to the realm of waking consciousness and are eager to get back into the darkness from whence they came, not unlike the fish on the hook struggling to get back into the water. They don't fit in with the rules of the waking world. Clarity and logic are not congenial to it. Temporal sequences seem jumbled and juxtaposed in strange ways. Unbidden and sometimes strange characters, and even stranger animals, invade our psyche. It is easy to let these mysterious events recede and vanish. They have a more difficult time escaping once they are on paper.

As far as the work in the group is concerned, no writing is absolutely required. In the first stage, however, I recommend that the group members write down the dream.[2] In this way, they will be sure to have all the details as given in the dreamer's own words. To accommodate the writing, the dreamer has to tell the dream slowly. Some groups prefer to hear the dream first in a natural conversational tone and then have it repeated more slowly. Either way is acceptable. The important thing is to get all the information contained in the dream across to the listeners as clearly as possible. This should be done without interruption, the only exception being if someone has not heard or not understood something the dreamer said.

In response to the request for a dream, it is important to distinguish between appropriate and inappropriate responses. Appropriate responses are along the following lines:

- "The dream does feel important to me, and I would like to share it."
- "This dream has images that puzzle me, and I would like to share it."
- "I feel very frightened in the dream. I would like to know what's going on."
- "I've had dreams like this over and over again. I really would like to know what they mean."
- "I would like to share it, but I don't feel I have to."

Inappropriate responses that come into play at this time arise from pressures from without or within.

From without:

- Others in the group may look questioningly at someone who hasn't shared a dream or hasn't shared one recently.
- Someone might say something like this to a friend in the group: "On the way here this evening, you told me a dream you had this morning. Don't you want to share it?"
- A group member might turn to someone and say, "I didn't have a dream. Did you?"
- A group member might put someone on the spot by saying outright, "You haven't shared a dream in a long time."

From within:

Feelings of obligation and guilt may move someone to share a dream under circumstances in which they would prefer not to:

- "I haven't shared a dream yet (or haven't shared one recently). I ought to."
- "I won't feel like a real member of the group until I share a dream."
- "No one else is volunteering. Maybe I ought to share mine even though I'd prefer not to."
- "Anne knows I've had this dream. We discussed it last night, and she urged me to share it with the group. What will she think of me if I don't?"

Situations arise when one wants to share a dream but hesitates for reasons that are not valid:

- "My dream is too short. It's only a fragment."
- "My dream is too long."
- "My dream is too old."
- "My dream is so dull (boring, uninteresting, meaningless, crazy)."
- "I remember only a little bit of a longer dream."
- "I know what it means. There's no point in sharing it."
- "I can't remember anything about what happened the day before the dream."
- "I didn't write it down."

Even in an ongoing group in which the members are familiar with the ground rules, the process occasionally strays off course. This is the case when for one reason or another a particular member is put on the spot and implicitly or explicitly made to feel he should share a dream. All eyes may turn to someone who has not yet shared a dream. This is an implicit invitation and should be avoided. Or more explicitly and innocently but still inappropriately, one member might turn to another and ask, "Did you have a dream?" No one, for any reason, should ever be maneuvered into feeling obliged to share a dream. That impulse should come freely from within. One has the right to remain silent in a dream group when it comes to the question of sharing a dream.

Confidentiality

Personal names may be a source of puns or double entendres that may be important for the message of the dream. In the interest of maintaining confidentiality, a judgment has to be made about revealing the name of a person appearing in the dream who is known to one or more members of the group. To do so may be a breach of that person's confidence. This is not so much a problem when the character in the dream is cast in a favorable light.

The Safety Factor

Obviously, a dream group can function only if a dream is presented. Whatever constraint is operating to share a dream affects everyone equally. Any pressure on any one person is to be avoided. There has to be a clear understanding that it is acceptable to have a dream and not wish to share it. The safety factor depends on the dreamer's having the freedom to decide whether or not he wishes to share the dream. That decision in turn rests on the dreamer's assessment of the discomfort that might follow in the wake of any self-revelation compared to his interest in the dream and what it might be saying about his life. The importance of the safety factor cannot be overemphasized. The group's ability to help the dreamer is directly proportional to its ability to ensure his feeling of safety. Any breach of this principle raises the anxiety level of the dreamer, mobilizes defenses, and impedes the process unnecessarily.

In a formal therapeutic relationship, the therapist is prepared to help the client recognize and deal with her defenses. In a dream group, however, the client-therapist relationship doesn't exist. The group's most powerful tool is to see that the dreamer's curiosity about the meaning of the dream is given free reign to unfold in as anxiety-free a field as possible. Although it is natural for some anxiety to accompany dream work, its provocation by any intrusive maneuver by someone in the group must be avoided. Keeping the anxiety level low is essential if the dreamer is to find the courage to follow the path the dream has taken. If that sense of safety is tampered with, the dreamer will pull back to the defensive modes she uses to maintain her sense of safety in the world. It's one or the other. Either the group is successful in providing a new social realm of safety, or the dreamer retreats into the personal one she has worked out for herself. We all have such safety valves at hand. We rationalize, we suppress, we deny. We engage in any number of ways to wall off painful feelings. In making a decision to share a dream, the dreamer is ready to test the safety net that the process promises to provide. Paradoxically, knowing that it is perfectly acceptable not to share a dream she may have had can be the deciding factor in resolving any ambivalence about sharing and lead to the decision to share the dream.

The Discovery Factor

Bear in mind that up to this point in the process the group members have not actively responded to the dreamer. They have not gone beyond giving the dreamer their attention and their interest. The fact is, however, that on occasion, the simple act of telling a dream aloud to a receptive audience is enough to trigger an insight that wasn't there before. The reason is simple. The decision to share the dream is based on a readiness to lower one's defenses. There is an inverse ratio between lowering defenses and seeing more. It is as if something within us realizes that if we can surmount our fears and allow more of the truth about our lives to become visible, it would be to our advantage to do so. Indeed, the truth does set us free.

Stage 1B:
Clarification of the Dream

The group now has the opportunity to ask about any aspect of the dream that did not come across clearly. To avoid the questioning's getting out of hand, certain precautions have to be observed. The dreamer is told that, in responding to a question, she should not go beyond what is in the dream. Care should be taken not to give associations or meanings (see note 1 again). For the moment, we are concerned only with being as clear as we can be about the dream as the dreamer dreamed it. There is a problem here that group members must be aware of. It is characteristic of dreams to have parts that are vague and difficult to translate into words, illogical sequences, strange and puzzling images, and actions that seem to make no sense. In putting questions to the dreamer, we have to respect these features of dreams and not try to clarify something that defies further clarification. We seek to clarify what can be clarified and accept what is unclear and puzzling to the dreamer.

Information that can be helpful includes the following:

- If people appear in a dream are they identifiable people in the dreamer's life? If they are, the dreamer is asked to state very briefly their relationships to the dreamer (e.g., friend, spouse, relative, etc.).
- If the dreamer hasn't described his feelings in the dream, he may be asked about them.
- One might ask if the dreamer was aware of any color in the dream if color wasn't specifically mentioned.
- There are times when we cannot be certain about the age of the dreamer in the dream; one can then inquire about it.
- Sometimes when there are structures or spatial arrangements that are difficult to describe, the dreamer may be asked to sketch them.
- Sometimes the time of day in which the dream is taking place is not clear from the context and can be asked about.
- In telling a dream, a dreamer may report that the dream woke him up. One can then inquire what the feelings were on awakening. When a dreamer recalls having had the dream sometime during the night without awakening, it is best not to ask this question because this is apt to take the dreamer into his waking reflections in the dream. What we are interested in is what feelings in the dream were insistent enough to wake the dreamer up and persist on awakening. We are not concerned at this time with the dreamer's waking reaction to the dream.

Problems

Problems with regard to questioning the dreamer are more apt to arise with a group that is new and inexperienced. In general, there is a tendency to overdo the questions, to look for more precise clarification of an image than it is possible for a dreamer to give. The questioner may be trying too hard to fit a confusing sequence into a logical cause-and-effect sequence such as we are accustomed to.

The questioning may go on for too long. This is particularly true for a new group that may use the question period to elicit the dreamer's associations rather than simply clarify the dreamer's description of the dream. A new group also lacks perspective on how the time available for the entire process should be allocated and the importance of not taking up too much of that time with the questioning.

Notes

1. The reason for this is to avoid tracking the contributions of the group in Stage 2. The imagination of the group has a freer reign if not limited by the dreamer's associations at this point.

2. The group members soon take to this recommendation because, except in the case of a very short dream, it is practically impossible to do an effective job in reading the entire dream back to the dreamer in the playback (Stage 3B.2).

3
■

Stage 2

The Group Takes Over

The second stage provides the group with its opening strategy in helping the dreamer. The leader begins this stage with instructions both to the dreamer and to the group.

Instructions to the Dreamer

The group is going to make your dream its own. They are going to work with it as their dream and try to do two things. First, they are going to see what feelings they can bring to the imagery of the dream. Then, they are going to see what possible meanings they can think of that would fit the imagery. They will, in effect, try to bring out some of the potential meta-phorical meaning that lies embedded in each image. Whatever feelings or meanings they come up with are to be considered their own projections and are to be seen as such by you.

We have no basis for telling you what your dream means. In the course of this exercise or game, we may come up with something that you feel is true about yourself generally or, more specifically, in connection with the dream. Whatever your reactions are, you are free to deal with them as you see fit. They are your private reactions. Later on, when you will be asked to respond to the work of the group, you will be the one to decide which of those reactions you wish to share with the group. In other words, you are free to do whatever you like with whatever you are made to feel. Much, if not all, of what comes out in this stage will, indeed, be our own projections. Remember that you have the freedom to accept or reject anything we come up with. If anything strikes you as significant, you may wish to write it down. This is recommended but is not obligatory. It can make it easier later when you are formulating your response to what you have experienced during this stage.

Throughout this stage, you will be actively listening to all that goes on but not actively participating. There are only four indications for you to interrupt the work of the group:

1. Someone is under a misimpression about an image or segment of the dream. You should correct any distortions that arise. We are free to build on an image or amplify it, but we are not free to change its basic character. If, for example, you mention that in the dream you are going someplace by car without mentioning any specific details about the car, we can amplify that image any way we wish as long as it doesn't conflict with the context in which that image appears: For example, someone can say, "It's an old car I once had," or "It's a new car I like very much." But we are not free to change the car into an airplane.

2. As we begin to work with our projections, it not infrequently happens that you recall more details and even more scenes in the dream. If this happens, you should share the additional material with us. It is important that we work with all that can be recalled about the dream.

3. If something said by a member of the group is not heard or understood, you can interrupt to ask that it be repeated or that it be clarified.

4. You may be curious as to how someone's projection relates to your dream. You are free to ask.

Instructions to the Group

You are now asked to try to make the dream your own. In some instances, you will find it relatively easy to superimpose your own past experience onto

the dream and share the feelings and meanings that emerge. In other instances, this may not be easy. In that case, just use your imagination to see
what you can do with the imagery. Pretend you are an actor or actress being
given a part to play. Cast yourself in the role of the dreamer and look at the
dream from her standpoint. The important principles to keep in mind are
these:

1. From whatever point of view you approach the dream, either in its
possible implications for your own life or as you try to put yourself in the
dreamer's shoes, the fact is that whatever you have to say about the dream
is your projection. You are in no position to say anything to the dreamer about
what the dream means to her. You don't know where the dreamer is coming
from at this point, and you have none of the dreamer's associations. You are
to talk about the dream in the first person, thereby emphasizing the fact that
you are the one making up whatever you have to say about the dream.

2. Throughout the time you are working with the dream as your own, it
is imperative that you not address your thoughts to the dreamer. You are to
share them with each other and leave a clear space around the dreamer. This
emphasizes the fact that you are leaving the dreamer free to accept or reject
anything coming from the group. Make a conscious effort not to look at the
dreamer as you offer your projections. This isn't as easy as it sounds. There
is the realization that this isn't really your dream and, in coming up with your
feelings and ideas, you are hopeful they will be of help to the dreamer. If you
are not careful, you will unconsciously act this out by looking at the dreamer.

Specific Instructions to the Group

Stage 2A: Working With Feelings

You are to begin your work with the dream by asking yourself, "If this
were my dream, what feelings am I experiencing as I make it my dream?" If
you are not responding at a feeling level, then what feelings might you have
if you were in the predicament described in the dream? What feelings might
you imagine you could have in those circumstances? As you make the dream
your own, you will inevitably begin to get ideas about the possible meaning
of some of the images. Keep those in abeyance for the time being and ask
yourself what feelings underlie these thoughts about the dream. To separate
the feelings and meanings this way may seem arbitrary, but there is a reason
for it. Left to your own devices, there is a tendency to respond to the seduc-
tive way that dream images have of stimulating ideas about their possible
symbolic significance. If you hold this tendency in abeyance for the moment

and try to make explicit whatever feelings the images suggest, you might hit on a feeling that a dreamer may have had in the dream and not have recognized until you conceptualized it for him or her. Be as inventive as you like in describing the feeling quality of the dream: for example, "There is a fairy tale quality to the way this dream makes me feel," or "I have the feeling I'm watching a Grade B movie." Such responses convey implicit felt reactions.

Stage 2B: Working With Meanings

You will now try your hand at transforming the metaphorical potential of each image in the dream into a metaphorical meaning that links the image to a relevant bit of real-life experience. The dream presents us with images that have potential symbolic meaning. The symbolic meaning can best be considered as the metaphorical expression of aspects of a dreamer's waking life experience. The feeling residues of these recent and remote life experiences are embedded in these images. It is up to each of us now, through the use of our collective imagination, to explore the possible directions these metaphorical images can take. It is, in essence, an exercise in using our creative imagination. We are self-consciously trying to be as creative as the dreamer was in unconsciously imbuing these images with meaning in the first place.

As you begin working with the possible meanings these images convey, other feelings may occur to your. Feel free to share them. Consider yourself free at this point to develop the dream further, either at the level of feelings or at the level of meanings. You can work with a single image at a time, with a sequence, or with the whole dream. Try not to suppress anything you consider as "too wild" or "too far out." Something someone else in the group offers may touch off a whole new set of ideas in you. Go with it. Feel free to give any symbolic meaning to an image that conveys meaning to you. Many of you have some background in Freudian or Jungian psychology. Feel free if you wish to cast the metaphors in Freudian or Jungian terms. Remember, they are your projections. They are not what Freud or Jung or any other authority would have necessarily said about the dream. Within the two constraints of owning the image and working with the image as given, you are free to say anything you are moved to say.

The Safety Factor

This is built in through the assurances that the dreamer remains in charge of whatever it is he may feel as the group members offer their projections.

If something feels true, he retains the freedom to explore that feeling in his own way with no obligation to share it later if his preference is not to do so. Good feelings and insights are generally easy to manage. When uncomfortable feelings or painful insights are touched off, he may or may not wish to or be able to acknowledge them. In other words, he is free to continue to use his tried-and-true defenses that make their presence felt in the face of anything potentially threatening. The hope is that if the dreamer's privacy and need for safety is respected, he will examine whatever it is he has been made to feel. The point of the exercise is to initiate some feeling response in the dreamer while, at the same time, respecting his right to deal with those feelings in any way he wishes. He is in charge of the movement away from or toward whatever feelings are set in motion.

In talking to each other and not to the dreamer, the group members make it easier for the dreamer to function in his own private space. Thus isolated, he is free to consider any contribution coming from a member of the group as that person's projection. He is in the position of possibly benefiting from the work of the group without having any responsibility toward the group other than what he himself freely assumes. Paradoxically, it is the group's respect for the dreamer's privacy, by not imposing any obligatory responsibility to respond, that moves the dreamer in the direction of experiencing an inner sense, not of imposed responsibility, but of wanting to give back something to the group.

The Discovery Factor

It is often quite a surprise to those new to the process that others, working with the dream as their own without any of the dreamer's associations, can in their free play with the dream, come up with feelings and meanings that are experienced as so personally relevant to the dreamer. The fact is that in most instances, and regardless of whether or not the group comes up with anything that is specifically on target, the result of this exercise is to bring the dreamer closer to the dream. A number of things go on at the same time that account for this.

Not infrequently, the group comes up with direct hits. The feelings or ideas they share with each other have specific meaning for the dreamer. When you think about it, it's not so strange at all. Our dreaming consciousness gravitates toward issues that are part of the common experience of all of us— issues pertaining to authority, concern over being for oneself or for others, independence versus dependence, activity versus passivity, issues around self-identity, and so on. Furthermore, the imagery that finds its way into our dreams is social in origin. We may combine, distort, and alter these images in highly idiosyncratic ways, but it is our way of life as social creatures that has created the available images in the first place. You won't find an airplane in the dream of a primitive tribesman who never saw one. The fact that we move about in the same social arena and share a common social heritage makes it possible and even likely that a member of the group could come to the meaning of an image that feels right to the dreamer.

Another helpful factor comes into play during this stage. The group members talk of the dream as their own, all the time remaining fully cognizant of the fact that it isn't. Even as they are trying to get into the dream and make it their own, there remains some distance from it. This distance gives them a certain advantage over the dreamer. They have less at stake in saying things about someone else's dream than they might about their own. They are offering what they have to say as their own projection, but at the same time, there is the hope that it will be meaningful to the dreamer, and they try to shape it in a way that it will be. Having a greater distance from the dream allows their imaginations to roam more freely.

A number of other nonspecific reasons account for why the structured relationship between the dreamer and the group in this second stage is helpful to the dreamer. The fact is that the presence of the group working with the dream, taking the dreamer's dream seriously, applying it to their own lives, and, in so doing, sharing part of their psyche with the dreamer just as the dreamer in telling the dream did with them, all have the effect of moving the dreamer closer to the dream in a way that would not have been possible had the group not been there. The dreamer feels the nonintrusive support of the group. She now has allies in dealing with the mystery that lies before her. It has now become a social, not simply a personal, endeavor.

Problems

Because different problems arise at each stage of the two substages, let us consider them separately.

Stage 2A: Sharing Feelings

When the group is asked to confine their projections to the feeling tone or mood that they connect to the imagery, they often bypass this in their eagerness to work with the metaphorical meaning of the imagery. The leader should call this to the group members' attention and ask them to try to get at whatever feeling tone they would connect with the meaning they are giving the imagery.

When a group member protests that she has no feelings about the dream, simply ask that she use her imagination and explore what she might imagine feeling if this were her dream. You might draw the analogy referred to earlier that she is being assigned a part in a play, and even though the part doesn't fit her very well, she is to do the best she can with it. If she still can't come up with feelings associated with the dream, she need not—the offering of one's projections is not obligatory.

Stage 2B: Offering Meanings

At first, confusion is apt to arise as to what is expected of the group. How do you deal with the image as a symbol or a visual metaphor? Presumably, this has all been explained beforehand, but if necessary, it is clarified again. The task of each member is to ask, "What kind of life situation might I be in that would lead me to choose just these images in my dream?" The group members look at the images as metaphorical presentations of that experience. They can do this in small bits or by working with the dream as a whole. Not infrequently, someone asks if what he or she is doing is interpreting the dream, particularly if that person has made use of Freudian or Jungian formulations.

My answer is that you can call it interpretation if you like, but I prefer to limit the word *interpretation* to its technical meaning. It is more applicable in therapeutic situations in which a therapist, operating within a particular theoretical frame of reference, offers an interpretation based not only on the dreamer's associations but also on her knowledge of the dreamer's past. Interpretation in this sense goes beyond the data derived from the dream to become a more generalized formulation congruent with the therapist's theoretical orientation.[1] I prefer to see what we are doing as "appreciating" the metaphorical style of the dream imagery.

In this exercise, we are free to borrow from Freud or Jung, but in this context, what we are borrowing is their particular metaphorical view of a particular image. Through their writings, they have enriched our available store of metaphorical possibilities. By offering them to each other as our projections, we are not constraining the dreamer to take them more seriously than any other meanings that turn up.

Certain problems that arise are common to both substages of Stage 2:

1. There is a tendency for group members to forget to talk about the dream in the first person. Because it isn't really our dream, we have to make a conscious effort to remember to talk about it as our own.

2. By the same token, people will look at the dreamer and offer their remarks directly to him. Even though they may be using the first person, their intent is obviously to get something across to the dreamer. They are trespassing into the free space around the dreamer we spoke about.

3. A group member can turn to the dreamer and ask for a point of information concerning the dream if some part of the dream isn't clear. This can be misused, however, and become a way of trying to elicit associations from the dreamer.

4. The group should understand that no one in the group takes issue with anyone else's projections. All are free to shape their projections as they wish, no matter how strange or wrong others in the group might think them to be. We can build on each other's projections and amplify them in any way we choose, but we cannot challenge them.

5. A problem that might arise when the group is playing with the dream has to do with gender identity. An example of this is when a dream involves pregnancy and men are in the group. In developing their feelings and metaphors, they should attempt to work with the dream from the perspective of a woman. The reverse, of course, holds when a dream has distinctively male features (e.g., a reference to shaving).

6. Group members will tend to focus on what appears to them to be the most striking or most interesting imagery of the dream. If there are details in the dream they are not responding to, this should be pointed out by the leader.

7. If someone is too rambunctious, taking up too much space, interrupting others, and so on, this would require intervention by the leader. That rarely happens. What is more apt to happen is that in the excitement of developing their projections, people may interrupt each other, or in offering a projection, someone will offer it too vehemently as a point of disagreement with someone else.

8. Sometimes it is the dreamer who may stray off in the wrong direction. The dreamer cannot help at times but respond bodily, through an involuntary gesture or other nonverbal means, to something coming from the group that affects her in a powerful, interesting, or humorous way. That is natural and should not be inhibited. What should be checked, however, is any impulse on the part of the dreamer to begin giving her associations. She may do that without being aware of doing it. As an example, she might suddenly blurt out, "Oh, now I know why that image was in my dreams. I saw it on TV last

night." On the face of it, that is innocent enough, but if it isn't checked, there are apt to be more and more such interjections. It will then have the effect of tracking and thus limiting the free play of the imagination of the group. It will be counterproductive to the group's effort to explore the full range of metaphorical possibilities inherent in the imagery. If the dreamer is touched by something someone has said, she should check any impulse to offer a validating comment at this time.

The most serious error a dreamer can make is to react personally in a negative way to a particular projection made by a group member. For the purposes of this exercise, she has to respect the group members' freedom to formulate their own projections in any way they wish. That means that, although she may feel that a particular projection is directed against herself, the group member has the right to make it and she, the dreamer, has the right to reject it. Again, it would be counterproductive for the group members to be constrained to limiting their projections to only what they think the dreamer would like to hear. Group members have to have the freedom to say what they want within the basic rules of the game. The dreamer has the responsibility to view their statements as projections and to accept or reject on the basis of what she finds helpful to herself.

Remember in connection with the safety factor, we said that the dreamer is in control of the process at each and every stage. There may come a point in this second stage when the dreamer might feel so overwhelmed by all that is coming from the group that she feels there is more than she can cope with and she wishes that it would stop. It is perfectly legitimate—indeed, it is her responsibility—to take control at this point and ask that the exercise be terminated. She may wish to terminate the entire process at this point, but more often, it simply means she has had enough for the moment and is ready to go on to the next stage.

There are a number of other special points for a leader to keep in mind. One is the question of time. The group enjoys playing the game with someone else's dream and can go on and on with it. The leader has the responsibility for being the timekeeper. Stage 2 cannot be allowed to take up a disproportionate amount of time. More important stages follow, and time has to be reserved for them. At times, the leader must make an arbitrary decision about ending the second stage even when it is obvious that the group, left to its own devices, could have gone further. There are cues that can help a leader pick the right moment to shift from Stage 2B to Stage 3. When long silences ensue between contributions or when there is a good deal of repetition, it is a sign that the group has run out of things to say.

One way for the leader to avoid a disproportionate amount of time in Stage 2 is to have in mind a rough breakdown of the time that can be allotted to each stage of the process within the total time available. This will be further discussed once we go through the entire process. In general, Stage 2 time would vary from 15 to 20 minutes, depending on whether you are working within a 1.5- or a 2-hour frame.

As the leader feels the time for the second stage is drawing to a close, she should begin to give advanced signals to the dreamer that this is so. This is because a radical change of mind-set is required of the dreamer as he shifts from Stage 2 to the next stage. While the exercise is in progress, he is listening to what is coming from the group and is immersed in his own thoughts. At the invitation from the leader to respond, his focus is now turned outward to what he can share with the group. The signals can come in the form of the leader's asking the group several times before the end of the second stage, "Are there any further contributions before we return the dream to the dreamer?" Each time the leader puts this question to the group, there may be a few additional comments. At some point, however, the leader will have to make the decision to terminate.

Issues

A number of interesting and important issues have a bearing on the discovery factor involved in the second stage. The more I pursue dream work, the more impressed I am with how much help a group can be to a dreamer without knowing the relevant personal emotional context. I think that deeper and more subtle influences are at work, influences that elicit what might be called the *healing potential of the group.*

A dream is the most spontaneous and most honest story we are able to relate about ourselves. Animals act spontaneously and do not know what dishonesty is. So it is with our dreaming consciousness. I don't mean to imply that we regress while we are dreaming but, rather, that we have salvaged these two remarkable features from our animal heritage. The dream is always spontaneously presenting us with the naked truth just as a small child often will. So we might add to the virtues of dreaming consciousness the quality of innocence, a quality associated with an earlier stage in our development and never completely extinguished.

I call attention to these attributes of the dream to emphasize how rare such features are in the complexity of our waking lives. Being both virtuous and rare, they are appreciated when we come across them. We approach a young child with love, not judgment. So it is in our response to the dreamer who sets about to share her dream and engages honestly in dream work. Waking judgmental tendencies are set aside. They are not relevant to the task at hand. There is an implicit understanding that the dreamer has entrusted to our care a very private part of her psyche and in so doing has risked revealing herself as a vulnerable human being. This, in turn, evokes the group's capacity for concern, honesty, and empathy. Any waking judgmental impulse fades into the background, and there is the single-minded focus on the effort to be helpful.

Although these factors operate throughout the process, their effect in the second stage is to deepen the level of sharing and widen the imaginative range of what goes into the projections of the various group members. There is an implicit understanding that they have been entrusted with a delicate task, and they respond accordingly. Implicit also is an awareness that the dreamer, by sharing her dream, is creating the basis for an encounter with the group at the advancing edge of her growth potential. The dreamer is concerned with movement into a future that has not yet fully come into view, and she does not yet know whether she will arrive successfully or be deflected by pitfalls in her path. All parties to the enterprise, the dreamer and the group members, are involved in a sensitive and delicate operation.

In sharing her dream with the group, the dreamer has taken the first step in what might be called the *socialization of the dream*. Whenever we recall a dream, we capture something that arose during a different state of being— namely, our existence during the state of sleep. I have likened it to catching a fish on a line. We have to use specific social artifacts, such as a frying pan and stove, to transform the fish into an object that can then satisfy our need for food. The dream, too, is an alien in foreign territory when it is first recalled.[2] Capturing it on awakening is the initial step in the socialization process. There are times when a flash of understanding accompanies the recall. Analogously, some people eat raw fish. To push the analogy still further, the fish as food comes into its own when it is cooked, embellished with other delicacies, and enjoyed in the company of others. So it is with dreams. With practice and developing skill, one can go a long way toward appreciating the feelings and the information embedded in dream imagery. It is my contention that work on a dream, in a supportive and stimulating social context, is necessary to fulfill more of its inherent promise. In the second stage of the process, the members of the group are kitchen helpers who set up things for the dreamer so as to prepare the fish to her liking and for her benefit. At a later point in the process, they will help her serve it and, later still, will participate in the enjoyment of a meal so mutually prepared.

Helpful Hints

Circumstances arise that can be better managed by knowledge beforehand. Sometimes, relatives, spouses, or friends who have known each other for a long time may be in a group together. They will, of course, know a good deal more about each other than do others in the group. If one of them is the dreamer, and the other would like to include in her projections something she had previous knowledge of, the question of guarding the dreamer's confidentiality comes up. In this process, we work only with what the dreamer himself freely divulges. If the particular group member is absolutely sure the dreamer would have no objection to that information's being made public— that his favorite color is orange (and that color is prominent in the dream)—it can be offered if it is thought to be relevant. If, however, the group member is unsure, she should then check with the dreamer by passing him a note asking if she is free to divulge this private bit of knowledge in her projection. It is up to the dreamer to give permission or not. In this way the confidentiality of the dreamer is not compromised.

There have been situations in which the dreamer has been touched by many things the group has offered. When it comes to the next stage and he is invited to respond, he may be flustered and confused and might say something such as, "You've said a lot of things that were meaningful to me, but I can't remember what they were." The way to avoid this is to suggest in advance that the dreamer jot down anything he finds interesting. Some people do very well without taking a single note.

It is helpful to remind the group members that they can introduce any context into their projections that is known to all members of the group. This can include events in the news about which there is general knowledge. More important, it can include things about the dreamer's life that have been shared with the group in the course of the work done with earlier dreams of the dreamer in the group. The basic rule is to work only with what is known to all or, with the dreamer's permission, can be made known to all. In the session to follow, the context of being in a dream group was very much a factor in the dream occurring at the time it did.

An Illustrative Dream

In this and the succeeding chapters describing the various stages of the process, I have included an account of a session to illustrate the particular stage under discussion. Although, in general, the examples chosen illustrate the range and depth of the issues explored, they also illustrate the limitations of the process. In each of the instances to be cited, the work was done within an allotted hour and a half. This was generally adequate for the goal we had in mind—namely, to start the dreamer in a direction that felt right to him and hope that he could go further on his own. Dreams of any considerable length posed a problem, but even there, our goals for the dreamer were generally met. Because control of the process always remains in the hands of the dreamer, there is a respectful acceptance of whatever limits the dreamer's ability or desire to do more with the dream.

These accounts are reconstructed from notes taken at the time. At best, they give only a partial picture of what went on. It is by no means an easy task to capture the spontaneity and nonverbal subtle interplay between the dreamer and the group. In Stage 2 in particular, the exchanges between members of the group occur so rapidly that they are almost impossible to get down verbatim. I have avoided taping sessions because there is usually some resistance to the idea. The accumulation of tapes and the editing would also pose a practical problem.

Sarah's Dream

This is the first dream to be shared in a group by someone new to the process. It occurred in the course of a 2-day workshop in Edinburgh. When a dreamer is genuinely interested in her dream, an initial exposure of this kind can have a profound effect. It did in this instance. The dream was presented on the second day of the workshop. The dreamer had volunteered to present a dream on the first day but backed off when someone else offered a dream. The dream to follow was recalled on awakening on the second day.

Stage 1: Presentation of the Dream

> I walk past a signpost that is difficult to read. I pass two or three teenage boys. One turns around, faces me, and comes up to me. He tells me the sign referred to a group meeting taking place in a large space.
>
> I walk on and come to this room where there is a young male tutor from the art college. He is sitting on the floor in a Yoga position. There is a ladder there. All I can see is the bottom of it. It rests on metal plates. One of the plates moves a little, which makes the ladder more secure. The tutor tells me there are other designs of ladders.

> *I walk on until I come to the YWCA. I'm sitting in a square room talking to someone at a table. I go from there to someone at a house where I first lived in Edinburgh.*
>
> *I go from there past a clothes shop. I pause and look in the window but decide to walk on with the group of people I am walking with. I end up somewhere not far from the art college.*

Following the presentation of the dream, the group asked questions of the dreamer to clarify any aspect of the dream that was unclear and to learn if any characters mentioned in the dream are real people in the life of the dreamer. The questions disclosed the following:

"There were other people there with me at the shop window. I know the tutor briefly through my work at college. I didn't know anyone else in the dream."

Stage 2A: Projecting Feelings

The group members work with the dream as their own with the dreamer listening without actively participating. They focus first on the feeling tones suggested by the imagery. The projected feelings and meanings offered by the group that were of interest to the dreamer are italicized.

"*I feel like a pilgrim making a journey.* The ladder has a biblical feeling, as if it were Jacob's ladder."

"*I, too, feel I am on a journey. I'm grateful to the young teenager for directing me to a large meeting place. That feels like coming here today.* I feel comfortable seeing the tutor in the Yoga position. It's all so calm. *I'm grateful to him for telling me about the other ladders.* I seem to be searching for something. There was support and comfort."

"*I'm looking for guidance and there are people there helping me find it.*"

"I have a feeling of contrast between me as the young woman on a quest, searching for something, compared with the certainty of the young me and the Yoga teacher."

"I'm feeling very good about myself. I manage to move on getting the help and support I need. I'm confused at some of the places, but I feel safe."

Stage 2B: Projecting Metaphorical Meanings

While still working with the dream as their own, the group members were now asked to consider the various images in the dream and to ask themselves what kind of life situation would they have been in or imagine they might be in that would result in such imagery. They were also free to continue in their feelings.

"I feel relief after first coming upon the teenagers. The sign also conveyed something personal."

"The journey, like the various ladders, can go in many directions. I'm pleased at the choices I have."

"I feel I have lots of time and space. There is no rush. Everything is OK. There is a timeless feeling."

"The Christian association, the ladder, and the Yoga all have a religious connotation."

"I feel as though I'm facing up to something."

"I'm somewhat frightened when the teenager turns to face me."

"I feel confused. There is too much going on."

"There are lots of groups. Do I want to be part of any?"

"The square room feels very stuffy to me. I prefer the room the Yoga man is in."

"The sign and the reference to a group meeting has to do with coming into this dream group."

When it was over, the dreamer was invited to respond to the effect of the work of the group and to offer her own associations and ideas about the dream.

Stage 3A: Dreamer's Response

"I do feel I am on a *journey. I do feel I get help as I go along.* I seem to come to a point where I go back to the past, to my relationship to my father, where the ladder comes in. *I do look for help and guidance—at the tutor's place and the YWCA. The shape of a star comes to mind, as if I move out and then come back and keep doing it. I move out to take a look and move back.* It's a long path. It was most painful at the point where I saw the bottom of the ladder and at the house. I am interested in geometry. About the store, I feel I've been too interested in clothes.

"When I meet people, I feel apprehension. It's as if I go out and come back again. At particular points in the dream, I don't feel confident. I never give up, even though sometimes it's very difficult.

"The person at the table with me is a woman.

"I am interested in the work of this tutor. I find his work interesting. He puts stories in his pictures. His approach to structure is different from classical structures. There is a magic to them. He makes use of circles in them."

The dreamer finished at this point. She began to experience the opening up of the dream as she worked with the idea of a journey, seeking and getting help. She responded affirmatively when asked if she would like further help from the group. The group and the dreamer then entered into the dialogue, the first part of which was to explore the thoughts and feelings of the dreamer during the period immediately preceding the dream (the recent emotional context).

Stage 3B.1: Amplifying the Recent Context

Question Can you recall what your thoughts and feelings were at the end of the day at the point where you were ready to fall asleep last night?

Response I was out with friends and their children. We were talking about the college and how the structure there makes it difficult for students to learn how to paint. My friend's daughter wants to go to my college. I was not confident in expressing my feelings about it. I wasn't saying clearly what it was I meant. I felt anxious. I could see what was wrong but didn't know what to do about it. There was one tutor there, a woman, who helped me understand the problem. It had to do with the way the painting course was structured. Feelings and technique were too sharply separated. It made me feel confused.

Question Is there anything more you can say about yesterday that may have left you with any residual feelings?

Response Yesterday, in the course of the dream work, I felt I had an opportunity to ask a question and I held back. I didn't do it. I would have felt more satisfied if I had. It is not uncommon for me to think of something afterward that I should have said. I felt very good about the dream work yesterday, though a bit apprehensive. Even though I knew it would be safe, I felt a bit not confident.

Question Anything more about your reactions to yesterday's work?

Response I came with a great many dreams and wanted to find out about them. Then I realized I had to listen and learn how to go about it. So I came with a lot of enthusiasm but then realized how much I had to learn. I found the dreams that were shared interesting. I was determined today that I would share my dream. I do feel I have to value my dreams. I felt very relaxed here. I was touched by this dream and the many problems that go back to childhood and to my parents. These are painful thoughts. I have spent much time recently trying to look at my childhood and what my real feelings were. I look to my dreams for help.

Stage 3B.2: Reading the Dream Back

Again, the dreamer responded positively to moving on to the next phase of the dialogue. She was told the dream would be read back to her, scene by scene, by a member of the group in the hope that, as she now heard it in the light of all that she had so far shared, further associations to the imagery would occur to her. The first scene was read back, stopping at the end of the first paragraph:

Response It was as though I was going to a big meeting held in a big area with a lot of space, like a football field. The three boys were not aggressive. They were wearing dark suits. It was as if the sign was pointing to an alternative. The letters were handwritten, not Arabic but something like Arabic. It was a language I didn't understand. The whole thing was reassuring. There was no reason to be afraid.

The next scene was read back to the end of the second paragraph:

Response The ladder was familiar to me. It's the kind that was made near where I was brought up. It was of very good design and was the kind recommended by my father. There was one like it in our own house. The tutor suggested that I look at other types, particularly one I could hold on to. I didn't really want to climb that ladder. I felt somewhat sad about that. I realized with a sense of relief that there were other designs. The tutor sat there very calmly in the Yoga position. He was telling me I had alternatives. The ladder was located in between the teacher and myself. I didn't want to let that ladder go. Even though there was metal, it had an organic form.

Question Can you say more about the dilemma you were feeling about it?

Response My father had ideas for me that weren't really mine, were not what I wanted. It was a difficult decision to go a different way. I don't believe in hierarchical arrangements. The ladder implied something hierarchical.

The third scene was read back to the end of the third paragraph:

Response I think of the YWCA as a place where people come to when they have no other place to go. I have never gone there. I could see the room with a woman there. I was aware that if I needed help I could go there.

Question Can you say any more of the appearance in the dream of the first house you lived in in Edinburgh?

Response It was the first place I lived in after leaving home on returning from a year in North America. It was the first break with my family. It felt lonely and strange. I grew up in the countryside.

Question Anything more?

Response It was a Victorian structure. I didn't find myself in a very sympathetic environment. I didn't feel it was how things should be. The whole setting was rigid, with too much emphasis on order. Once I left the room, I felt very differently about the street and the part of town I was in. It was lively, and the group I was with has more to do than buying clothes. I was quite happy to go with the group. I felt much happier and much younger. Also, where we get to is also near the place I'm staying while I'm at college. The atmosphere is quite stimulating and multicultural.

Question Anything more?

Response It's a dream about movement, change, and growth. Move from loneliness to being in the company of people. There is a magic quality in the dream in the reference to the tutor's paintings and his use of circles.

It is not easy to convey the charged feelings that characterized her search for the meaning of the images. At several points she was close to tears.

Stage 3B.3: Orchestrating Comments

At the dreamer's invitation, a number of orchestrating ideas were offered to the dreamer. What follows are my own orchestrating comments.[3] In formulating them, I try to bring together what I've learned of the immediate life context of the dreamer, how the imagery metaphorically displays the issue being raised, and to what extent past and present are linked in the dream as the dreamer moves into her future.

> Let me begin with the sign you see as you start this journey, a journey I would characterize as the struggle to move closer to a feeling of authenticity about yourself. This is part of your effort to discover who you are, not who your father wanted you to be. The handwritten sign, in a language difficult to understand, pointing the way to a large space, suggests that you are talking about dreams, which do initially appear as a strange language and which also point to a larger dimension of the self. You mentioned, in introducing yourself, your interest in dreams and how many you recall and try to work with. "Enough to fill a football field," you said when you introduced your dream. There were two things that occurred yesterday that had the effect of pushing you back into your old pattern. The first was the way you initially volunteered to share a dream and then quickly withdrew in favor of someone else's. The other was the way you squelched a question that you wanted to ask and that later you thought would have been helpful to ask. It was as if you were afraid to show yourself and take the risk of being seen. You came here with many dreams and then with some feeling of frustration, realizing that to truly understand the language of the dream, much hard work had to be done in the way of self-exploration. It was almost as if you felt you had to start from scratch. I think you were relieved to find yourself in a group that was supportive, worked within a nonhierarchical structure, and recognized and respected your authority over the dream. The work was experienced in a lively and nonintrusive way. In your references to your upbringing and to the nonconformist approach of the tutor, possibly me, you are bolstered in your effort to work freely toward the values you genuinely believe in.

Before terminating, the dreamer was given the opportunity to give her own final impressions.

"What you said (referring to my summary comments) is true, particularly about not taking risks for fear of making a fool of myself. I'll have to learn how to do that. Thank you all."

On behalf of the group I thanked the dreamer for sharing the dream and working so hard on it.

Comment: Because the dream was worked through on the second day of a 2-day workshop, there was no opportunity for a later follow-up. That would have been the fourth and final stage of the process. I did, however, receive a note subsequently from the dreamer in which she said this:

> The dream came back to me again, and I realize how important it would have been for me to have had a follow-up on it. I then thought about the dream, and through subsequent dreams, it brought up the fact that I have been living too much in my parent's past in particular and not enough in my own present. That is not to deny the past, but not to live in it. I think that is how I would put it. Painful, but true.

This example illustrates the basic features of dreaming consciousness and how meaning is arrived at through the unfolding of the process. A concerted effort was made to help the dreamer explore waking experiences during the period just prior to the dream. What emerged as the recent emotional context of the dream was traced back to two sets of circumstances. One involved the way the discussion with her friend the day before touched on an area of great sensitivity—namely, her reaction to the way art was being taught at her college and how this connected with her lifelong struggle against superimposed pressure to conform. The other involved all the feelings she had in embarking on group dream work—anticipation, frustration at how much there was to learn, eagerness, annoyance at herself for holding back, and a good feeling at how the group worked to help the dreamer. Note how current concerns lead into the interplay of past and present so characteristic of dreaming. References to childhood and the appearance of parental images are quite common.

Notes

1. This is discussed further in Chapter 17.
2. This is a loose analogy. The point is made only to emphasize the qualitative difference in state between dreaming and waking.
3. The orchestration stage also posed problems for note taking. The ideas were sometimes developed at considerable length, and everyone was eager to participate. As the leader and trying to do two things at once—namely, listen to each orchestrating projection and its effect on the dreamer and at the same time trying to formulate my own thoughts—I could generally do no more than capture in writing a bare outline form of what I had to say. This was fleshed out as faithfully as I could in the typed version and then checked with the dreamer.

Stage 3A

Back to the Dreamer

The dream is now returned to the dreamer who is invited to share her thoughts with the group. This is the first step in a continuing interplay between the dreamer and the group, with the goal of deepening the dreamer's grasp of the dream. Only after the dreamer has completed her response, will the group actively and directly seek to further the discovery factor while operating within the constraints of the safety factor.

The Dreamer's Response

When the second stage is completed, the leader turns to the dreamer and orients her to this next step in the process. He will say something like this:

"We are now ready to return the dream to you, its rightful owner. We have worked with your dream as if it were our own in hopes of coming up with something that might be of help to you. That may or may not have happened. You are now free to say whatever you would like to say about the dream. You can start in any way you wish. You can begin by talking about the impact the work of the group may have had on you. You may wish to start with your own associations and your own ideas about what the dream means. In other words, you are free to develop and organize your response in any way you choose. Take all the time you need. No one will interrupt you. Remember that you are in charge of what is going on. That means you decide on the level of sharing you feel comfortable with. No one will push you beyond that level. You may need a few moments to collect your thoughts. Start whenever you are ready."

It is important that the group members understand exactly what their role is at this point. Naturally, they assume they are to listen to the dreamer. What they are not aware of is that they have to learn how to listen. Listening is a skill and is not as simple as it appears. It takes a deep understanding of the process and a good deal of practice and experience to learn how to listen in the most productive way. This will be considered further in the next chapter. Suffice it to say at this point that this involves a change in mind-set on the part of the group members from being involved with their own thoughts to now listening. Careful listening means taking in all that a dreamer says without prejudging its importance. Furthermore, it involves keeping all that she has said in mind, because it will form the basis for the dialogue that will follow.

The Safety Factor

The leader has to impress on the dreamer that she has the responsibility to monitor her own safety level. It is up to the leader, of course, to see to it that no one interferes with this self-monitoring. Two processes are going on at the same time. As the dreamer develops more of a sense of what the dream is saying, she must also evaluate how comfortable she feels about sharing these inner experiences. The freedom to share and the urge to share are sometimes there from the beginning. In others, it develops more gradually as there is increased experience with and trust in the process. One soon learns that the more one can share the more helpful the group can be.

The Discovery Factor

The hope is that the exercise engaged in by the group has set this factor going in the dreamer. In the course of her response and the bringing together of her associations, more and more ideas about the dream may occur to the dreamer. In fact, this may have developed to the point that, in the midst of her response, a sudden and genuine "Eureka!" feeling occurs when a felt connection is made to a dream. When that happens, the dreamer may feel relieved and satisfied so that she doesn't feel any further need to go on. If the dreamer so wishes, the process can be terminated at that point. In most instances, however, the dreamer's grasp of the dream is still fragmentary, and further work is indicated.

As the dreamer shares her thoughts and reactions with the group, she is laying the groundwork for the development of the discovery factor in the next part of the third stage. Her response will provide the leads for later exploration, keeping in mind that what the dreamer has said is a prerequisite for the group's ability to ask relevant questions in the dialogue.

Problems

The first time a dreamer finds herself at this stage of the process, she may feel uncertain and confused as to what is expected of her. Some of this may be resolved easily by repeating the instructions, emphasizing the dreamer's complete freedom to do whatever she wishes to do, to say anything she wishes to say, and to say as much or as little as she wishes. Such reassurance from the leader can help the dreamer get over the initial hurdle. Sometimes, she simply may need a little more time to organize her thoughts, and when she is made comfortable about that, she then can get started. As the second stage draws to a close, the leader should begin to give the dreamer signals that the dream is about to be returned to her. This alerts her to the fact that this is going to happen soon and gives her some time to begin to think about her response.

The dreamer may be unsure about how much she should say. Some dreamers mistakenly assume that they are to respond only to what the group has said about the dream. Some may wrongly assume that they are obliged to say something about all that has been said by everyone, regardless of whether or not it was meaningful. The dreamer should not feel under obligation to acknowledge each contribution individually. She should work only with what touched her personally.

In the orientation to the process, the dreamer has been made aware of the importance of exploring the recent emotional context and the role this plays in triggering the dream. This is sometimes mistakenly construed to mean that she is not to talk about the recent-day residue in her initial response but to take that up later on in the dialogue. Although it is true that the content will be explored in further depth in the dialogue, she should feel completely free to say whatever she wants about recent events in her life, regardless of how relevant these events may seem to be to the dream.

The dreamer may have a number of responses to the projections of the group. It will take some experience for the dreamer to separate the genuine from the spurious. By the latter, I mean the tendency to accept a projection intellectually without having any genuinely felt sense of its relevance. A very suggestible dreamer may be tempted to accept a response because it seemed to be emphasized by the group rather than because it genuinely feels right. A true response, in contrast to one accepted in this fashion, has an "opening up" quality. As it sinks in, it opens the dreamer up to further thoughts and insights about the dream. There is a gut reaction that cannot be denied, a feeling of something falling into place and paving the way for further discoveries. By way of contrast, a suggestible response begins and ends with some kind of flat acknowledgment—"I suppose it could be what you said about . . ."

A problem can arise when a dreamer has little or no response to offer the group or, as it happened in one instance, when a dreamer made it clear that she wished to stop the process before offering any response. She said, "You've said a lot of things. I'll have to think about it." Responses like that leave the group feeling frustrated, the dreamer in a state of nonresolution, and the leader caught in between. The important thing to keep in mind is that the dreamer is within her rights in giving little or no response and in wishing to terminate the process. A leader should make that clear and should refrain from trying to encourage the dreamer to go on. What I said to the dreamer who gave the preceding response went along the following lines:

> It's perfectly all right for you to stop the process at this point. That is the contract we made when we started out—namely, that you would control the process and that we would go no further than you wished us to go. We are here to be of help but only to the extent you want our help. We follow where you lead us. We do not lead you.

I said this spontaneously, not knowing what else to say in the face of mounting tension in a group that had worked very hard on the dream and was eager to continue with the process and with a dreamer who seemed to be pulling back and not allowing herself to get into the dream. What I said had a dual effect. For the dreamer, it was reassuring. It meant I genuinely respected her authority regardless of the feelings they generated in the group. For the group, it helped them live with the tension they were feeling. It helped them accept the fact that they were not there to get a return on their investment, so to speak, or to satisfy their own curiosity. They were there to help the dreamer to the extent that the dreamer called on them for help. Once I said what I did, the dreamer, much to my surprise, shifted her stance and said, "Perhaps there is something I'd like to say." She then proceeded to pour out her feelings, and the dream work continued to completion. It was obvious that she had been ambivalent about continuing and needed reassurance that we would respect her decision. This heightened her trust in the process and resolved her ambivalence in the direction of continuing.

In general, it is a good idea at the conclusion of a dreamer's response for the leader, speaking for the group, to acknowledge the response in a way that is genuine and appropriate. It should be meaningful, not just polite, and indicative of the fact that what the dreamer has shared has been heard. If the dreamer has worked well with what the group gave her, say so. If you feel moved by the dreamer's response, say so.

It cannot be emphasized too strongly that the movement from one substage in the dialogue to the next takes place only if the dreamer wishes it. We are talking about fall-back strategy with regard to the way the group members help the dreamer. They are not automatically invoked. It is up to the dreamer to invite the next phase of the dialogue. If the dreamer doesn't wish to, then the process is concluded on a note of thanks to the dreamer for sharing the dream and her response.

One further point before going on to the dialogue between the group and the dreamer: The leader should feel free to express an opinion as to whether or not he thinks such a dialogue would be helpful. He makes it clear that the decision still remains with the dreamer. He may say something such as, "You seem to have gotten a good deal from the group. Perhaps we can help you further through the dialogue." An experienced dream worker will have no difficulty making the decision. An inexperienced one may seem perplexed and at a loss about how to proceed. Not having prior experience with the dialogue, she has no idea of the kind of help the group has to offer. The leader might review for her what the goals of the dialogue are, reiterating that the final decision is up to the dreamer. Generally, the dreamer will be open to the dialogue. It does offer an opportunity to go deeper into the dream, even if the dreamer feels she has a good grasp of it by the time she finishes her response.

5

Stage 3B.1

The Dialogue Begins:
The Search for Context

Some general remarks are in order with regard to the substages of the dialogue that follow the response of the dreamer. This aspect of the process will make the most demands on the dreamer, the group, and the leader. It is the part of the process that requires experience and skill. When carried out properly, it is the most important and rewarding phase of the work. It's as if all that preceded it was a kind of tune-up, preparatory for what comes next. For the dreamer, it will be a lesson on how to use the group most effectively. For the group, it will be a lesson on how to interact with the dreamer in a way that helps elicit relevant information without ever going beyond the limits set by the dreamer. For the leader, it will be a continual challenge to see that the group never wrests control from the dreamer.

Before embarking on the dialogue, everyone should have a clear idea of his or her role and what the rules are. The dreamer has to bear in mind what I refer to as the Dreamer's Bill of Rights. These include the following:

1. The dreamer remains in control and is responsible for setting limits.
2. Questions put to the dreamer are instruments for the dreamer to use to explore his own psyche. He is free to deal with those questions in any way he wishes. If anything interesting occurs to him, it is his decision whether or not to share it. If he doesn't wish to respond, he is free to say so and go on to the next question.
3. The dreamer has the right to take as much time as he may need to consider the question. He need not feel any compulsion to provide an immediate answer to a question put to him.
4. The dreamer can terminate the dialogue at any point.

The following guidelines make clear to the group members both the opportunities and the constraints they must keep in mind with regard to the dialogue.

There are three different approaches to the dreamer in the dialogue, each with a different goal and each posing a different set of questions. We will go into the differences when we consider the various phases of the dialogue, but for the moment, let us consider what they have in common. The group is given to understand the full implications of the Dreamer's Bill of Rights. We don't ask questions in an "information-demanding" way. Every question put to the dreamer has to be considered as an instrument offered rather than one demanding an answer. (If you ask someone the time, you expect an answer.) The questions are put to the dreamer with the hope that they are information eliciting for him, with the understanding that he is free to respond or not.

There is one way of putting a question that is totally out of bounds and is to be avoided at all costs. I refer to the use of leading questions. Such questions purport to be questions but are, in fact, designed to get across to the respondent an idea in the mind of the questioner. They are "information giving" rather than "information eliciting": For example, "Wouldn't you say that older man in the dream was your father?" They are the kind of questions to which a lawyer might resort to influence a defendant or plant a thought in the minds of jury members. They are completely out of place in dream work (as they are in a courtroom). At the same time, it is in the nature of dream work as such to make it very tempting to frame leading questions.

What is so bad about a leading question? Might it not provide the dreamer with an idea that turns out to be correct? Sure, it might. If that happens and there is a good result, one might consider it a good thing to do. But hold on a moment and take a closer look at what is actually taking place and what other results might occur. A leading question *leads*. In this process, we *follow* the dreamer. We do not lead the dreamer into areas we think she should pursue. We only go into areas the dreamer has opened up to us. To do otherwise is to subtly take the control away from the dreamer. If this is done repeatedly, it erodes that control, and the authority over the dream will shift from the dreamer to the questioner. He may be skillful at it and, up to a point, even be helpful, but the questioner will have taken over the dream and relegated the dreamer to a dependent role.

Leading questions are risky. They may heighten the anxiety level of the dreamer. They may be perplexing to the dreamer. They may touch on areas the dreamer has not opened up and doesn't wish to open up. In her anxiety, the dreamer may wonder, "What does this person know about my dream that I don't?" Any increase in the dreamer's anxiety level is counterproductive to the whole thrust of the dream work we are doing. The success of the process depends on creating a safe enough environment so that the dreamer is able to allay her anxiety to the point that she feels secure enough to venture into new and unexplored areas. When anxiety is induced gratuitously from outside, it is experienced as a danger signal and disrupts the feeling of safety. Old tried-and-true defensive maneuvers are always ready to take over and block efforts to hear what the dream has to say.

The ability of the group to manage the dialogue depends on its mastery of two important skills. We have already spoken of the first skill: framing the question properly. To know what questions to ask requires another more important skill—namely, to learn how to listen to the dreamer so that you really grasp all that the dreamer has already said. Listening may not seem so difficult a skill, but much is involved if you are really concerned with where the dreamer is and being able to identify with her. It involves the following:

1. Listening to and remembering all that a dreamer has shared from the time she first volunteered the dream through the completion of her response (Stage 3A).

2. Listening to what she said with emphasis and feeling.

3. Listening to what is not said—what aspects of the dream or the recent context have not been touched on in the response. If we haven't listened carefully in this regard, we will not be clear about what areas have been covered by the dreamer and what areas need further clarification.

4. Listening without bias as to what the dream means to the dreamer. This is the most difficult of all. The work in Stage 2 has stimulated many ideas in your mind about what the dream means. Fine! But keep them in the back of your mind—far back. They might be very wrong. Remember, the dream is coming out of the unique life experiences of the dreamer, not out of your life. If you are to be successful in helping the dreamer get at those experiences, your orientation has to be to the life of the dreamer, not to

self-satisfaction with the way you are reading the dream. Careful attention
to her story is the only way. It is a humbling experience to learn how to rely
more on what the dreamer is sharing with us and how to stimulate that sharing
rather than relying on our preconceived ideas about what the dream is going
to turn out to mean. It's so easy to develop preconceived ideas and so tempting to short-circuit the more laborious learning-from-the-dreamer route. The
dream work rests on our facilitating the work the dreamer has to do and
disabusing ourselves of the idea that we can do it for her.

There are a number of other important things to learn about the questions.
These will be taken up in relation to the specific phases of the dialogue.

The leader participates in the dialogue in the same way as do other members of the group. With a new group, the leader will have to take more of the
initiative and do a good deal of modeling of the questions until the group
feels knowledgeable enough to participate more actively.

The common aim of all three stages of the dialogue is to elicit the data the
dreamer needs to work out the dream. At some level, the dreamer has felt a
sense of why those images are there. After all, she created them in the first place.
Our goal is to help her discover and relate to that knowledge while awake.
The remainder of this chapter will deal with the first part of the dialogue.

The Search for the Recent Context

A dream starts in the present. Although it doesn't end there, it's the jump-
ing-off place for the direction that dreaming consciousness will take. Some
recent emotional residues remain with us until the moment we fall asleep.
They resurface at the time the brain gets the signal to start dreaming and
influence the thematic unity of the imagery to follow. What is there in the
nature of these residues that enables them to play so important a role in
shaping the content of our dreaming consciousness? They derive their power
because of their connections with more significant and still unresolved emotional residues from our past. None of us grows up perfect. All of us carry
about unresolved aspects of our emotional heritage. As a consequence, we
move into our future not only faced with the unknowns of that future but also
dragging along these "windows of vulnerability," thus creating a situation of
double jeopardy. It doesn't take much to touch off one of our vulnerable
areas. One such vulnerability many of us grow up with is a constraint on the
free and appropriate expression of justifiable anger. Some recent event may

have left us feeling annoyed. Perhaps that annoyance conceals anger that could not be acknowledged either because the circumstances wouldn't permit it or because of a long-standing problem in showing anger. In both instances, we are left with a tension in the face of circumstances we can't control. Emotional residues of this nature are the ones that are apt to show up in our dreams. The free play of a spontaneous feeling has been blocked.

When, through no fault of our own, outside circumstances block the feelings they give rise to, we are left feeling compromised, hurt, angry, helpless, and frightened. These feelings will then find their way into our dreams. Sometimes, events leave us with some residual discomfort because they have touched an area of strength or some positive resource we have not yet owned up to. We can shy away from the good as well as the bad in ourselves. Because these emotional residues can be both positive and negative, I prefer to refer to them by the neutral term *tension*. If we talk of emotional residues as exposing some conflict, the tendency is to give a negative connotation to the term *conflict*. If we refer to the emotional residue we go to bed with as a residual tension, we bypass any judgmental attitude toward it.

We have used the term *recent* in describing this residue. How recent is recent? The term is used loosely. The specific events involved may have occurred 2, 3, or more days before the dream, but their repercussions last and resurface the night of the dream. Sometimes, no specific external event is easily identifiable, and the residue seems to rise up from within. Unconscious ruminative activity begins to make its presence felt through the vague feelings or tensions that result.

How do these residual tensions influence the development of the dream? The specific feelings involved seem to function as a magnet that has the power to evoke bits and pieces of our past that have some emotional connection to the issue at the heart of the tension. If enough of a dream is recalled, these references to the past are often explicit: For example, "I found myself in the house we lived in when I was a child." Sometimes, they are merely alluded to when, for example, an unidentified character in the dream has some quality of a person the dreamer knew in the past.

Why does the dreamer go to all that trouble? My explanation runs something like this: A recent event has touched off unfinished business from the past. The dreamer then goes to sleep and temporarily disconnects from the world about him (this is relative; bodily or external stimuli that are intense enough can gain representation in the dream). At certain repetitive phases of the sleep cycle, dreaming consciousness occurs. Waking or dreaming, consciousness as we experience it is the way we have of appraising our present situation so as to have as much to say as possible about the way we move into our own future. We are, as Korzybski (1941) put it, "time-binding" creatures. We have a sense of our own past and the ability to look into our own future. The more we know of our past, the better position we are in to guide our future.

How does this apply to dreaming consciousness? Let us try to put ourselves in the position of the dreamer who, at the end of a period of seeming consciousless sleep suddenly experiences consciousness. Being conscious implies being conscious of something. There is no new sensory input to respond to, evaluate, and act on. What is there that can occupy the dreamer's consciousness? Only whatever memory, by virtue of its recency and intensity, is strong enough to intrude into consciousness and become the focus of the dreamer's attention. What we have described as the recent emotional residue is this intrusive event. If we bear in mind the fact that the dreamer asleep as well as awake is moving into his own future, we can better understand what happens next. How is the dreamer going to assess this recent intrusive feeling? He has to assess its implications for the immediate business at hand—namely, the continuation of the sleep cycle. The question he is confronted with is, "Is what is happening to me now something I can manage to contain within the sleeping state, or is it of such a nature as to induce the waking state where it can be managed better?" The dreamer cannot consult any outside source to find the answer to that question. The only avenue open to him to find out more about this intrusive event is to scan his own past and work with whatever memories and remote residues come out of that past that connect at a feeling level with whatever issue is surfacing in his life at that moment. Again, as in waking consciousness, a more accurate knowledge of where he has been is the most reliable guide as to where he is apt to be next.

If the feelings he comes up with are containable within the imagery created, the sleep cycle can continue undisturbed. If, on the other hand, they are above a certain threshold in either a good or bad way, dreaming consciousness will be interrupted and the waking state will ensue.

Let me say a bit more about the importance of ferreting out the recent context, the specific inner or outer events that triggered the dream. By the time we are adults, we may have a general idea of some of our shortcomings. We may be aware, for example, of being too passive or too dependent. This knowledge, abstract and general as it is, is of little use to us. When we do dream work and make a connection between the imagery and the specific contextual situation out of which it arose, we experience that behavioral trend quite differently. We uncover it in its concreteness and particularity, whereas before it was known to us as an abstract generalization. How it made itself manifest in the particular situation was not known to us. We had no leverage on something that had a disturbing hold over our lives. What has been operating in the dark is now exposed to light. It can no longer be the same thief in the night, robbing us of control over an aspect of our behavior. He has been caught in the act. He is apt to try again, but having discovered how he operates, we will be prepared for him the next time.

It can be most useful to the dreamer to reconnect with those emotional residues. This is the first task in the dialogue. Preparation for this task involves establishing as accurately as possible the date of the dream. This should be known even before the dream is told. If, for example, a dreamer has difficulty dating a dream that occurred several weeks prior but is able to place it, for example, sometime around a weekend, this fact can help focus the efforts of the group and the dreamer, to discover the relevant context.

As we listen to the dreamer's response to the work of the group in the third stage (3A), we must pay particular attention to any references made to recent events in the life of the dreamer. The group will help the dreamer review these events in this first part of the dialogue to see if there is more he can say about them. There is usually a good deal more that can be said, and the dreamer is given every opportunity to do so.

Let us first consider a dream that was dreamed the night before the group met, from a dreamer who has not made reference to any recent happenings in his life. I like to begin the questioning by working backward, starting with the last thing the dreamer can remember before falling asleep. Not infrequently, this can provide an important clue. The question can be formulated in several ways:

"Do you remember the last thing you thought of before falling asleep?"

"Can you recall what was on your mind when you were in bed and about to fall asleep?"

"Can you recall what feelings you were left with at the end of the day and that remained with you as you fell asleep?"

Almost always, additional material comes forth. As you listen to the dreamer's response, it is important to give some thought to whether or not a follow-up question is indicated before going on to another line of inquiry. What are the indications for follow-up questions, and what purpose do they serve? Let us suppose that included in the dreamer's response to the initial question were the following observations:

"My mother called me last night."
"I watched a program on TV."
"I read for a while before falling asleep."

The dreamer has shared these facts with us. We don't know the significance of these facts. What we do know is that dreams don't come out of facts. They come out of the way facts make us feel. Let us focus on the first of these for a moment. In this case, then, a follow-up question would be this:

"Let's go back to this telephone call. Can you recall what feelings it left you with when it was over?"

We are staying with something opened up by the dreamer. Once a dreamer opens up an area we can, if it seems indicated, ask if there is anything more he wishes to say about it. There is nothing to lose and sometimes much to gain by asking if there is anything more. We follow rather than lead the dreamer: For example,

"Can you say something more than you have already said about feelings that call left you with?"

When the dreamer is given time to explore these feelings, important information may come out that immediately connects with the dream. Even if it doesn't, it is to be regarded as potentially important data that may fall into place at a later time. Here's another example along the same line:

"I watched a program on TV."

Follow-up questions might be these:

"Is there anything more you can say about the program or what feelings it left you with?"
"Did the program touch you in any way?"

One can watch television and have no particular emotions, or one can respond quite emotionally. It may set something going in the dreamer that he was hardly aware of and subsequently forgot, until our question brought him back to that earlier moment when he was watching the program. Another example:

"I read for a while before I fell asleep."

Again, further questioning is needed to see if that fact can be transformed into the feelings that accompanied it:

"Can you recall any particular reaction to what you were reading?"
"Did it leave you with any feelings when you finished?"

This kind of inquiry applies to all subsequent questions in the dialogue. It is important to complete any indicated follow-up before going on to the next question.

When the yield is meager up to this point—and even if it isn't—it can be helpful to question the dreamer further about the recent emotional context of his life. Questions such as the following are in order:

"As you look over all that you did yesterday (the day before the dream) does anything else come to mind that touched you emotionally, that left you with any particular feelings?"
"Did anything happen at work, in your private life recently, or was there anything you may have heard through the media that touched you?"

And finally, one might ask what I refer to as a general fishing question:

"As you look back over your life recently, is there anything else that occurs to you that you haven't yet mentioned that may have left you with any residual feelings?"

The importance of the recent emotional context of the dreamer's life in setting the stage for the nightly dream that ensues cannot be overemphasized. Here is an example.

The following dream depicts tensions felt by the dreamer in connection with her responsibility to organize and prepare for the dream group I was to lead the following day. She is a woman who held a high administrative position and who, at the time the group was to meet, was facing a number of oppressive personal and professional problems. The dream was short and is reproduced in its entirety.

The dream is just about a teapot, a large beige terra-cotta pot that holds enough for ten people. It was an amazing shape. (She later made a sketch of it, showing a decorative pattern of ten rectangular shapes

*about the top.) At first I did not like it. Then I found myself in the kitchen
of a little house on a moor. There was a very large woman in the kitchen
who exuded warmth. She offered me tea from this teapot. As the dream
went on, I saw the beauty of the teapot. I looked at it differently at the
end. I had the tea and woke up.*

The lady in the dream exuded a motherly feeling and at a later point in the
process was identified as her grandmother, whom she recalls with great
warmth. She spent a lot of time with her as a child: "She gave me space to
be myself."

The teapot was to provide for ten people, the exact number participating
in the dream group. Burdened down with certain administrative responsibilities and other issues in her life, the dreamer was not sure she could handle
it all. As she reflected on the image of the pot, her associations emphasized
its earthiness, its warmth. She felt it represented a "mothering principle" as
she recalled the strength she drew from her relationship with her grandmother. This in turn gave her the courage to enter an unfamiliar house on the
moor (the dream group) and to share her dream. She was in need of that
comfort and nurturing and drew on her earlier experience to provide it for
herself.

If this dream had been worked on at a later date, the relationship to the
immediate residues having to do with the dream group and other issues in
her life would most likely have been lost.

Problems

In a new group, there is an almost irresistible impulse in the dialogue to
go directly to the dream and to ask the dreamer about certain images in the
dream. It is hard to get across the idea that in this phase of the process we
are not directly concerned with the dream. Our aim is to reconstruct the
dreamer's private experience in its feeling aspects. Our hope, of course, is
that as she comes to these residues, connections to the dream will occur. We
use direct questions to bring the dreamer back to that experience. In the next
phase of the dialogue, we will use the elements of the dream to facilitate the
emergence of connections to the dreamer's life, present and past. Here, however, we are attempting to bring the dreamer back in time to the general tenor
of her life at the time of the dream's occurrence and to the specific preoccupations and feeling tones she took to bed that night.

This effort becomes more difficult the further back in time the dream occurred. It is important, however, to make the effort to help the dreamer bring back whatever she can from the period around the time of the dream. I have often been surprised at how much information can be recalled. One must use some judgment as to how specific one can be in questioning the dreamer when a dream is months or years old.

The most frequent problem is to fail to ask a follow-up question when one is indicated. It may take several follow-up questions before the dreamer can get to the heart of what a specific experience has meant to her. Intuition rather than rules provide the guide to when follow-up questions are indicated. At best we can point to certain general indications:

- When the dreamer refers to an incident with someone important in her life but hasn't gone beyond the bare facts
- When one detects a feeling tone in the dreamer's reference to a specific event without elaborating on it
- When a dreamer's response to a specific event seems confusing or inappropriate
- When one might expect more of a reaction to a specific event than the dreamer indicated

Failure to ask a follow-up question may be due to one of the following:

- Preoccupation with another question you wish to ask
- Interruption by someone else who has another question he wishes to put to the dreamer

What is the end point to follow-up questions? When do we stop and move on to a new question? The most satisfactory end point is when the follow-up questioning results in an obvious "Aha!" response, an awareness that something relevant has been uncovered. Short of this, we stop whenever the dreamer has nothing further to say.

There is one other important indication that no further questions along this line should be put to the dreamer. When we are about to ask a question relative to the response given by a dreamer, we have to first ask ourselves, "Are we being invited in further, or are we being invited out?" This, of course, depends on an intuitive sense that we may have touched on areas the dreamer prefers to keep private. If we are unsure whether this is so, we can check with the dreamer, saying something such as, "This may be something you prefer to keep private or work with on your own. This is your privilege and we can go on to other areas if you like."

In contrast to the failure to ask a follow-up question, the questioning can become too persistent, getting down to too much minutiae to the point of being repetitious and boring. This also can result in spending too much time on this part of the dialogue at the expense of the next two phases. In sum, questioning should be systematic, respectful of the dreamer's privacy, and not intrusive.

Issues

Awake, we do not think in the same metaphorical fashion as we do asleep. We do not ordinarily view our waking experience from the point of view of its potential for translation into visual metaphors. This presents us with a considerable gap between the way we are talking about ourselves asleep and the way we ordinarily experience ourselves awake. To help the dreamer bridge the gap between these two related but quite different forms of consciousness, he has to be helped to gather up all the possible relevant bits of information that can provide him with a clue. That clue comes in the form of a feeling, one that is recalled in the act of reconstructing his recent subjective experience. The dream image is the visual representation of that feeling, and its recognition as such sparks the recognition of the image as a metaphor. What then occurs is in accord with the power of metaphor to effect an emotional release of some kind. There is an expansive, opening up feeling, a sense that something has been made to fit in a puzzle of great interest to us.

Because the dreamer isn't thinking metaphorically while awake, he doesn't always know where to look for the missing pieces to the puzzle. It's as if he were working with a jigsaw puzzle with many pieces turned wrong side up. Our questions serve to turn the pieces right side up, thereby providing him with a greater opportunity to see how they fit together. Although there may be certain pieces he doesn't wish to turn over, in the main, this is not the problem. He needs our help in turning them over, not so much because he wishes not to but because he is unaware of where to look to find the pieces that should be turned over. The cooperative enterprise begun by the group and the dreamer is one of exposure and discovery in which the dreamer is a willing, curious, eager, and helpful partner. It is more truly seen in this light than in the usual dynamics of undoing repressions.

One cannot elicit the relevant components of the recent emotional residue by simply asking the dreamer what he thought the day residue was. It takes investigative effort to bring the dreamer close enough to the living feeling context of the period just before the dream. Skillful questioning is needed to re-create enough of the context to allow for this to happen.

Helpful Hints

A dreamer may awaken in the middle of the night, not recall a dream, go back to sleep, and recall a dream on awakening. Our task is to help her explore not only the feelings she went to bed with but also the feelings on awakening during the night, her reactions to not having a dream, and her thoughts and feelings on going back to sleep.

In the case of dreams months or years old, one can possibly provide a clue to the timing of the dream by asking,

"Do you recall whether or not it occurred around a holiday time? Or a family occasion of any kind?"

"Do you recall any general circumstances around the time of occurrence of the dream—for example, where you lived at the time, any important moves in your life at the time, and so on?"

In the dialogue, everyone should feel free to participate in the questioning. It is a good idea, however, for whoever initiates a question to be given the opportunity to ask any follow-up questions that may be indicated. After that, if someone else has a follow-up question in mind, he can then ask it.

The dialogue should be carried out in a lively way with the group's actively engaging the dreamer. This means that when a dreamer has been given all the time she needs and has finished her response, too long a time shouldn't elapse before the next question.

Remember that the questions are offered to the dreamer as instruments for her use in her search for relevant data. That kind of inward searching requires time. Not infrequently, when a question is first put to a dreamer, her immediate answer may be, "No, nothing occurs to me." That, in fact, may be the only answer. If you observe the dreamer closely, however, you may detect signs that she hasn't let go of the question and is still mulling it over. If, indeed, this is happening, it is important to recognize it and not allow any interruptions to occur or further questions to be asked until one gets a second—and this time, a clear—signal that the dreamer has completed her response. That quiet period can be most productive, ending with the dreamer's unexpectedly coming up with much new information. It simply took time for the dreamer to get in touch with it. When any of us are asked a question, we feel called on to give an immediate answer. In dream work, when an immediate answer may not be on hand, the dreamer is apt to reply in the negative. A "no" answer in this case often does mean, "No, I don't know at the moment, but if you give me time I'll look for an answer." Using the question you put to her, the dreamer then goes to work.

Bear in mind that in a new group a dreamer may need to be reminded of his rights. For a member new to the process, it may be helpful to offer the reminder that the primary purpose of the questioning is as a stimulus to self-discovery and that he is under no obligation to share everything that occurs to him. The freedom to share is contingent on the degree of trust and comfort the dreamer feels in the group. Of course, the more the dreamer can share, the more help the group can be. Openness pays dividends in dream work, but it has to come naturally. It can't be forced. A cautious attitude on the part of a dreamer has to be accepted by the group even though it may result in a feeling of disappointment because of the limitation it places on the group's ability to help the dreamer.

Before leaving this phase of the dialogue, be sure that in addition to asking the routine questions about the recent life experience of the dreamer, any allusions to recent experience touched on by the dreamer in her initial response (Stage 3A) have been picked up and explored. The dreamer, for example, may have made mention of a particular friend who had been on her mind or a movie she'd seen several days before that stayed with her. She may have made passing reference to an incident that occurred the day before the dream but not have thought it important enough to mention when questioned about her activities on that day.

Finally, keep in mind that the various phases of the dialogue are not automatically evoked. They are fall-back strategies to be engaged in only if the dreamer wishes to go further. At the end of this phase of the dialogue, the leader checks in with the dreamer for a decision as to whether or not to continue.

An Illustrative Session

In the following account of a session, the section having to do with the search for the recent emotional context of the dream is italicized. Had this dream been worked on weeks or months after it occurred, much of the recent context would have been lost.

Michael is a young man with AIDS who has been in the group for several months. The dream occurred on the night of the prior session of the group a week earlier. True names are used at the dreamer's request.

Stage 1A: The Dream Is Shared

There is a beautiful bird. The wings are silvery and trimmed in blue. There is also some red and black and yellow. No one color predomi-nates. The combination of the colors and the gracefulness of its flight make the bird an exquisite beauty. Everyone around (vaguely, some people from work) is impressed with its beauty.

I watch her flight and I'm very anxious. Very suddenly, she drops straight down (as if shot, but she wasn't shot) from a real height, landing in a sitting or nesting position. Just plops on the grass.

I notice she looks kind of fat. In fact, she looks more like a plump chick with a lot of bright yellow down on her belly. The bird spontane-ously lays two eggs, one after the other. She was pregnant. Among others, Laura and David are there, and somehow there is a connection between them and the bird's getting pregnant. They're taking credit for it, in a largehearted kind of way, beaming. My old very good feelings about Laura return.

Stage 1B: The Dream Is Clarified

Michael identified the people in the dream: Laura is a former student and then colleague of his, and David is her fiancé. Michael also added that, in his dream, he (Michael) was very impressed with the colors of the bird.

Stage 2A: The Group Shares Feelings

"I want to fly free as a bird."

"I have the same feeling of freedom I had in reading *Jonathan Livingston Seagull*."

"There is something magnificent about a bird. I would like to be a bird in a future life."

"I feel responsible for the bird."

"I'm angry at the bird. She can fly out the window and I can't."

"I really want it and am frightened when it went away."

"I am concerned over its life cycle. First there is the beauty of the bird, then the laying of eggs. That's what life's all about."

"Only a young chick has down and yet she is pregnant."

"I feel flight. I feel like taking off."

"I'm puzzled because it's usually the male bird that has the bright colors."

Stage 2B: Meanings Are Offered

"The bird can stand for spirit or soul."

"The bird is an aspect of myself that wants to escape."

"My dream reminds me of Icarus flying high and then falling to earth."

"The bird may be my colorful imagination."

"The colors represent highlights of my life."

"The eggs give me a sense of life continuing."

"Birds are beautiful and sing, but they are elusive. You can't communicate with them."

"The bird may be a parrot, and that brings in the idea of parroting."

"In my dream, there seems to be some gender confusion."

"My bird has been helped to grow up and is now launched."

"I can't understand how Laura and David managed to get the bird pregnant."

Stage 3A: Michael's Response

"The most important thing for me was that the bird was going to survive. The bird looked like one from these parts except for its incredible colors. Since the bird was very delicate, I was very protective. You're right about the sense of freedom. Its flight was so graceful you just had to look at it. In the dream, it does seem to change from an it to a she. When she dropped down, I was afraid something awful would happen. Her appearance changed. She was fat, and two eggs came out. She was like an Easter chick.

"Laura and David are a happy young couple I know. The wedding is in October, and Rafael, my partner, and I are both invited. There are some old feelings connected with Laura. For a few years, we were very close. I was a mentor for her and helped her to be open to her spiritual side. Our times together seemed to help temper her very strong materialistic values. Since she became aware of my illness, it seems like she has been pulling back. Our closeness has diminished. Yet I remember how very wonderful and close our old feelings were. I feel neglected by her. I want to confront her with my feelings. I'm having trouble connecting this with the dream.

"I remember what happened the night of the dream. A call came through at midnight from the doctor who takes care of Rafael, saying that the biopsy showed something serious, something life threatening, a form of tuberculosis. The doctor said he would have to get intravenous antibiotics immediately. It made me terribly upset. I didn't tell Rafael until the morning. When I did tell him, he said he felt like a Mack truck had hit him. He was hospitalized. He was awfully sick and delirious. I was in a state of tension and worry. I feared the worst and was anticipating loss. I felt in limbo. Perhaps it's the anxiety I felt in the dream about the bird.

"The eggs were a good omen, a very potent symbol. Birds do represent spirit. It was so beautiful. Its beauty could reach into the soul. Meditation and getting in touch with spirit is important to me. But my anxiety still snowballed. In the dream, the bird survives. I'm torn by the fear she won't survive. I feel responsible.

"There is a feeling of androgyny about the bird. I'm happy about the eggs. I feel like parents do beaming over a newborn. It was certainly my bird. I felt strongly connected to it and so impressed with its beauty.

"Laura is a person with a great deal of inner beauty. Her fiancé is a real dream of a guy, well-rounded, genuine, and decent."

Stage 3B.1: Amplifying the Recent Context

Michael welcomed the dialogue, the opening phase of which is to further explore the recent thoughts and feelings that led to the dream. He had earlier made reference to the dramatic events of the night before so that in questioning from the group very little more came out. He did say more about the disturbing telephone call and how shaken he was by it. He hardly slept that night. The only other thing he brought out was a loving and supportive conversation he had had with a woman friend of his.

Stage 3B.2: Playing the Dream Back

Michael invited the playback. The dream was read aloud by one member of the group to the end of the second paragraph. Michael added the following:

"Blue is my favorite color. The combination of blue and silver stands out. Now I recall there was a blue car in the dream parked in my parents' driveway close to their home."

The remainder of the dream was read back:

"She (the bird) looked so beautiful and free, but I'm aware of feeling anxious. That's the way I felt that night. The fall was very strange. It looked like a dangerous fall, but she survived and was productive. Her pregnancy and the two eggs were good omens. With regard to Laura and David, I feel good about their happiness together. My partner and I had thoughts about being a twosome and of parenting with a couple of female friends and living in a collective together. This is no longer a possibility."

Question Anything more about Laura and David being the parents in the dream?

Response It was a nice feeling seeing them. They made a happy and successful union as I believe my partner and I do. All four of us come from very different backgrounds.

Stage 3B.3: Michael Invites the Orchestration

An orchestrating comment by one member of the group called the dreamer's attention to an earlier shared dream of his that involved a plane going down and that turned out to be a dream of resurrection.

In my orchestration, I likened the sudden fall of the bird to the impact of the unexpected midnight telephone call and the suddenness of the felt sense of the imminent loss of his partner. It was as if he had a "bird in hand" and was about to lose it. The dream ends with the fantasy hope that his life with his partner will continue and get to the point where their union will be as happy and productive as that of Laura and David. The practice of meditation and the dream work he was doing were both necessary to keep his own "spirit" soaring.

Michael's final comment:

"The work here has helped me to experience and behold the beauty in my life."

Stage 4: The Follow-Up

Subsequent to the session in which the dream was presented, Michael offered the following with the group the next week:

"Bird is spirit. The spirit of the relationship between Rafael and me. I think of our relationship because it is like a bird of many colors and have often envisioned ourselves as, indeed, many many colors coming together. So many colors, a union of many opposites: white and brown, Puerto Rican and Irish-German, Catholic and Communist, middle class and working class, inner city and suburban, introvert and extrovert, lover of poetry and dance, and lover of music and architecture . . . finally, lovers of each other.

"The silver of the wings tells me something of the preciousness of the relationship, tempered by blue, some felt sadness due to the loss of friends. The red, of course, is passion and the fire within. The black has been the facing of our own darkness, whereas the yellow symbolizes our inner light.

"The people in the dream who are watching the bird are our many friends who hold us up as role models, in a manner of speaking, for a successful relationship.

"The car is a cage, symbolizing perhaps the restrictions we have placed on ourselves in the last couple of years of high stress. Showing less affection has been one restriction. Illness is also part of the cage. The caged bird, of course, won't sing and seeks a liberation.

"Bird is freedom. Being in my parents' driveway is significant on a few levels. Literally, the very few times Rafael and I were ever together in my parents' home, we felt *very* restricted. And freedom was always a major theme in my life—one way I found it: being-in-relationship. More figuratively, the driveway symbolizes the entry into something 'close-to-home,' close to my heart, indicating an issue of great importance.

"The sudden fall is the urgent telephone call from Rafael's doctor and the impending hospitalization. Will the relationship survive the fall? She just plops on the grass. This is the first clue as to survival. The grass—feeling the earth, nature, our groundedness.

"The transformation from the slender, beautiful bird of colors to a fat, yellow, downy-feathered chick makes me think of Easter and resurrection. What looks like could be certain death instead results in new life. The two eggs symbolize Rafael and myself and a completely new phase of our relationship. Potential. They also suggest a time of fragility.

"Laura and David, another admired, successful relationship, indeed another true union of opposites, symbolize that part of us that is happy, youthful, and keeps our dreams for the future alive. These are the parts of ourselves we especially need to nurture in order both to survive and to enter this new phase of our development. The 'old very good feelings' about Laura symbolize revitalization.

"Some of the group's initial comments included, 'I love this bird'; 'the bird is very strong'; 'the eggs indicate life is continuing.'

"Bird of spirit, of freedom, of beauty and survival. I am left with two questions.

"What (life) is inside of those eggs?

"When are they going to hatch?"

6

■

Stage 3B.2

Playback:
The Dream Itself

The point of the playback is the same as the search for context—namely, to elicit more data from the dreamer and thus facilitate more felt connections to the dream. The way we now go about doing it, however, is quite different. The dream itself, rather than any direct questions, becomes the instrument. The following instructions are given to the dreamer:

> The dream will be read back to you one scene at a time. This may very well jog your memory a bit. You are invited to take a second look at the scene and all the images in it to see if there is more you can say about it. As you work once more with the imagery you have at your disposal, keep in mind all that you shared in your initial response when we returned the dream to you and the additional information you made available as we helped you reconstruct your recent life experience. The idea is for you to play the imagery back against all that you have brought out to see if any further associations occur to you. The question you might begin asking yourself as you listen is, "Why did I choose just those images the night of the dream?"

You are not being asked to repeat anything you have already said but only to see if there is more you can say. Whoever reads the scene back to you will first read the scene in its entirety. After you have responded to that, specific images in the scene will be called to your attention if you have not yet addressed them or to see if there may be more you can say about them. Don't be concerned if you can't. There is always the chance that more may occur to you as we get into subsequent scenes.

In an effort to be of help, whoever reads the dream back to you may refresh your memory of what you have already said about a particular image, in the hope that it may stimulate you to say more. Feel free to take whatever time you need to gather your thoughts.

The Safety Factor

The Dreamer's Bill of Rights is fully operative. The dreamer remains in control of what is shared with the group.

The Discovery Factor

The dreamer now has more information to work with than when the dream was first returned to him. On that basis alone, this second look tends to be more productive. There is another factor operating here that isn't obvious but is of great importance. Notice that in the playback, we are not asking the dreamer to play the scene back silently to himself. Instead, the scene is repeated out loud by another person. Confronting a dreamer with his own dream in this way can have a powerful impact. It concretizes the dream. It makes it more real. The dream becomes something "out there," separate and apart from the dreamer. The difference between hearing the dream in this way and just thinking about it to oneself is analogous to the difference in feeling between stroking one's own skin and having someone to whom you are sexually attracted stroke it. The same touch receptors are involved, but there is quite a difference in the way it is experienced! In the case of the dream, were the dreamer to do it alone, there might be a tendency to skim over or discount certain details. This is the result of unconscious judgments we tend to make when left to our own devices as we look at the dream from the waking state. When someone else renders the dream, a neutrality enters into it that can work against any biases on the part of the dreamer. He is presented with what he created, and the dream is now experienced with a greater sense of reality.

The Technique of the Playback

There is a technique to reading a scene back to the dreamer. When you read a dream back, you are actively confronting the dreamer with its drama and mystery. A bit of that sense of drama and mystery has to enter into the way it's played back. A simple monotonous repetition of the bare details is to be avoided. The one reading the dream back becomes an actor or actress reading lines that he or she hasn't written but reading them with feeling and with regard for their dramatic potential. The dreamer related the dream in the first person. When the dream is read back, however, substitute "you" for "I" and address the dreamer directly. You can take certain liberties with the text of the dream as given, as long as you don't omit any details and don't stray from what the dream is saying. Any amplification is only for the purpose of highlighting, emphasizing, pointing up incongruities, underlining the imagery that has not yet been considered by the dreamer, and in general, respecting the quality of mystery that is so much a part of the dream.

In initiating the playback, the group itself has to keep in mind all that a dreamer has thus far shared. This will vary a great deal. In some instances, the dreamer in her response may have attempted to address all the images. In other cases, she may have made very little mention of the dream. When a dreamer has said a good bit about the images, it may help to call attention briefly to what has been said before embarking on the playback to stress the fact that the dreamer is not being asked to repeat anything. When some of the specific images are brought to the dreamer's attention and nothing else comes to mind or when the response falls short of clarifying the connection of the image to her life, it may be of help to remind the dreamer of what she has already specifically said about that particular image. Sometimes, it helps to recapitulate all of the details in the dream related to that image. A reminder that the imagery was triggered by recent late events may also jog loose further associations.

Anyone in the group may initiate the playback. It is better if the one who has read the scene back is also the one to initiate the exploration of the specific images in that scene. When that person has gone as far as she can, then others may have further questions they wish to put to the dreamer. Sometimes, the way the dreamer talks about an image or sequence of events in the dream appears to bear no relationship to the way the image is used in the dream or what the sequence appears to be saying. It soon becomes evident that what the dreamer is saying doesn't seem to relate to what is going on in the dream. This should be called to the dreamer's attention: "But in the dream it didn't happen in the way you have just described it." Or, "The feeling about that image in the dream was quite different from the way you are talking about it now." In other words, the dream is our instrument, and we use what occurred in the dream as a way of helping the dreamer keep the associations on track. We are responsible for confronting the dreamer with the entire content of the dream. The dreamer can manage that confrontation any way she pleases, but it is up to the group to make every effort to help her work with the dream as she dreamed it.

It is helpful to point out to the dreamer that, although the dream sequences may seem very disparate and not connected in any logical way, they do represent a further development of both feeling and content of what went before. The story initiated in one scene is further developed in the next scene, even though the sequences show no obvious or logical connection to the earlier one. The connection is at a feeling level.

The decision as to what constitutes a scene may present a problem. Usually, the scenes in a dream are clearly demarcated. Not infrequently, the dreamer in reporting a dream will say, "Then the scene suddenly shifts." The only other guideline is to think of it in terms of what constitutes a unit of action in the dream. In general, it is better to take bites that are too long rather than too short. The scenes should be taken up in their proper sequence. This creates the possibility that the associations elicited in one scene provide the dreamer with more information with which to work in the subsequent scene. The dreamer, of course, is always free to jump ahead to later scenes as connections spontaneously occur to her.

Problems

We have indicated some of the areas where problems may arise. If the scene is read back to the dreamer without expression, without highlighting the still unclarified images, it will have more of a soporific than a stimulating effect. If the segment taken to be played back is too small, it may leave the dreamer with too little to work with. If it's too big, it may be too much for the dreamer to handle all at once. If the leader doesn't caution the dreamer against repetition, the dreamer may feel called on to offer the same associations he gave earlier.

Inexperienced leaders do have difficulty going for the specifics. That means helping the dreamer say as much as he can about every image and going after details that may seem minor or trivial to an outside observer. One has to strike a balance between confronting the dreamer with all that is in the dream in as complete a way as possible and, on the other hand, wearing the dreamer out with questions. Insensitive persistence is counterproductive.

I mentioned earlier that in the playback, one can try to stimulate the dreamer's thoughts about a particular image (if none come spontaneously) by referring back to what the dreamer has already said about the image. If this is done, it should be in as neutral a way as possible. That means including all the dreamer has said about that image without giving undue weight to any one association. If, instead, you select or emphasize one thing at the expense of another, the dreamer may experience this as your trying to lead him in a particular direction. This tends to occur when someone in the group feels that the dreamer's associations have clarified the meaning of an image without the dreamer himself being aware of it. Aside from whether the group member's assumption is correct or not, it is a practice to be avoided. Were it to persist, it would move the process in the direction of group members' attempts to make more and more connections, albeit indirectly, instead of focusing exclusively on deepening the dreamer's own associative range. There is a time in the final phase of the dialogue when such connections can be directly offered for the dreamer's consideration.

Perhaps the most common error is failure to bring the dreamer back to what the dream is saying. A dreamer may feel satisfied in the way he has handled a particular scene, but if what he says is at variance with what is taking place in that scene, then that discrepancy has to be called to his attention. The dream is the only instrument the group has, and it has to be used effectively. A dreamer may be seduced by rationalizations that have a certain intellectual appeal but that do not capture either the feeling or the content of a particular scene. Bringing him back to the dream keeps the dreamer honest.

Issues

The way in which we concretize the dream by playing it back to the dreamer puts the dreamer into quite a different relationship to it than she was before. It is as if the dream once again takes on a life of its own, but this time as a social event, known to others as well as the dreamer. Much to the dreamer's surprise, this new way of experiencing the dream produces new insights. It is not uncommon to hear something such as this after the dreamer has responded with a fresh insight: "I don't think it would have occurred to me if you hadn't read it back in the way you did." Reading the dream back in a way that emphasizes its special features as a dream—that is, its original and dramatic content—deepens the dreamer's own appreciation of the dream and, with that, intensifies her interest in and openness to it.

The playback produces more data. The way has been prepared for this to happen by all that has gone before. When the dream was returned to the dreamer at the end of the second stage, she was given all the time she needed to thoughtfully bring together her spontaneous associations. She was further helped with the insights she gained from the greater clarity about the emotional context of her life at the time of the dream through the questions put to her in the first phase of the dialogue. Finally, she was helped to experience the dream in a fresh new light by the way it was read back to her.

As more and more data emerge, the likelihood is that the dreamer will begin to make connections between her waking life and her nocturnal reflections of that life depicted by the imagery she created. This way of proceeding fosters a dependency not on an external authority who, in some mysterious way, knows how to interpret a dream but on what the dreamer herself can salvage from the information she put into the dream at the time she dreamed it. The dreamer becomes attuned to the fact that the answers lie within and that, given the proper instruments to work with, she can get at the information she needs. Dream work is demystified. It remains work but without superimposed authority of any kind.

Hints

In a new group, you, as the leader, will have to do a good deal of modeling to get across to the group how a scene is read back, how specific images in that scene are further developed, when and how to ask follow-up questions, how to determine what constitutes a scene, how to stimulate the dreamer's associations by reference to material brought out earlier, how to help the dreamer work back from a feeling expressed in a dream to the source of that feeling in waking life and, in general, how to help a dreamer discover why that particular dream was dreamed on that particular night.

In an ongoing group, the playback is the responsibility of the entire group. It is up to the leader to encourage others to undertake that responsibility and to guide them in learning how to do it. It may take very active modeling to bring a group to the point where the playback can be handled skillfully. The strange, incongruous twists and turns in a dream, the subtlety of expression of feeling, the potential significance of seemingly minor details, the punning that may be connected with names or words that appear in the dream, the possible significance of characters, known and unknown in the dream as well as the incongruities in their appearance, all have to be gotten across to the dreamer by the person reading back the dream. This is a way to orient a dreamer to the task he faces and a way to provide as much help as possible as he tackles it.

Sometimes, it can be helpful to the dreamer to view the dream as a drama in which there is an opening scene that sets the issue he faces, a middle section that explores the issue in its connections to the past and its implications for the future, and a final act in which there is some attempt at resolution based on what light has been shed on the interplay of both resources and vulnerabilities.

At the end of the playback, the dreamer may very well have a sense of closure and feel content to stop at this point. The leader will check in with the dreamer to see if this is so or if the dreamer would like to go further and invite the next phase of the dialogue—the orchestration.

An Illustrative Session

Lila's Dream

In the dream to follow, the group's projections in Stage 2 were not recorded. Those that had meaning for the dreamer were incorporated into her response and are represented by bold italics. The playback itself is italicized.

Lila, a young woman who had been in the group for several years, presented the following dream, which occurred on a Sunday night. The group worked with the dream the following Thursday.

I remember being in an outdoor plaza with a female friend of mine. We go into a restaurant that has a gargantuan screen like a video or movie screen. It seems translucent. Daylight comes through it. There are waves of increasing intensity crashing against the back of it. We can see them through the screen. Along with the visual impact, there are auditory acoustical effects; in fact, it involves all the senses so that you know they are real waves and not something on video. It is a tidal wave.

Then we start to feel a rumbling as if the wave is shaking the foundation. I'm terrified. Yet we are just sitting there at lunch and having a normal conversation while this is going on. I'm trying to be calm and pretend it doesn't affect me that much.

I calmly say to my friend—'Oh, that's a tsunami. Do you know what that means?' I do this in an attempt to appear really calm. It is calming for me to talk this way.

The plaza in the dream was real. It had a garden and was located near where Lila lived. She was aware in the dream that *tsunami* referred to a tidal wave. She believes the friend with her was a woman named Lucy.

Stage 3A: Lila's Response

"I came across this word tsunami at work the previous Tuesday and looked it up. It refers to a huge wave brought about by an underwater volcanic eruption.

"What was said about *the idea of hanging on to what you know when you don't know what is really happening* struck me as very important. Saying that word tsunami was like an anchor. It was as if it were a magic word. I love playing with words. They are alive. I do copyediting and proofreading and I really love it.

"Another thing that struck me was the remark about *feminine energy* (someone likened the tidal wave to feminine energy). Lucy is a good friend as well as a coworker. She had me to dinner several months ago, and we had a fascinating conversation in which she gave me some insights about myself. What she said was amazing. It started me looking back over my life, going all the way back. It was very powerful, thought provoking, and intriguing.

"I had a bad flu the week before the dream and was very sick. I tried to go back to work and couldn't. On Sunday, I started to feel a little bit better. I spent that day with my boyfriend. We visited his parents whom I love. That night was very unusual because I didn't do very much. I know I was concerned about my apartment and the decision whether or not to buy it or go on renting. I was thinking of how I'd renovate it if it were mine.

"I was also thinking of my future. When you're sick, you sort of feel like taking stock. Then there were the ongoing themes in my life. I think a lot about what's happening now in Communist countries. I feel an overwhelming kinship to people fighting for their freedom. This is very important to me. I always hoped this would come to happen.

"I have a constant awareness that life is very short. It is so precious and so fragile. That's like the foundation being shaken."

Lila invited the dialogue.

Stage 3B.1: Amplifying the Recent Context

Question Can you say more about the visit?

Response It's always wonderful. They treat me like a daughter. My parents died many years ago. My mother was my best friend. I lost her when I was 20. My boyfriend's father knows of my interest in words and saves words for me. On Friday night, I picked up a screenplay I was to edit. I had an interesting meeting with the author. We discussed religion. I was concerned with when I'd get to do the editing. Also thinking of getting the ball rolling again at work, being out a week.

Question Anything more about your boyfriend?

Response He wants to live with me. I like my freedom and independence. I'm happy with the situation as it is. I don't know where the fear is coming from. At some level, there is the fear of losing him. If I lose him, I also lose my "family." There is also the ongoing fear of losing the place I live in. I had a talk with the landlord just before the dream.

Stage 3B.2: Lila Invites the Playback

The first scene, the setting of the dream was read back, ending with "daylight came through it [the movie screen]":

"The plaza part is almost identical with the area near my house. I go there a lot. It's one of my favorite places. When I'm there, I feel very happy."

Question *Anything about Lucy's being in the dream?*

Lila had nothing to add at this point.

Question *The screen?*

Response *As someone said, it feels like a giant barrier. I can see through it. It was like the Berlin Wall. Simultaneously, I was able to see the wall of defenses while at the same time using it, my defenses, to overcome something equal in force to my ability to fight.*

Question *Think of Lucy's appearance in the dream either in terms of any feeling about her or what she might mean in your life (coming back* *to the image of Lucy in an effort to help her see various ways of thinking about it—for example, literally or as an aspect of herself.)*

Response *She is very loving. I enjoy talking to her. She loves words in the same way I do. She is an outstandingly good writer and a very spiritual person. I love and admire her. The only thing I don't feel good about Lucy is that she is in an unhappy marriage.*

The remainder of the dream was then read back to Lila. Her first comment (not at all unusual in dream work) was that she had nothing more to add. She paused for a moment and then began to talk about what turned out to be powerful and revealing feelings:

"There is in me a terror of losing my new family and my boyfriend (again a pause) . . . except that the terror I felt in the dream was more like the terror I felt at losing my real mother. Maybe the dream is showing me how powerful it could be if something does go wrong and I lost them. It hasn't occurred to me as a real possibility. As someone said, in life sometimes something can happen that suddenly changes everything."

Stage 3B.3: Lila Invites the Orchestration

Several helpful points were made by members of the group about Lila's concern with maintaining her freedom at the risk of losing the boyfriend and the newly found sense of belonging to a family.

My own orchestrating comments are given as nearly as I could reconstruct them. Although they were built on the basis of what Lila shared that evening, there was added emphasis on the impact of her mother's death based on the work she had done on earlier dreams:

The dream seems to reflect a deep sense of crisis, arising in connection with the challenge you are now experiencing to your current lifestyle with its emphasis on being independent and completely free to make your own choices. The appearance of the plaza seems to epitomize that lifestyle, a lifestyle in which you are completely free to do the things that give you joy. The question is why should that lifestyle be threatened by a loving relationship and a loving family coming into your life? The only way to understand this is to go back to the loss of your mother and the terror you spoke of in connection with that loss. It's as if your passionate concern with the issue of personal freedom and an independent lifestyle (feelings that emerged through earlier work with dreams in the group) was your way of protecting yourself against ever experiencing that kind of terror again. It resulted in seeing relationships as constraining (as in the case of Lucy) and hence making you shy away from permanent commitments. So many feelings came together to play into this dilemma. You had a particularly loving time with your boyfriend and newly formed family, a family you found congenial in every way, even down to your interest in words. The issue was joined when your boyfriend indicated he felt it was time for you to live together.

You raised the issue of the Berlin Wall and the deep meaning the struggle for freedom of people in Eastern Europe had for you. It is as if you had fought hard for the personal freedom you had achieved in your life. The foundation of that lifestyle was being shaken by powerful instinctual forces beating against the barrier of defenses. For the first time, the hidden forces have become visible. The barrier is transparent. Your only way of coping with it seems to be a desperate effort to appear calm by invoking the magic you attach to words and knowledge.

Lila was visibly moved. She became tearful. At the end, she asked me how I could have known from the dream and the work done with it that she was protecting herself through her lifestyle. "It's incredible, and I am shocked that you were able to deduce that from one dream. I'm very grateful. I don't want to repeat the devastation I once felt. That was the ultimate devastation."

I went over the highlights of what she had shared to show her in her own words how she, step by step, had led the way herself to this conclusion. Her bout with the flu had, in a timely fashion, given her pause to reflect on her life as had the recent meeting with her friend Lucy. That day she had felt a stronger pull to find the right family for herself than she had ever felt before. It had set in motion a powerful force, a tsunami, that was threatening to overwhelm a lifestyle characterized by her ideal of personal freedom, an ideal that left no room for commitment to another.

She was mystified by the dream before presenting it. Much that came out of the group's early projections began to stir things up. She became aware of the feeling of threatening forces within her that she had long since lost sight of. As a very self-possessed person, the recent illness, falling behind at work, and the anxiety about the apartment all played into feelings of vulnerability.

In the first part of the dialogue, the recent context was further elaborated, emphasizing the extent to which she felt accepted as a daughter by her boyfriend's parents and delighted by the way they responded to her own intellectual interests. She brought out the critical fact that her boyfriend confronted her by saying it was now time for them to live together. There was not a happy response forthcoming from her. Instead, it made her aware of how precious and important her personal freedom was and how happy she would be to simply go along as they had been. She felt fear—the fear of losing and the fear of upsetting her present equilibrium.

The playback sharpened her insights. She became aware that she resorted to the same defenses in combating the threat as were under attack by the threat. She herself referred to those defenses as her intellectual ability and her knowledge—for example, the meaning of the word tsunami.

Most important, in connection with the playback, was the dawning insight that behind the current concern about the possible loss of her new family was a far deeper and far more painful fear connected with the loss of her mother.[1]

There is another point of interest in connection with the playback. The first time she was questioned about Lucy, nothing occurred to her. Only after she was helped to think about her feelings about Lucy were relevant connections made. Here is someone who in many ways was an idealized mirror image of herself, except for one thing. Lucy's life was constrained by a bad marriage.

The question arises, did I "hit the nail on the head," as Lila subsequently remarked about the orchestration, because I fell back on psychoanalytic expertise, or is this way of putting things together a teachable skill? My experience does count for something, but there is nothing mysterious at work. With experience, one learns how to help the dreamer come to and share the relevant information. One learns how to listen to the feeling accompaniments of the information and how to extract what seems to be the underlying theme that ties things together. It does take experience to get to the point where things do fall into place and where the orchestrating projection is on target. No matter how forthcoming a dreamer may be, it is in the nature of dream work that a final integration made by others, offered as their projection, is more often than not the final touch in disposing of any remaining discomfort should the dream still elude her after so much effort has been put into it.

Comment

It is hard to convey the deeply felt impact that the work had on Lila and the gradual and incremental way in which sufficient information emerged to lay the groundwork for the imagery to come to life against the backdrop of life events in so powerfully dramatic a way. Here is a woman who has prided herself on her ability to maintain a highly independent lifestyle, free to pursue her own interests, able to give generously of herself to others in their struggle to be free of their own historically engendered burdens, and yet possessed of a deep wariness when it comes to the issue of a close relationship leading to a long-term commitment to a man she feels she loves very much.

A general point of interest illustrated in this dream is the way we harbor seemingly minor items of daily experience until the time is ripe to realize in a dream their metaphorical potential. The encounter with the word tsunami and its meaning were in her head for some time before its appearance in the dream. Only the special concatenation of events transformed that memory into the powerful metaphorical meaning it carried in the dream—the magic power of her intellectual curiosity and the satisfaction it gave her on the one hand and, on the other, how impotent it might prove to be in the face of the reality behind the word.

Sometimes, what is most puzzling to a dreamer is the discrepancy between the mood the night of the dream and the feelings described in the dream. This was illustrated earlier in another of Lila's dreams. She had just left her job to become a freelancer. Her presleep mood was one of excitement and exhilaration at the freedom this offered. In the dream, she found herself in a hotel room with a man. "I was terrified. My fear was that I had stupidly gotten myself into a very dangerous situation. I would end up being assaulted and raped." The dreamer was puzzled by the unexpected terror and desperation that she felt in the dream. This is a woman torn between commitment to a relationship with a man and her compelling need to pursue her own career free of any constraints, real or imagined. The upsurge of freedom she felt in undertaking freelance work touched off hidden fears she was beginning to experience in a relationship that was becoming more and more serious.

Note

1. She added this at the time she reviewed the dream for publication: "I later realized something significant. My mother was born in Germany (as were my grandparents). Freedom for her country is something I wish she could have lived to see. This is very powerful for me."

7
■

Stage 3B.3 and Stage 4

Orchestration—Harmonizing Image and Reality—and Follow-Up

Definitions

I use the term *orchestration* to refer to the effort by the group members to organize the associative material given to them by the dreamer in a way that offers a more focused sense of what a dream may be saying about the dreamer's life. It is an attempt to bring image and reality together in their metaphorical unity. It may be complete or partial. A *complete orchestration* is one that tackles the dream as a whole in an effort to reveal the metaphorical logic of the images and of the sequential way in which they unfold. A *partial orchestration* is one that limits itself to one or more images rather than working with the entire dream.

By the time the playback has been completed and all the relevant questions have been asked and answered to the extent they can be, the dreamer may, and usually does, know a great deal more about the dream than she did before. There may even be a sense of closure at this point. More often than not, there is more work to be done. Data elicited in the first two phases of the dialogue may emerge in too random a way for the overall meaning to become apparent. Connections made by the dreamer are in turn sporadic and leave too many gaps to be bridged. Something more is needed. That something is the orchestration. At the request of the dreamer, group members are invited to offer the connections they see between the images in the dream and those aspects of the dreamer's life that have been shared. Orchestration seems an appropriate metaphor because what is attempted is to separate the melody from the cacophony of sounds that have filled the air. The group member becomes the conductor at this point but uses only the notes supplied by the composer-dreamer. The unusual arrangement he comes up with may or may not be the music the composer had in mind. She may have used the notes to create a different melody, which is why the connections offered by the group members are always considered as their orchestrating projections unless validated by the dreamer. The intent is to order the associative data (the notes) presented by the dreamer in a way that gives metaphorical meaning to the imagery (the melody). The imagery is made to stand out more sharply and dramatically in its possible connection to the life of the dreamer.

In Stage 2, we offer our projections without knowing the relevant life context of the dreamer. They are truly our projections, which we offer to each other while the dreamer listens and assesses their fit. By the time we get to the orchestration, we know something about the life context of the dreamer. In this third and last phase of the dialogue, we assume that the dreamer has shared all she can or wishes to at the moment. Our job now is not to seek further information but to use what has already been given, to work with it and attempt to pull things together. If we do it successfully, we accomplish two goals. We help the dreamer see more deeply into the nature and source of her own behavior. We are at the same time conveying to the dreamer that she has been heard, that what she has had to say has been taken seriously and used productively.

This phase of the dialogue begins with the answer to two questions: Is an orchestration needed? If so, does the dreamer want it? The answer to the first question is generally obvious. The dreamer may have acknowledged certain gains but continues to be puzzled by various parts of the dream or by the dream as a whole. There are clues that point to the need for orchestration. The dreamer may repeat herself or appear to be stuck. The point has been reached where further questioning is counterproductive and where the need now is for an effort at integration. The answer to the second question depends on her wishes. Let us assume that the answer is yes.

Instructions to the Group Members

As you listened to all that the dreamer shared with us, you may have developed some idea of the metaphorical meaning embedded in the imagery. If you feel the dreamer hasn't yet seen connections that have occurred to you, now would be the time for you to offer them to the dreamer as your orchestrating or integrating projections. You are sharing what you feel are connections between what the dreamer has said and the way they are being represented metaphorically in the imagery of the dream. They are offered as your projections because they are and remain your projections, unless they have felt meaning for the dreamer. It is you who select certain things from all you heard the dreamer say, and it is you who are making the connections to the dream. All this is filtered through your psyche, and so it is to be considered as your projection unless validated by the dreamer. In trying to do this, you may address any image in the dream, any group of images or the dream in its entirety. You don't have to put it in the form of a question, but it is to be considered as a question to the dreamer.

In formulating your orchestrating projection, you must base it only on what information has been provided by the dreamer and not on ideas of your own that open up areas not touched on by the dreamer. The principle of following, not leading, the dreamer is as important here as it was in the previous parts of the dialogue. This can be a hard limit to set for yourself. You are being asked to use your imagination to come up with something new that can be helpful to the dreamer, but that something must be implicit somewhere in all that has gone before. It isn't that you would necessarily be wrong in overstepping that mark, but it would be inappropriate for this process. You are not being given free reign to express your ideas about the dream. You are being asked to help in fleshing out the metaphorical potential of someone else's dream, based on information you have been given by that person.

Address your orchestrating projection directly to the dreamer. Working with both context and image, our projection now has a greater chance of reflecting back to the dreamer something about the dream that she missed. As in the case of our earlier projections in Stage 2, it remains a projection unless it feels right for the dreamer. The dreamer is free to accept or reject it in whole or in part. This is not something you are obliged to do. Nor is it anything you can suddenly produce on demand. Orchestrating ideas are those connections that occur to you spontaneously as you listen to the dreamer. They are not suddenly there at the end of the playback.

A common error is to continue to think of the dream as your own and to base your orchestrating projection not on what the dreamer has shared but on the continuing thoughts about your own life set off by the dreamer. Another is to put further questions to the dreamer to validate an idea you had about the dream that the dreamer's associations have not substantiated.

If there is uncertainty about whether or not to proceed with the orchestration, the dreamer can always be asked directly how close she is to a sense of closure. She may not have reached closure but feels she has gotten enough and does not wish to go any further. In most instances, the orchestration is welcomed.

Instructions to the Dreamer

You are free to respond or not to any of the orchestrating projections at the time they are offered. They are to be considered as questions. Only you can judge whether or not what is being offered feels right. Don't feel called on to respond to each speaker. Save your comments for what feels like a true fit. When everyone has had a chance to offer his or her projections you will be given the last word.

* * *

The orchestration is a creative act that involves skill and discipline. Some of the skills are similar to those involved in the conduct of the other stages of the dialogue. These include the art of listening to and retaining (in memory or in written notes) everything a dreamer says, listening without prejudging the importance of any of it, not allowing one's preconceptions of the meaning of the dream to get in the way and, of course, being sensitive at all times to the feelings and points of emphasis conveyed by the dreamer. Having at hand all the dreamer has shared is essential before any effort can be made to tie things together.

The discipline involved lies in structuring and limiting the play of one's intuition to the imagery and input of the dreamer. This often presents considerable difficulty. Someone may come up with a version of an image or a scene that has not been justified by anything the dreamer has said, and yet it feels to that person as if it has to be right. If the image cannot be linked to any of the shared context, then despite one's enthusiasm and confidence about it and despite an honest intent to be helpful, it is best to exercise restraint. Even if someone may be right about what he or she has to say, if it were said, there is too great a risk of opening an area that has not yet been opened up by the dreamer or one that she does not want opened. For those with a background in psychology and psychotherapy, there is another impulse that has to be checked—namely, to offer generalized theoretical formulations that go far beyond anything justified by what the dreamer has said.

The Art of Listening

One has to learn how to listen not only to the expressed content but also to the unconscious rumblings that go along with it. As you listen, part of you is always trying to sense connections between what is said and its possible metaphorical translations into imagery. Lots of ideas may occur to you, but all have to be tested against the dream as the template. Only those that survive the test and have something to offer that the dreamer has not come to by himself are the ones to be included in the orchestration.

Our thoughts continually move back and forth from the associations the dreamer presents to the way these may be reflected in the play of the dream imagery. As the dreamer shares information with us, more and more ideas may occur to us about the images in the dream. The point is to let these ideas be generated from the information that comes forth rather than clinging to preconceived ideas in the hope of validating them. In focusing your attention on what the dreamer is saying, you are also tuning your ear to clues about any feelings that are emerging. Something said in passing and offered as if it were of no importance may, for example, be accompanied by an embarrassed smile. One has to be sensitive to the background music, so to speak, accompanying the words being offered.

One soon learns the value of careful listening. Any dreamer who seriously wants to acknowledge the message of the dream will, if given the opportunity, reveal the information needed to accomplish that. Often, the dreamer will say a great many things without seeing their relevance to the dream, until they are brought together later in the framework of an orchestration. A dreamer gives much more information about a dream than he is aware of at the time or, for that matter, than anyone else is. As you continue to listen to the dreamer, you may suddenly get a glimmer of a metaphorical connection based on something the dreamer said earlier, a connection that may have escaped the dreamer. Connections of that kind form the basis of later orchestrating projections. Obviously, the data on which it is based must be readily available. I find I can't keep all that the dreamer has said in my head, so I resort to extensive note taking.

I find it helpful to think in terms of what question the dreamer took to bed that night and how that question is being addressed in the dream. As I listen,

I try to build a picture in my mind of what the dreamer was feeling at the time of the dream. What were his thoughts and feelings just prior to falling asleep? What need was rising to the surface? What underlying vulnerability was being exposed? What kind of predicament was the dreamer in? What emotional forces were converging that gave rise to these particular images that night? Can I identify the concern, tension, dilemma, preoccupation, uncertainty, conflict, or anticipation in the dreamer's mind as he fell asleep? In this connection, the setting or opening scene of the dream is important, both as a prelude to what follows and in the light it might shed on the precipitating life context. Sometimes, the very opening comments a dreamer makes as he begins his response in Stage 3 to the work of the group provide an important clue to what was uppermost in his mind at the time of the dream and what is now being reflected in the dream.

The Technique of Orchestration

In the early stages of my work with this approach, I was ambivalent about encouraging orchestrations by the group members. Although I found it a natural and effective way of pulling things together for a dreamer, I was unsure about whether this was a skill that could be taught or whether it could come only from my many years of clinical work with dreams. I came down on the side of encouraging people to try their hand at it. The result was mixed. I was surprised both at how eagerly group members took to making the attempt and how much difficulty they had at first in doing it in a way that was effective for the dreamer. Coming to an orchestrating idea that really moves the dreamer is an interplay of intuition, the ability to listen to a dreamer and discern the appearance and flow of feelings, openness to the material the dreamer has shared and *all* that has been shared, and finally, sensitivity to metaphor. These are the ingredients; then one has to hope for that unpredictable flash of insight that brings it all together. When this is on target it is experienced by the dreamer as a true fit. We all know what the truth feels like. Whether we embrace it with relief or recoil from it in pain, it feels real. Its very reality provides us with the opportunity to engage with it and grow in our struggle to come to terms with something new about ourselves. Dream work is a very direct way to provide us with such opportunities. Even if the orchestrating insight falls short or fails altogether, it can still have a salutary effect. It is offered as a projection, and just as in the second, or game, stage of the process, a wrong projection helps a dreamer define what she doesn't feel or what an image doesn't mean. In defining what it doesn't mean, she often comes closer to what it does mean.

An effective orchestration requires preparation. It requires the offering of projections in a qualitatively different way than when the group members made the dream their own (Stage 2). Let us look more closely at how one goes about developing an orchestrating projection.

At the point where the group members are invited to share with the dreamer the connections they have made, it isn't as if at that moment a sudden insight forms in the mind of a group member and becomes the basis of an orchestrating projection. It may possibly occur that way, but it is more likely that an effective offering has an antecedent incubation period. This begins with the occurrence of spontaneous insights into the possible meaning of the imagery as one listens first to the dreamer's response and then to the succeeding two phases of the dialogue (the search for context and the playback). Often, members of the group feel called on to render an orchestrating comment when no such spontaneous response has occurred. It then has a forced or intellectual tone in contrast to a spontaneous insight, one that is imbued with a feeling of freshness and novelty.

The more one learns how to listen to the dreamer, such spontaneous insights are more apt to be on target. Ideas begin to form about what the images might mean. One doesn't hold on to these ideas rigidly but tests them against the continuing flow of information from the dreamer. This means shifting one's point of view to be in better accord with the emerging data rather than the reverse—for example, being selective about the data to fit in with one's ideas.

To the extent that it is appropriate and within the ability of the person offering the orchestration, it should be a felt response to the very personal and moving experience that sharing a dream is for the dreamer. There is a palpable sense of drama in the dreamer's struggle to get close to the dream. We try to work with the feelings we have picked up from the dreamer, reflecting them back, often with emphasis, to point up a connection the dreamer may not yet have seen. Orchestrating projections may focus on puns, double entendres, or the possible meaning of numbers that appear in dreams and thus come up with new and often striking connections that were overlooked by the dreamer. Unusual imagery in a dream or inappropriate reactions to ordinary imagery may be the telltale sign of what the dream means. Often, helping the dreamer see the self-referential potential of objects or other persons in the dream can effectively widen the dreamer's horizon.

Clarity about the task is of utmost importance. The goal is to effect a systematic transformation of the dreamer's input into a knowledge of the issue being raised, how the current context of the dreamer's life set that issue in motion, how that issue is expressed metaphorically in the imagery of the dream, and how that imagery reflects the dreamer's way of exploring and dealing with the issue. The question put to oneself is, Considering all that the dreamer has said, what light has been shed on each element in the dream and on the sequences in which they occur? Intuition and insightful flashes play a role here, of course, but the chances of their being helpful to the dreamer depend on the skill with which one has listened both to the words of the dreamer and the emotional nuances that have accompanied the account, the ability to detect metaphorical connections, and the ability to render an orchestrated version using as many of the dreamer's own words as possible. This last point is important. The closer one stays to the dreamer's words, the more likely the success of the effort. We are offering a projection in the hope that it isn't a projection but is, rather, a reflection of the meaning of the dream as felt by the dreamer. To do this, we order the content given to us by the dreamer in a way that parallels the ordering of the images in the dream. It should be offered as concisely as possible, so as to give everyone a chance within the time available. A good orchestration should clarify or even identify what the dreamer was feeling.

Finally, in our efforts to look through the connection between image and meaning, have we been able to identify any specific unifying issue? Issues such as the following are common stumbling blocks in the path of our evolving maturity and are apt to show up in a dream:

- How well do we handle feelings such as anger on the one hand and tenderness on the other?
- How susceptible are we to feelings of guilt, self-depreciation, and self-denial?
- How aware are we of our own need for nurturing and support?
- To what extent are we oriented to the needs of others at the expense of our own needs?
- To what extent do we blindly accept personal, social, and institutional arrangements that limit or do violence to our own humanity?
- To what extent do we deny or suppress what is truly alive in us?
- To what extent are we being carried along passively by the tide of our life?

There is still another aspect to the orchestration. A dreamer may feel very much in touch with the meaning and feelings conveyed by the imagery of the dream and still invite the orchestration. In this case, the need for something more has nothing to do with the further clarification of the imagery. The dreamer gets something else from the group's orchestrating efforts: She gets the sense of having been heard and, with that, a sense of having her own feelings validated. Up to the point of hearing the responses of others, the dreamer is alone with her feelings and, as genuine as they may be, she may not let herself feel that sure about them until she sees them reflected in the orchestrating comments of another. The feeling that what has been given has been received is important, often more important than the actual content involved. To have shared something so deeply personal and then to have it resonate so deeply in others leaves the dreamer more comfortable with herself and grateful for its having happened. One can generally tell from a dreamer's response how meaningful the orchestration was. Nonverbally, the dreamer may nod, smile, or in some way, reveal an "Aha!" response. One sure sign of an orchestration's success is its capacity to elicit further corroborating data from the dreamer. One or more details might be clarified for the dreamer, or a whole new meaning of the dream may suddenly spring into view.

To recapitulate, there are two important points about the orchestration:

1. The orchestration is an implicit question directed to the dreamer. It is offered as your projection and remains just that until and unless it is validated by the dreamer. We are simply testing the waters when we offer an orchestration. We are, in effect, asking the dreamer if what we have to say brings her any closer to the dream. We might not put our comments in the form of a question, but that is the intent.

2. Keep in mind the differences between projections offered at this stage and the projections shared in Stage 2 when group members made the dream their own. In both instances, the projections are for the benefit of the dreamer, but now they are offered directly to the dreamer and are built up on the basis of what the dreamer has told us.

Other questions to keep in mind as you review what the dreamer has said include the following:

- Can any further insights occur as you note the movement in the dream from beginning to end?
- Does a comparison of the mood at the beginning and the end of the dream fit with anything the dreamer has disclosed?
- Can viewing the characters in the dream, real or otherwise, as aspects of the dreamer, shed any additional light?
- Can later sequences of the dream be seen as attempts to resolve issues raised at the beginning of the dream?

- Do the images in successive parts of the dream, different though they may be, seem to be expressing and developing the same theme?
- Is there a sense that the dream is touching on different levels of the dreamer's personality? Can you detect this by looking at the dream as a longitudinally structured statement of the dreamer's life?
- A number of themes, common to all of us, occupy our dreaming psyche. Do any of the following themes seem to fit?

   a. Concern over identity: Who am I? What is there in life for me? What do I really want?

   b. Passivity versus activity: Does the dream point to an inappropriately passive or active stance with regard to the predicaments the dreamer finds herself in?

   c. Being for oneself versus being for others: Is the dreamer raising questions about the degree to which her life has been oriented to meeting the needs of others at the expense of recognizing and meeting her own needs?

   d. Freedom versus constriction: A sense of freedom is an essential quality of life. Is the dream dealing with the way this freedom is being placed in jeopardy by constraining circumstances? Is the dreamer struggling to develop a sense of freedom about her life?

   e. Dependency versus being independent: To what extent is the dreamer struggling with the unwarranted assumption that she is dependent on more powerful others and the fear of taking a more independent stance?

From all that I have said, the task of orchestrating may seem a difficult and complex undertaking. Again, this is more apt to be true at the beginning before one has had time to develop the skill necessary to retain and work with all the information offered by the dreamer and before one has learned how to reorder that information so as to embed the images of the dream in the life context of the dreamer. If the dreamer has been open to exploration of the dream and the group has done a good job of eliciting the data, this reordering will begin to evolve in a natural way. We are detectives on a trail, learning to make use of every possible clue and learning how to distinguish true clues (feelings and data from the dream) from false clues (ideas we superimpose on the dream).

The Safety Factor

Even though we base what we say in our orchestration on what we get from the dreamer, the way we put it together and relate it to the dream makes it our projection. This must be understood clearly by the dreamer. Just as in the second stage, he is free to accept or reject any orchestrating ideas. When

I complete an orchestrating attempt, I make it clear that it is my projection and is offered as a question that may or may not be of help.

The Discovery Factor

An orchestrating projection may fall short and have no import for the dreamer or it may be on target and elicit a deeply felt response. Sometimes, it opens up a flood of relevant new and confirming associations. This kind of response makes a fitting close to the dream work. The dreamer is left with two feelings—one, the satisfaction of feeling in touch with what the dream is saying, and two, the sense that what he had to say registered with others and that he was heard. After the last orchestration has been offered, the dreamer is invited to make any closing comments.

The process draws to a close with the dreamer having the last word and the leader then thanking the dreamer for sharing the dream and for the work he did on it.

In most instances, this final step in the dialogue brings the dreamer to a point of closure or close enough to it that he can go the rest of the way himself. On those occasions, when the dream still hasn't come together for the dreamer or when there is no time for further exploration, there is another technique that can be resorted to, the delayed orchestration to be described shortly.

The session is formally over with the completion of the orchestration. It often continues informally in what I have called the "driveway syndrome" where participants gather in my driveway and cluster about the dreamer following the session to offer further ideas about the dream that occurred to them but did not come up in the course of the process. After the process is over, the dreamer is on his own as are the members of the group. I do not know of any instance in which such spontaneous exchanges have bothered the dreamer, and on occasion, something comes out that is very helpful to the dreamer.

Problems

The most serious difficulty arises when someone uses the orchestration as a way of rendering personal feelings about the dream with little or no attempt to base what he or she is saying on what the dreamer has said. In effect, that person is still playing the game (Stage 2) and is talking about the dream as his or her own. It is difficult for some to realize that, once we return the dream to the dreamer at the end of the second stage, it is no longer our dream. They lose sight of the fact that they are to try to connect what the dreamer said to what the dream is saying. It is not an invitation to freewheeling interpretive activity.

A dreamer may have actually arrived at a sense of closure but may invite the orchestration out of a feeling of obligation to the group. A typical answer in this case might be, "OK, if you [the group] wish it." It is up to the leader to point out that the only valid indication for an orchestration is if the dreamer desires it.

A dreamer may not have reached closure but feels uncomfortable about going further. If the leader senses any hesitancy, he should again intervene and reassure the dreamer that it is perfectly acceptable to stop if he so wishes.

Failure to listen carefully can result in an orchestrating connection that the dreamer was already aware of.

Frequently, therapists in the group resort to terminology derived from their own theoretical orientation that is not justified on the basis of what the dreamer has said. The question is not whether they may eventually be proven correct but whether the material from the dreamer has justified their theoretical formulation.

Sometimes, there are those who are so influenced by the pain or distress felt by the dreamer that they will offer an orchestration geared not so much to making connections as it is to offering the dreamer reassurances. They forget that the best reassurance is to help the dreamer be in touch with what the dream is saying. Any other well-intended reassurance will fall short of that. The dreamer may appreciate the effort, but he won't be brought any closer to the dream.

Helpful Hints

1. As you listened to the information coming from the dreamer in the preceding phases of Stage 3, what feelings have emerged and what points have been emphasized by the dreamer?
2. Can you reconstruct the feelings the dreamer took to bed the night of the dream?
3. Can you relate what you have heard about the recent triggering context in the life of the dreamer to the metaphorical potential of the dream imagery?
4. Taking into account all the information shared by the dreamer, can you identify a central issue around which the dream images seem to focus?

5. To the extent possible, are you offering the orchestration in the dreamer's own words?
6. Are you giving the dreamer the opportunity to respond to an orchestrating comment should she wish to do so?

Traps to Avoid

1. Orchestrating projections should be based on spontaneously generated ideas. They should never be forced or put together simply because the time has come to offer orchestrations.
2. Avoid making theoretical generalizations that are not warranted by what the dreamer has said.
3. The dream is no longer yours. Avoid talking about how the dream work has made you feel. It is not an opportunity to further work with the dream as you did in Stage 2, when you made it your own.
4. Be modest in your attempt at orchestration. Don't be too expansive. Try to think through your remarks in advance and be as concise as you can in the connections you make between life context and imagery. It is better if the orchestrating comments that come from the group are fewer and shorter and more on target.
5. Avoid offering orchestrations that repeat what the dreamer knows.
6. Avoid being repetitive if someone else covers what you had in mind.
7. Avoid asking further direct questions of the dreamer. That should be completed by the time the playback is over and not continued into the orchestrating phase.
8. Avoid the temptation to use the orchestration primarily as a way of reassuring the dreamer. An accurate orchestration that finds its mark is the only genuine reassurance needed by a dreamer. This is true whatever feelings it may leave the dreamer with. The impulse to reassure a dreamer can be very strong, but if that is what shapes the comment at the expense of a more objective approach, it is apt to be obvious to the dreamer and to be counterproductive. When it comes to dreams, only the truth is genuinely reassuring.
9. Don't rush in with your orchestrations without giving the dreamer a chance to comment on the last one.
10. Finally, be sure the orchestration is both needed and wanted. If it is not necessary, it can be repetitious and counterproductive.

An Illustrative Session

Ann is a woman in her early 60s whose husband had died a year before she joined the group. The dream reveals her ongoing struggle to deal with the painful sense of loss. A very talented and creative woman, she is attempting to rebuild a new life for herself. The orchestrating comments are italicized.

Ann's Dream

Ann introduced this dream by saying she had an idea of what it was about, but some of the imagery puzzled her. It had occurred a week ago (on a Thursday):

> *I was in what I thought was my apartment. I thought I came out of my bedroom, but when I came out, it wasn't my apartment at all. It was like there was a lot of space, broken up as if apartments were being built, each having three walls. One wall was not there so you could see in. I wondered where I was. I remarked to myself, "Where am I?"*
>
> *I looked into one of these semi-apartments. A redheaded woman was painting the wall a terrible green color—chartreuse. I said it was entirely the wrong color. I showed her what color she should use.*
>
> *Then I turned to look for my apartment. I saw a very distorted image of this room [referring to the living room of her apartment where we were meeting]. It was as if there was a circle cut out from the center of the floor, but lying on top of a floor. It had this rug [pointing to the rug on the living room floor] on it. Part of the rug was pulled up so that you could see the lining of the rug.*
>
> *Then I walked into my bedroom, and my chest of drawers was missing. Someone said they have locked it in the basement. My heart was pounding so that it woke me up."*

The group's projections in Stage 2 were not recorded. That some were helpful is obvious from the dreamer's response and these are represented by bold italics.

Ann's Response

"Some of the things were obvious to me. Some were not.

"***The rug being pulled out from under me***—that's exactly the way I felt last Thursday night about my life. Last week, it felt as though I were going through a turning point. I keep hitting a new bottom when I'd like to think I'm on the way up. That day, I was feeling very hopeless. The rug turned up in the dream—it was ready for someone to pull it up and leave me nowhere.

"What was said about the ***chest being a reference to heart*** seemed right to me.

"*The basement as the unconscious domain*—has to do with the final issue, the final acceptance of my husband's death. He is now in my unconscious domain, and I have to let it rest there.

"*Also, about being disoriented and disconnected from feelings*—after his death, everyone thought I was great in how I was handling my feelings, but I was really not admitting what I was really feeling. I wanted to appear strong and together. The fear I felt in the dream about going out into this semi-apartment[1] was that it was as if I had come to the point where I was saying to myself, 'Get out there and move! Stop making excuses.'

"There was a big exhibition last week in connection with my business. I hadn't tested myself this whole past year with regard to showing myself in public. I'm well-known in the business.[2] Last Thursday, I wasn't sure if I had the guts to go out. I felt shaky and disoriented.

"At the same time, I was concerned about the relationship with this man I had spoken about before. I had come to the point where I had to do something. I knew I was using him as a crutch, and I was aware that was not a good idea. At the same time, I felt I would be unprotected if I broke it off. It had come to the point where I couldn't respect myself if I didn't take some action. I don't know how this was reflected in the dream. Breaking that relationship was another pulling of the rug from under me.

"I have no idea who the redheaded woman was. She did look something like a woman I know, but I can't see how that could be connected to the dream. She is a very theatrical type. I saw her at a party 4 weeks ago. She came with her husband, who is a dwarf. This came as a surprise, as I hadn't known about him before. It overwhelmed me, but I don't know what it has to do with the dream.

"I felt the dream was very significant since it affected me so strongly subsequently. I began to make a log of progress going out into the world and getting this relationship in order. I did go out into the world this past weekend and began to feel as if I were not all dried up and all used up. Maybe I'll be in a position of having choices again.

"I handled the relationship well. I didn't want to end in an unfriendly way. Now it's much better.

"Finally, I've gone from staggering around in the unknown to saying to myself, 'Stop all this shit! Get with it!' I never thought much about dreams before coming to this group, but now I feel how amazing it is to work with them. After I had this dream, I absolutely could see how it gave me the shove I needed to get going on a path. The feeling of returning to life is the strong effect of this dream.

"But why the rug cut in a circle? I'm a very visual person, so I saw myself standing before a painting, disoriented and out of focus, trying to get it into focus. It has all become real to me these last few days. Friday, I straightened out the relationship problem. Saturday, I was back in the business world. I made some good contacts that gave me my self-confidence back. I had no more fear about my abilities. I don't know why I had to go through all that despair before getting here, but now I don't question it.

"At first, I was confused by the dream. But then all these things happened, and it became clear it had to do with my going out into the world. I still don't understand about the redheaded woman and the round piece of rug."

Ann Invites the Dialogue: Amplifying the Context

Question Can you think back and say anything more about what the experience of that Thursday left you with?

Response Last Thursday was very upsetting. I felt alone in the world. No one loves me. I'll never be able to handle this relationship. I was having physical problems. I felt I was ready to be thrown away. I really was a mess, a bereft person.

Ann Invites the Playback

The first scene was read back, ending with her wondering, "Where am I?"

Response Now I can relate to it. I had created certain safety measures in my life. I had thought I was secure. Now I had to think of breaking out into the world without the security of my husband and my whole past life. It was more overwhelming than I had expected. My bedroom is my safety box. I walked into my living room, but the safety box wasn't there. I found myself going out into the world again.

Question What about the small apartments with only three walls?

Response It makes me think of the way exhibits have displays in cubicles with three walls. I had the feeling, "Oh, my God! Can I get myself to go to the show?"

The next scene was read back with her showing the redheaded woman the color she should use. As soon as the scene was read back Ann exclaimed, "I know! Now I have the very strong feeling it was this woman I mentioned.

She is kind of overwhelming and overpowering. Then I found out she was married to a dwarf. My feelings completely changed, and I began to have a terrific respect for her. I realized what a difficult situation she had been strong enough to live with. Seeing what she had overcome made me feel I can be strong enough to get rid of all this namby-pamby stuff."

Question To get back to the dream—in the dream, she is doing something wrong, and you are correcting her.

Response She is involved as the director of a project that interests me. I thought some of the things she was doing were not of the quality that it could be. I felt we could upgrade the quality of what she does if we were to work together. I could be helpful.

The rest of the dream was read back:

Response I now connect the chest of drawers with my heart. It was pounding. It has to do with my heart now in the basement—acceptance of the fact that my husband is no longer in the bedroom. He is gone and I have to continue to live. His death pulled the rug from under me. I don't know why the rug was cut in a circle."

At this point, I suggested that she no longer try to focus on the circle itself, which seemed a dead end, but take into account the entire image—namely, that although a hole was cut out, there was a solid floor underneath. This change of perspective made her eyes light up:

"Maybe I could look at it positively. Even though there was a hole there, I wasn't going to fall through it. I couldn't fall through it. Last week, before the dream, I couldn't think positively. After the dream, it was as if all this negative thinking had changed into positive thinking."

Ann Invites the Orchestration

One projection in connection with the circle suggested that Ann had come full circle and was now ready to start again.

One began with a reference to The Lost Weekend, *suggesting that only when one reaches rock bottom, as she did last Thursday, does one begin to discover and use one's own strength and resources. Only then was she able to get rid of her crutch and the addiction to her grief.*

I then addressed a reason the redheaded woman appeared in her dream. Her feelings of respect and admiration for her led her to question her own weakness. At a symbolic level, the woman, too, was married to a "diminished" man. Ann, impressed by the strength of this woman, could also go forward even though the role played by a man in her life was diminished by the death of her husband. I concluded by saying to Ann, "You are beginning to recognize the depth of your despair and the way this had been camouflaged by the 'butterfly syndrome.' Always an up person, you felt nothing could ever get you down. Your creativity and the originality and excitement of the new venture you have undertaken are a counterbalance to the anxiety you feel. You have taken to dream work, are good at it, and recognize in it another manifestation of your creativity."

Ann's Closing Comment

"It's always amazing. It is true. After all, I shared what I felt was a perfect relationship with a man. I wasn't aware of the extent I wallowed in the grief. After his death, I thought I was terrific in the way I went about living, but it wasn't real. I was going through the butterfly syndrome, able to get right up and fly again, but in a world of fantasy—not reality.

"I feel extraordinarily better. There is so much difference in the way I felt last week and this week."

For further examples of illustrative sessions of orchestrating comments the reader is referred to the dreams offered in Chapters 1, 2, 3, 5, and 6.

Delayed Orchestration

In those instances in which time has run out before orchestrations could be formulated (this may happen if the dream is long and complex, if the dreamer has provided too much material to work with in the time frame available, or if there has been time but no one has been able to pull the loose ends together in a way that was helpful to the dreamer), one can resort to what I refer to as a *delayed orchestration*. This simply means doing an orchestration after the session is over at some time before the next meeting of the group. The general idea is to reassess all that the dreamer has said about the dream and to see if further light can be shed on the images and their sequential arrangement. Any member of the group can attempt it. It is then offered to the dreamer at the subsequent session (Stage 4). The delayed orchestration is the exception rather than the rule.

The essential prerequisite for the delayed orchestration is to have available the information given to us by the dreamer. When an orchestration is undertaken in the session in which the dream is presented, you may be able to rely on your memory or notes you may have taken. When there has been a delay of one or more days before attempting the orchestration, I find it necessary to have on paper as much as I can of what the dreamer has said. The material is not as fresh, and I need rather elaborate notes to be able to bring back the entire experience.[3] This, of course, involves me in the onerous task of ongoing note taking as I listen to the dreamer. I find that helpful in preparing an ordinary orchestration and essential should a delayed orchestration be necessary.

The advantage of a delayed orchestration is that one can go about it in a leisurely fashion. There is not the press of time as there is in a regular session. It may take an hour or more for a detailed working through of the material. I have often been amazed at how many clues the dreamer has given to the meaning of the dream that were overlooked at the time and only picked up later on in a more careful review. The subject matter for this review includes the following:

1. As complete an account as possible of what the dreamer has said in his response to the work of the group in Stage 2
2. All that came out in the course of the dialogue
3. Whatever context may be known to all but not yet introduced by the dreamer
4. Observational data—for example, feelings displayed by the dreamer

When I have all this down on paper, instead of relying on what remained in my head, then the only task is the reordering of the data. Although the principles are the same as for an immediate orchestration, a more elaborate technique is needed to bring out the necessary connections. I work with legal-sized paper divided into three columns. Paper this size is generally large enough to accommodate an account of the dream in the left-hand column. One can foreshorten the account a bit, omitting words that do not affect the meaning. It includes all the details in the dream in their proper sequence. I then go over all that I have written down that the dreamer has said, earmarking each comment as to its possible relationship to the images in each

Table 7.1 Excerpt From Notes for a Delayed Orchestration

Image	Dreamer's Comments	Metaphorical Reference
Bed	Someone linked the bed to dreaming. That resonates. I come here from an experience in group psychotherapy. This is a totally new experience. It's like being in England and having to learn to drive on the left side of the street.	This image is highlighted in this scene. It has meaning for her at several different levels. Superficially, it reflects her very positive response to the dream group process and the deep response she had to the work with someone else's dream.
	I'm very excited about this process.	At another level it represents the very personal space she needs in her life right now.
	It's very important for me now to pay that kind of attention to myself. . . . I'm better at caring for others. I felt a tremendous sense of excitement yesterday in the work with Anne's dream and excitement at what for me is a new process.	In this new feeling about her life, she feels very positive in her discovery of a place where she can entrust her dream to a "collective."
	I'm amazed at how it can work. The structure is so pure and so protective of the dreamer. The process unfolds by itself. Bed is a very personal place for me. It's where I do a great deal of my work.	She was relieved to replace the couch with the bed. This signified the new surge of energy she felt last night after the dream group.
	I feel this process is very important for my dream life and that I can trust sharing it with a collective. Putting the bed where the couch was was integrating that need. I feel this dream is opening up new possibilities.	

scene, noting these connections in the second column. In the third column, I note as I go along what might be a clue to the underlying issue or theme developing. I often see metaphorical connections I missed at the time the dream was presented.

Table 7.1 illustrates the development of one of the images in the dream of a very creative woman who finds herself in a living room, in an attic that is sparsely furnished, containing only a couch and a bed. The space is full of sunshine and very bright. In the dream she is trying to figure out how to put the bed in the place of the couch. The dream occurred during the course of her participation for the first time in a workshop of mine. In the dream, she refers to aspects of the process I use, its emphasis on the safety of the dreamer, and the respectful nonintrusive way the members of the group try to help the dreamer.

One may have to review the dream and the corresponding productions of the dreamer several times before finding something that seems right to say about the dream. It is a process that cannot be rushed. As you engage in this review, you are incubating the creative metaphorical potential in yourself in the hope that it will lead to a gratifying insight. Of course, it is your own insight, still to be validated by the dreamer. It has been my experience, however, that when the delayed orchestration is done with care and results in what seems like new insight, it will often prove helpful to the dreamer. In most instances, the dreamer has provided enough information to successfully orchestrate the dream. The delayed orchestration simply provides the time needed to pull things together.

Stage 4: Follow-Up

Ongoing dream groups meet at intervals, weekly, biweekly, or longer. The dreamer is invited to take a second look at the dream in the interval between the session in which the dream was presented and the subsequent session. This gives her the opportunity to take a fresh look at the dream after some time has elapsed, when incipient thoughts and reactions stimulated at the time the dream was worked on have had time to rise to the surface. This, plus the fact that the dreamer is not under any tension she might have felt while in the group, might be sufficient to bring about new insights. The interval also provides the dreamer with the opportunity to modulate or change reactions she might have had during the dream work, reactions she might have tried to make fit but that really didn't. Time is set aside at the beginning of the session for any additional comments she may wish to make. Our aim has been to give the dreamer a push in the right direction in the hope that she will go further herself. The extent to which this happens is quite variable. She might have become so caught up in her life that she gave the dream no further thought. At the other extreme, there might have been continuing reverberations and a profusion of new insights that the dreamer can hardly wait to share with the group. Accordingly, one can expect a variety of responses. The dreamer may simply register satisfaction with the work that had been done with the dream and have nothing further to add. He may note that some parts of the dream still elude him. He may be eager to share additional insights that occurred to him, insights that may provide a more satisfying sense of closure or even recast the dream in an entirely different light. Sometimes, a dream occurring subsequent to the session in which the dream was presented sheds further light on the original dream or seems like a logical follow-up to that dream. Sometimes, the dreamer reports engaging in a novel bit of behavior or making a decision as a consequence of the dream work.

The delayed orchestration can be offered to the dreamer at this time, but it is not rendered until after the dreamer has had a chance to share any additional thoughts about the dream. Such information may be so congruent with your orchestration as to make it unnecessary or, if not, may suggest some change in the orchestration. Remember that you are offering it as your projection. As such, it is a question to the dreamer and not a statement about what the dream means. A delayed orchestration often results in a greater feeling of completeness to the dream work, even in instances in which the dreamer may have felt that the dream work at the prior session accomplished a good deal.

When there are any delayed orchestrating projections by either the leader or the other members of the group, they are to be seen as finishing touches and are not to be construed as opening the dream for further exploration.

The group should also be receptive to any other group members who wish to share exciting new insights to dreams presented earlier to the group or new developments in their lives that they attribute to the dream work.

Here are two brief examples where further insights were shared by the dreamer in Stage 4.

A long and complex dream of a young man dealt with the fear of his destructiveness toward women. One image in particular spoke to this fear. "Someone shot a gun. Out of the gun came a Doberman pinscher who began to attack the woman." The dreamer had had a fear of dogs since an early childhood encounter with one in which he was severely bitten. One of the orchestrating projections dealt with his fear of the violence that could come out of his penis if it were used heterosexually. This didn't register at the time, but after reflecting on the dream during the week that followed, the full significance of the image hit him. On returning to the group the following week, he excitedly exclaimed, "My God! The gun really was a phallic symbol, and the dog coming out of it was my fear that making love would harm the woman." It was an emotional insight that had escaped him the previous week.

In the next example, a key triggering residue didn't occur to the dreamer until several days after the initial dream work had been completed. In one scene in the dream, she was looking for a new pair of high-heeled black shoes. The following associations emerged in the dialogue: "I felt I could never be that kind of woman. I never express that part of me." When invited to say more about "that kind of woman" she added, "I have to work hard for everything, and you can't be a hard worker wearing high heels." When she returned the following week, she shared her later awareness of where the image came from. There had been a meeting the night before the dream of a group embarking on a new project together. A woman was there, elegantly dressed, wearing high heels and fancy earrings. She also learned that this woman, in contrast to herself, was married and had a child. This encounter made a very deep impression and had the effect of undermining some of the rationalizations that kept her from owning up to the envy she felt toward someone who could more publicly display these particular qualities of femaleness.

Very few problems are encountered in Stage 4. Sometimes, the dreamer's postscript can go on too long and impinge on the time available for a new dream. This is not apt to happen once attention is called to it.

Notes

1. At a later point, in writing up this dream it occurred to me her use of the word *semi-apartment* may refer to the loss of her husband.

2. Prior to her husband's death, Ann had been involved in arranging exhibits.

3. I do try to capture the gist of what the dreamer says at each stage of the dialogue. Having available what was said about each image makes it easier to catch on to the metaphorical messages being conveyed.

8

■

The Leader

As we go into the role and responsibilities of the leader in greater detail, it will be apparent that an almost infinite variety of problems and issues may arise. Not all can be anticipated, and only the most common ones will be considered. The best preparation for dealing with such problems is a thorough grounding in the rationale for each stage of the process.

The role of the leader is subject to some variation depending on whether the group is ongoing or new. It also depends on whether an experienced leader is working with a group or whether peers come together to do dream work, setting up a rotating leadership arrangement, and learning together about the problems as they are encountered.

Before dealing separately with each of these circumstances, let me make some generalizations about the leadership role. I have touched on these in an earlier section but, at the risk of some repetition, will amplify them further here.

The Dual Role

The special role of the leader is to lead the group through the process, facilitate the transition from one stage to the other, and see that the group

113

adheres to the structure. The other role is that of a participating member of the group, entering into each stage of the process in the same way as the others do, including the option to share a dream. A new leader struggling to carry out the various responsibilities entailed in leadership often has difficulty in balancing the two roles. As she becomes more and more comfortable in the leadership role, there will be greater ease and freedom in carrying out the role of participant. It takes some time for a group to feel comfortable with the process, and it is during this initial phase that proper leadership skills are most important.

The task of leading a dream group is not a simple one. A number of different concerns have to be kept in mind at the same time.

Leading the Group Through the Stages

There is a natural ending to each stage and each substage of the process. The leader acts as the spokesperson for the group in determining when that point is reached. Clear directions are given to orient the group and the dreamer to what is to happen in each successive step. These directions have already been noted. They should be given clearly and completely in the early sessions of a group. Even with an experienced group, however, the group and the dreamer should be reminded of the essence of what is to occur at every stage. Without that clarity, even experienced dream workers can get mixed up. It is up to the leader to see to it that everyone knows exactly what is expected of him or her at every phase of the process. This implies clear and explicit directions from the leader. Inexperienced leaders sometimes lose sight of this and simply announce in a perfunctory way the onset of the next stage, assuming that the group is clear about what that stage is.

Keeping Track of the Time

A single session of dream work takes place within a time frame generally of 1.5 to 2 hours. It is up to the leader to keep that time frame in mind in the effort to encompass as much of the process as is possible. At times, this might involve arbitrary decisions to move on even though it is conceivable that more work could have been done at a particular stage if more time had been available. Only rough guidelines about timing can be offered. With experience, a leader will get to know how best to distribute the time. As a general rule, it is a good idea in an hour and a half time frame to allow 50 to 60 minutes for the dreamer's response and the dialogue. The latter requires time and is usually the most important phase of the process. It is perfectly possible, of course, that the dreamer may have gotten enough from Stage 2 to have a sense of closure and feel no need for the dialogue, in which case the process ends with the dreamer's response.

All of the process that precedes Stage 3 has to be covered, therefore, within 30 to 40 minutes (closer to the former being preferable). This includes any further remarks by the dreamer who presented at the last session, obtaining and clarifying a dream, and the second stage, in which the group members work with the dream as their own. Sometimes, Stage 2 has to be curtailed in the interest of leaving time for the dreamer's response and the dialogue. A new leader often has problems with this, hesitating to cut the group off. The most common misjudgment is to spend too much time in Stage 2 and not have enough time to manage Stage 3 properly. A leader can do a number of things to expedite matters.

Limit the clarifying questions (Stage 1B) to only those that are essential. A dreamer can sometimes be pressed for details that were not in the dream or for clarity where the dream was unclear or diffuse. When spatial arrangements or the form of an object seem important, the dreamer can be invited to make a rough rendering of the image. This can short-circuit a number of questions.

When the sharing of feelings (2A) is going on too long, the leader can always make the decision to go on to Stage 2B while reassuring the group members that their feelings are not being cut off. She might say something such as this after feelings have been shared:

> It is time to move on to Stage 2B where we will be working with the metaphorical possibilities of the imagery. If you have further feelings you would like to share, feel free to do so. You are now free to develop the dream further at the level of feelings and at the level of the meanings you can give to the imagery.

An inexperienced leader will tend to leave the termination of this stage too much up to the group. Dream imagery is intriguing, and a group can play with it indefinitely. The leader has to alert both the group and the dreamer that the time is drawing close to when the dream is to be returned to the dreamer. The latter needs some advance signaling of this by the leader so as to have the time to change her mind-set from listening to the group and pondering the reactions she is experiencing to one in which she begins to prepare to respond to all that she has experienced. The question the leader puts to the group when she feels the need to move on is, "Are there any further contributions before we return the dream to the dreamer?" The question might be asked two or three times before Stage 2 is terminated. An inexperienced leader keeps asking the question over and over again, hoping there will be no further responses so that she can move on to the next phase without anyone's feeling hurt. The problem is that, as long as the leader keeps asking the question, someone will find an additional comment to make. The time spent in each stage has to be commensurate with its importance. Stage 2 is intended as a starter, one that we hope will begin the process of the dreamer engaging with her own dream. Most often, it is just that. We don't know in advance which stage will be most helpful to the dreamer, and so we have to leave time for all the stages. In most instances, it works out better that way.

There is usually no difficulty in keeping to the time frame with a short dream. With a longer dream, there is a way of telescoping the process that can save time with a minimum amount of loss of help to the dreamer. Stages 2A and 2B can be combined so that feelings and metaphors are worked on together, and a time for this is set so as to allow enough time for the dialogue. Even if there isn't enough time to get to the point of closure, the likelihood is that the dreamer will have gotten something from whatever was done.

When, as occasionally happens, the dream work is completed or ended for whatever reason early enough in the time frame to have 30 to 40 minutes left, a decision has to be made about whether or not to consider another dream. Although that is not time enough to work through the entire process, some helpful ideas can occur. I leave the decision about whether or not to go ahead with another dream to the dreamer and the group. If a dream is offered, I inform the dreamer that there may not be time to do full justice to the material. It is, of course, far more preferable to have a sense of leisure in going about dream work regardless of the length of the dream.

Keeping the Process on Track

In what ways can the process get off the track? What are the things to be alert for? Aside from the misuse of time and a number of specific problems still to be mentioned, the main challenge to the integrity of the process occurs when anyone, be it leader or group member, functions in a way that takes the control of the process out of the hands of the dreamer. This can come about at any point in the process and can occur quite openly or quite subtly. Even in the very first stage when questions for clarification are being asked of the dreamer, they may be put in such a way as to seek more information than was in the dream, obviously with the aim of supporting some idea of the questioner. Any time a dreamer is left to wonder what is going on in the mind of the questioner after a question has been asked, there is a sense of his control being undermined. With that may come a rise in the anxiety level. As has been emphasized, the success of the process is contingent on helping the dreamer maintain the lowest possible level of anxiety.

In the second stage, when the group members are making the dream their own, problems occur when the freedom to say whatever one wants to say about it is misused. The group members are always aware in reality that the dream is not their own and that through their projections, there is the hope that they can be of help to the dreamer. The difficulty arises when they assume their projections are going to be helpful and address them directly to the dreamer instead of to the other members of the group. This is an invasion of the dreamer's private space and compromises his ability to view it as the questioner's own projection. Similar problems arise in the third stage in connection with the first two phases of the dialogue. This is when the group members often find it difficult to restrain themselves from offering interpretations and asking leading questions in the hope of validating any interpretation they have in mind. Lost sight of is the fact that in the first two phases the goal is to help the dreamer bring out, in as neutral a way as possible, relevant data without our biases entering the picture. Despite its being well-intentioned, any bypassing of this data search in favor of making premature connections once again compromises the dreamer's autonomy and shifts the control of the dream to the person trying to make the connection.

Asking a leading question is the key offender, because this is used as an instrument to get across one's own idea about the dream. Such a question leaves the dreamer wondering, "What does she know about my dream that I don't know?" Discomfort and defensiveness are apt to ensue. The center of gravity has swung away from the dreamer. It is very difficult at times to refrain from asking such questions when one feels so certain about being on the right track. What you have to realize is that even if you ultimately turn out to be right, you are on the wrong track when you try to make connections before you have given the dreamer every opportunity to come to them on his own. There is a place for you to make what you feel may be a correct link between the dream and waking reality, but that place is in the third phase of the dialogue, the orchestration. Before then, one's efforts are directed exclusively to eliciting information, not making connections. This is a hard message to get across. The impulse to feel free in interpreting someone else's dream is very powerful.

The problem in the orchestrating phase is somewhat different. The group members are invited to make connections that are offered as projections, and they are asked to respect the constraint that they not go beyond what the dreamer has shared. Here again, there is the temptation to come in with one's own interpretations, developed with little regard to their justification in what the dreamer has said. Someone may give meaning to an image that doesn't connect with anything the dreamer has said about it or that has no connection to the way the image is used in the context of the dream. Some group members may go so far as to forget that the dream is no longer their own, making no effort to connect the dream to anything the dreamer has said, building an interpretation on the basis of the meaning the dream has for them. Sometimes, this phase of the dialogue is used not to offer a connection as a projection but to further question the dreamer in the hope of arriving at one. By now, the time for questioning is over. The dreamer has made whatever connections he can make spontaneously. Now the rest of us should attempt further connections for him if they are so indicated and if we can.

There is another common way of misusing the orchestrating phase. As mentioned earlier, it is natural to have a sympathetic response to the dreamer's struggle. This often leads to an effort on the part of group members to view the imagery selectively so as to offer reassurance to the dreamer. In doing this, they overlook what the dream may actually be saying and, more important, overlook the fact that the only genuine reassurance arises out of the dreamer's ability to see all that the dream is saying. It is honesty, not reassurance from the outside, that is called for.

Managing Tensions That Arise in the Group

If the process works as it should, interfering tensions rarely arise. There is always the possibility that they may, and the leader has to be prepared to deal with them.

People in the dream group who already know each other sometimes bring preexisting tensions into the work. These may influence the degree of freedom experienced by one or the other for fear of the exposure that may occur through dream work. Hidden rivalry and competitive strivings may emerge and have an adverse effect. Although occasional instances such as these do occur, they have been rare in my experience. I have had many situations in which a husband and wife, two close friends, or even a parent and child were in the same group and there were no difficulties at all. The only general rule as far as prevention is concerned is that if any two people are aware of preexisting tensions (of any significant degree) they should not be in the same dream group. This process is not designed to resolve personal tensions within the group. In dream work, people come together to be of help to the dreamer and to work cooperatively toward that end. They are not there to work out the ongoing tensions between any two people in the group. In my weekly groups, people contract for only four consecutive sessions, renewable as many times as they wish. This has proved to be a fortunate way of resolving difficulties of this kind, because it becomes apparent within that period of time that the dream group was not the answer to the problems in the relationship, and one or the other or both usually drop out.

There is another kind of preexisting problem that may come to light only after the group starts and two members of the group discover that they are in therapy with the same analyst. This did occur on one occasion and created a problem for both but only until they learned to trust the process and to realize the control they had over what they wished to share with the group. In this instance, both participants remained in the group for several years.

The dream group is subject to all the emotional vicissitudes of any group, and sometimes two people rub each other the wrong way. They either succeed in doing good dream work despite this, or one or the other eventually leaves the group.

More important are tensions that arise as a consequence of the process itself. A good example of this is when the dreamer is so profoundly moved by what is going on that she breaks down in tears. This can happen at any stage in the process, and when it does, it is up to the leader to stop the process long enough for the dreamer to recover. The silent support of the group is usually all that is needed, occasionally augmented by the offer of a tissue or other nonverbal gesture. Providing the dreamer with the freedom and time to handle her own reaction results in a gradual release in tension and a readiness to continue. This, of course, also holds true if anyone else is so powerfully affected by the dreamer's dream that he or she breaks down.

A tension can arise in the group on the rare occasion that a dreamer abruptly desires to bring the process to a close. Again, this can happen at any stage in the process, but only when it occurs early in the process is it apt to give rise to some tension in the group. The momentum of the work is brought to a sudden and unexpected halt, leaving everyone with a feeling of incompleteness. The leader has to see to it that the dreamer's wishes are respected and reassure her that she has the right to terminate the process in accord with the basic contract. Being in control of the process means being able to stop it at any point. The dreamer is under no obligation to justify her decision. The feelings of the group, be they frustration or anger, have to be assuaged by the reminder that the group is there to be of help to the dreamer only to the extent the dreamer wants its help. Generally, it is only in the course of a first encounter with the process that a reaction of this kind occurs. It is exceedingly rare, in my experience, for a dreamer to abort the process once she stays with it beyond this initial effort.

Tensions between participants can arise when errors are made, directions are not clear, or there is persistent misunderstanding about proper role and procedure. In Stage 1, for example, someone who may have offered to share a dream and then withdraws in favor of another for inappropriate reasons when she really wants to work on her dream might regret her decision and experience an undercurrent of frustration and rage. This is best handled by anticipating it beforehand and handling it prophylactically. When more than one person volunteers, the leader has to get across to them how important it is that they be honest about the wish to be the one whose dream is worked on. If someone feels any discomfort about withdrawing in the face of some-one else's expressed wish to share a dream, that person should opt for having the decision made by the toss of a coin or the drawing of lots. No matter how strongly someone wants to share a dream, he or she will accept being given a fair chance at it.

In the second stage, group members often have to be reminded not to take issue with each other's projections. This can result in a defensively tinged dialogue escalating between two participants. It should be stopped abruptly with the reminder that what we have to offer is our individual projections. These are to be regarded as such and are not open to debate. Nor do they ever need to be defended. By the same token, this caveat applies to the dreamer when in the third stage he begins to respond to the projections of the group. If they are helpful, fine. If not, the dreamer has to respect the fact that they are offered as projections. It is no more appropriate for the dreamer to adopt a judgmental or critical attitude toward these projections than it is for group members to be critical of each other's projections when they were working with the dream as their own. It is important for everyone to be clear about this. Projections are always acknowledged as such and are never to be judged or challenged. They are to be accepted or rejected simply on the basis of how helpful they may be to the dreamer.

During the dialogue phase of Stage 3, the group may have the tendency to push too hard with their questions. This may happen when the dreamer is unable to offer the clarifying information being sought by the questioner. The dreamer begins to feel uncomfortable. He may feel inadequate, as if in some way he is failing the group. Becoming aware of a tension of this sort, the leader has to temper the group's persistence and to reassure the dreamer that he is under no obligation to satisfy the group's curiosity and that he has the power to call a halt. In a situation such as this, the questions have gone beyond the more modest goal of being instruments for the use of the dreamer and instead become aggressive tools in the hands of a group member seeking to validate his own ideas or simply to satisfy his curiosity.

Another point that should be mentioned is inappropriate levity in the group. Although humor, properly applied, can lighten what otherwise might be too serious an atmosphere, when inappropriate, it can result in the dreamer's discomfort or resentment. Often, ludicrous or seemingly funny images appear in a dream, or something comes up, usually in the second stage, as the group works with the dream that strikes a humorous note. The important thing about the group's laughter is to make sure the dreamer is also enjoying whatever has been regarded as funny. Otherwise, it may run counter to the way the dreamer is feeling about it, in which case the laughter could be resented by the dreamer. The only way to prevent this from happening is to take a clue from the dreamer. Such clues are not too difficult to pick up from what the dreamer has said in presenting the dream and from his demeanor as the group is working on it. There are times when a leader has to remind a group that dream work is a serious undertaking with a dreamer's exposing potentially sensitive and vulnerable areas.

The more experienced one is with the process, the less the likelihood of interfering tensions arising. This is because when the process unfolds properly, it does not generate the conditions for interpersonal tensions. Our sights are set exclusively on the dreamer's struggle to get closer to the dream. Despite the fact that an interpersonal field is bound to occur in any group, it is not the focus of our attention. We do not engage with this interpersonal field. Instead, we orient ourselves to a much narrower field, the intrapsychic field of the dreamer, a field that represents the distance between the information the dreamer put into the dream while asleep and his grasp of that information once awake.

In our discussion of the tensions that may arise, we saw that some are self-resolving and some require intervention by the leader. With regard to the latter, the leader is faced with a number of decisions. Is the tension severe enough to attend to? If it is, is it localized between two participants or does it involve the entire group? If it involves two people, it is best for the leader to suggest that the individuals concerned deal with it after the session. In that case, the leader has to make a judgment as to whether or not he should be involved.

If the tension involves the whole group and is serious enough to hamper the ongoing work, the leader has to stop the dream work and engage in group process to resolve the difficulty. This has happened only once in my experience, when a group member accused another member of being there under false pretenses—namely, that she was a journalist and not an ordinary group member and that she was using a tape recorder. Neither charge was correct, but the person accused was very upset, and time had to be set aside to resolve the issue. In fact, she was a journalist, but she was there as a participating member to learn more about the process for an article she was writing and with the clear proviso that she would not include any of the dream material she was privy to. I had told her she could tape my orienting lecture to the group but not record any of the dream work itself. She had kept her part of the bargain, and once this was made clear, the feelings generated were dissipated.

It should be obvious by now that the process can work properly only when there is a spirit of ease and trust among all the participants and when all are oriented to the task of helping the dreamer. We are not there to work through our individual processes in a group context. The dreamer is in a very special position vis-à-vis the group. He is there to benefit from the group's work. He is the one whose inner life is on display. Much can happen to other members of the group in the course of working with someone else's dream, but it is incumbent on all the participants to contain and manage whatever reactions the dream sets off in them. On those occasions when someone other than the dreamer encounters difficulty, it can be taken into account and, if necessary, the process can be stopped for a few moments. That person should not, however, seek to shift the focus of attention to himself or herself.

Concern With Completeness

The leader has the responsibility to see to the completeness of the work before moving on to the next step. In Stage 2, where the group members have made the dream their own, there is a tendency to focus mainly on the more striking images and to overlook what are assumed to be more details. Such details are there for a reason and may even be of critical significance. It is up to the leader to call attention to anything in the dream that has been overlooked and to encourage attempts to respond to such images. Even when there has been some response to an image, the group should be encouraged to continue working if the leader feels that more could be said. If the group has difficulty relating to a particular image, it sometimes helps for the leader to highlight the image by reminding the group of all the details given in the dream about that image.

In the search for the recent context in the first part of the dialogue, the most frequent error is the failure to ask appropriate follow-up questions when indicated and to stay with such questions until the dreamer cannot or does not wish to go further. The same is true in the playback phase of the dialogue. It is not enough to read a scene back in its entirety. This is only the first step. What follows is an examination of each individual image in that scene if the metaphorical connection to waking life has not yet been established. In confronting the dreamer with these images, one hopes the dreamer can say more without implying that more can or must be said. At times, it can be helpful to recall what the dreamer may have said previously about an image in her initial response in the hope that this can stimulate further clarifying associations. Another helpful technique is to invite the dreamer to reexamine the image in the context of the dream in which it is embedded to see if that provides any additional clues. Finally, one can invite the dreamer to play with the image in terms of whatever thoughts or feelings she might connect with the image from any time in her past experience. This frees her from too close a focus on why the image turned up the night of the dream and may provide a wider range of associations to work with. When an answer by the dreamer seems unrelated to the image or even is different from the context in which the image appears, the discrepancy should be pointed out to the dreamer. What is in the dream is true. The dreamer awake is trying to get as close to that truth as possible. Sometimes, the truth of an image continues to elude her. This may be due to a simple failure in memory to recall at that moment the relevant associations, or it may be due to the hold that her defensive operations have over her in that particular area. In the first instance, it is not uncommon for the relevant associations to surface soon after the session, in which case they can be shared with the group at the following session. In the second instance, the defensiveness is apt to diminish with more dream work.

Just asking the dreamer for any feelings at all suggested by the image may be what is needed to produce a sudden insight between the image and feelings she was experiencing the night of the dream.

By now it should be obvious that to pursue a dream as completely as possible requires time, an unhurried atmosphere, patience, and persistence. Dream work cannot be condensed. Like a symphony, once it starts, it should be played out to its natural finale. One difference between the two is that a symphony is played out for the satisfaction of the audience; a dream is played out primarily for the satisfaction of the composer.

Being the Spokesperson for the Group

Many people have asked me if a leader is still necessary if the group is very experienced with the process. The answer is not so much that it is absolutely necessary but, rather, that it is very advisable. There are many points in the work when it is better for one person to act as spokesperson rather than risk having the process stall with no one to take the initiative when shifts and movement need to occur. It is better for one person to sense where the group is and to take that initiative, particularly in seeing that the movement from one stage to the next takes place within an appropriate time frame. At the end of the session, it is good for one person, acting on behalf of the group to thank the dreamer for sharing the dream and for the work done with it.

In a group in which everyone is starting out at the same level and for which there is no experienced leader, it is still a good idea for one person to act as a spokesperson. This can be arranged on a rotating basis if the group wishes. The group members have to know where they are at each stage of the process, and it is better for one person to provide that orientation. This prevents a good deal of vague looking about and wondering what to do next.

Furthering the Group's Responsibility

As a group works together over a period of time, everyone should begin to assume responsibility for keeping the process on track. It is not up to the leader to do all the work necessary to ensure the best possible outcome, but it is up to the leader to see that the work does get done. If the leader is experienced in the process and the others are not, she does have the additional responsibility for teaching the process.

On Sharing a Dream

It's a good idea for the leader to take the opportunity at an appropriate time to share a dream. This has a number of positive effects on the group. Her openness encourages openness in the group. As she shares her feelings, she comes across not as an authority but as a peer, a fellow dreamer. Technically, it reduces any transferences toward her that may be generated in the presence of authority (feelings toward a current authority springing from earlier encounters with authority figures). This helps establish the reality that we are engaged in a flat rather than a hierarchical structure, a democratic rather than an authoritarian one. Although the leader's participation as a member of the group in all the other aspects of the process has this effect to some extent, it isn't until she shares a dream that the group really feels that her authority rests only on her knowledge of the process and that in all other respects she is there as one dreamer among other dreamers. A skilled leader can share her dream and lead the group at the same time. With an experienced group, leadership can sometimes be turned over to someone else in the group.

An outline of the various aspects of the leadership role is considered in the succeeding chapter.

Final Comments

There are many different kinds of responsibilities in the role of leader. The primary function is to see that the process unfolds as it should, that as much as possible is done to be of help to the dreamer, and that no one steps out of line in a way that would be hurtful to the dreamer or that impedes the process. The important point is that there is a need for some one person with a clear understanding of the principles of dream work to assume that role.

The role is more complex and difficult than at first glance. Ever since I started working with dreams this way, I have held leadership training workshops designed to acquaint people with the nature of the problems that are encountered in work of this kind and to help them become more knowledgeable about the difficulties inherent in the leadership role. In the interest of extending safe and serious dream work into the community and placing it in the hands of any group anywhere that wishes to work on its own dreams, I have tried to describe in detail the role of the leader and the kinds of problems I have encountered. My aim has been to provide a general orientation as to how to deal with problems when they do arise.

The dream work I have described departs sharply from the historical and cultural context in which such work has generally been carried out. Traditionally, those involved with dreams have always been aware that the dreamer working alone often had difficulty grasping the message of the dream and needed help from another person. The other person, finding himself in the position where he could be of help to the dreamer, moved easily into the role of the expert, the dream interpreter, someone with knowledge of the symbolic value of dream images and of their meaning for the dreamer. In the modern era, fortified by psychoanalytic theory and our knowledge of personality growth and development, this expert role now centers on the person of the psychoanalyst.

Starting from the same position—namely, that the dreamer needs the help of another or others—I have redefined the nature of that role, not as expert in any sense, but simply as the helper who places certain natural resources we all have at the disposal of the dreamer. The leader does not step into the expert role. The only expert knowledge he is expected to have is about the principles and structure of the process to be followed. Whatever knowledge he may have about dreams still does not place him in an expert role vis-à-vis the dreamer, the dream, or the symbols that appear in the dream. He need not necessarily be the one in the group with the most experience in dream work. He is simply the one knowledgeable enough about the process to undertake to lead it. In all other respects he functions exactly as do other members of the group. He participates in the same way as others in every phase of the process and shares his dreams with the group when he so desires.

9

A Manual for Leaders

It should be obvious by now that the role of leader encompasses many different concerns, ranging from simply changing one's seat to be better able to keep the dreamer in view to orienting a new group and modeling the process until the group feels ready to take over. To hammer home the points that have been covered, here is a reminder list that a leader can refer to from time to time. Some of the problem areas noted are rare; others turn up quite frequently. They also vary in importance. Problems that are not recognized and that persist may tend to shift the center of attention away from the dreamer to the leader or to the group. In general, the leader does a good bit of explaining, encouraging, modeling, reassuring, and participating. The following list spells this out for ready reference.

General Considerations

1. Are you sitting so as to have an easy view of the dreamer as well as a view of all the members of the group?
2. Are you keeping in mind the importance of leading and participating at the same time?

3. Are you keeping close enough tabs on the dreamer to pick up any early signs of upset?

4. Are you keeping close enough tabs on the other members of the group to pick up any early signs of upset?

5. Are you keeping the time frame in mind as you move the group through each of the stages?

6. Are you giving clear directions with each stage change?

7. Are you striking the proper balance between guiding and participating?

8. Are you being sensitive to any signs of tensions arising in the group?

9. Are you clear about how to manage the situation if someone does break down (stopping the process, giving the dreamer time, not questioning the dreamer about the cause of the distress)?

10. Are you staying with the rule of never interrupting a dreamer unless something said was not heard or not clear?

11. Are you succeeding in getting to the point where the group no longer places undue reliance on you but has come to see the process as the meshing of everyone's contribution?

12. Can you handle someone who is obviously a misfit in the group?

13. Do you know enough about dreams and dreaming to answer some of the common questions about dreams that arise from time to time? For example, Do dreams the same night have any connection with each other? Are dreams always symbolic? What is a nightmare?

14. Are you sure enough of yourself to step in and intervene when something goes wrong?

15. Are you aware of the limitations of the process?

We move now from some of these general issues to the ones associated with specific stages of the process.

Stage 1A:
Sharing the Dream

1. As the leader, are you prepared to share a dream of your own? Although it is not appropriate for this to occur at an early point in a group's history, it is advisable at some point. A dream group feels most comfortable after everyone, including the leader, has shared a dream.

2. What do you do when no one volunteers? In a new group, one simply has to wait it out in the way described earlier. In an ongoing group, this is an opportunity for a leader to present his or her own dream.

3. Do you take pains to see to it that only the people who volunteered to share a dream are the ones involved in making the decision about who is to share and that the decision feels comfortable to those concerned?

4. Is it clear to the dreamer that he is to give the dream in as detailed a way as possible, including any feelings in the dream?

5. Is the dreamer aware of his responsibility to be truthful about the dream and to present all that he remembers about it?

6. Is he aware he can make a sketch that may be helpful to clarify any spatial arrangements?

7. Is the dreamer aware that after the first session he can offer any dream regardless of how far back in time it may have occurred?

8. When an old dream is presented, have you alerted the dreamer to some of the limitations the group may face in working with the dream?

9. With regard to a long dream and the time factor, have you alerted the dreamer to some of the limitations the group may face in working with the dream?

10. Does the dreamer know he has the choice of reading the dream or telling it spontaneously?

Stage 1B:
Clarifying the Dream

1. Is the question appropriate?

2. Is the dreamer being pressed for greater clarity than is possible when the image itself is not clear?

3. Have the characters in the dream been identified as real or not?

4. If the characters are real, is the dreamer going beyond a brief statement of their relationship to her?

5. Has the dreamer been asked for the feelings in the dream if not given spontaneously? The appearance of color in the dream?

6. Are questions being asked that have already been answered?

7. Is too much time being taken up with the questions?

Stage 2A:
Working With Feelings

1. Have clear instructions been given to both the group and the dreamer about their roles at this point?

2. Are the group members and the dreamer clear about staying with their feelings and not addressing what the images mean?

3. Are group members talking of the dream as their own and talking to each other, not to the dreamer?

4. Are group members sneaking in metaphorical meaning under the guise of offering a feeling?

5. Is the dreamer aware of the circumstances under which he can interject a comment? (See Chapter 3, p. 33.)

6. Is this part of the game going on too long?

Stage 2B:
Working With Metaphors

1. Have clear instructions been given to the effect that the group members can now come up with the meanings that they can give the images as well as adding any further feelings they may have?

2. Are group members aware of the possible meanings that they can give to unidentified characters in the dream—for example, as possibly representing some aspect of the dreamer?

3. Are group members aware of the possible meanings that they can give to identified characters—for example, as representing themselves, figures from the past, or some aspect of the dreamer?

4. Are group members aware that they are free to use any context known to all in the group in arriving at the meaning they give to the images?

5. Are group members being too literal and not working with the dream metaphorically?

6. Are group members trying to say something about every detail in the dream?

7. Are group members aware that they can base their response on a single image, a scene, or the whole dream?

8. Is this stage going on too long?

9. Are group members sensitive to the issue of confidentiality when someone in the group knows more about the dreamer than the others do?

10. Are group members aware of the different sources (their own lives, identifying with the dreamer) out of which they can develop their projections?

11. Are you as leader bringing in your projections?

12. Have signals been given to a dreamer that the dream is about to be returned to him?

Stage 3A:
The Dreamer's Response

1. Have you taken a moment or two to orient the dreamer fully as to the freedom and range she has in formulating her response?

2. Have you reassured her that she may take as much time as she needs and asked her to let you know when she is finished?

3. Are the group members aware that they are not to interrupt the dreamer?

4. Is the dreamer under any misimpression—for example, that she is to respond to all the projections of the group, right or wrong, or that she is not to give her own thoughts about the recent context until asked about it in the dialogue?

5. Are you prepared to give the dreamer the time she needs even though there may be extended pauses?

6. When the dreamer finishes have you checked with her as to whether she wants to go into the dialogue?

7. If the dreamer does not want to continue, have you acknowledged her sharing the dream and the work she has done?

8. Have you expressed an opinion as to whether or not a dialogue might offer further help?

9. Have you left the decision up to the dreamer?

Stage 3B.1:
Search for Context

1. Are group members aware that their questions are to be simple and direct with a view to helping a dreamer recall more of the emotional climate of her life just prior to the dream?

2. Do you see to it that questions start with the last remembered events prior to falling asleep, then move backward to the evening, the day, and if necessary, an even more extended period before the dream?

3. Is the dreamer's recall being stimulated with specific questions about what was read, seen on TV, phone calls, and so on prior to going to bed?

4. Is the group aware of the impact of being in a dream group as a powerful anticipatory day residue (touching as it does on feelings of exposure, problems in sharing oneself, sense of vulnerability, feelings of being judged, fear of being victimized, defensiveness, feelings of competition, exhibitionistic needs, etc.)? In a first dream being presented by a dreamer new to the group, has anyone asked about anticipatory feelings of coming into the group and possibly sharing a dream?

5. Are you giving the dreamer enough time to use the question as a tool in exploring her psyche?

6. Are relevant follow-up questions being asked?

7. Are you countering any premature tendency to start asking questions based on what is in the dream rather than keeping the focus on the recent context?

8. Is the group aware that if a possible recent context is known to all, questions can be put to the dreamer about it?

9. Have you asked a general "fishing" question?

10. In short, is it clear to the dreamer that the group is trying to help her recover any recent thoughts, feelings, or preoccupations around the time of the dream?

11. Is the group aware of the kinds of question not to ask? Questions to avoid include these:

> Information-giving questions
> Information-demanding questions
> Questions that are not obvious to the dreamer
> Questions going into areas the dreamer has not opened up herself
> Pursuing questions when it is obvious the dreamer doesn't want to go any
> further

12. Are you keeping the time factor in mind, limiting the questions if necessary so as to leave time for the remaining parts of the dialogue?

13. At the completion of this phase, have you checked with the dreamer about going further with the playback?

Stage 3B.2:
Playback

1. Have you taught group members how to conduct the playback? Are they clear about what constitutes a scene? Are they dramatizing the scene as they call the dreamer's attention to it, emphasizing seeming incongruities, unusual imagery, and so forth? Are they offering help to the dreamer, recalling related material already shared by the dreamer, and inviting the dreamer to look at the scene in its possible connection to the scene before?

2. Have you reassured the dreamer that this is being done to elicit new material and not to repeat what has already been said?

3. Has the scene been played back in its entirety, including every detail given by the dreamer?

4. Has the dreamer then been confronted with specific images in that scene that have not been fully developed?

5. Have appropriate follow-up questions been addressed to the dreamer?

6. Have enough "anything more" questions been asked?

7. Have you been reasonably persistent without being insistent?

8. As the dreamer gives his response, is it congruent with or divergent from what the dream seems to be saying, and if divergent, has this been called to the dreamer's attention?

9. Has the dreamer been given enough time to gather his associations?

10. Has the dreamer been helped to view the dream symbolically and not literally?

11. Has the dreamer been confronted with the feelings in the dream?

12. Have you been reassuring to the dreamer who cannot come up with any further associations?

13. Have you seen to it that everyone who has questions to put to the dreamer has had the opportunity to do so?

14. Keeping in mind the time, will there be enough time for the orchestration and completion of the process?
15. Have you checked with the dreamer as to whether an orchestration is desired?

Stage 3B.3:
The Orchestration

1. Does the group see its role now as offering connections between dream and reality and not one of asking further questions?
2. Are group members staying with what the dreamer gave them and not offering formulations of their own that are not related to anything they heard the dreamer say?
3. Are group members talking to the dreamer about her dream and not slipping into the error of talking about the dream as their own?
4. Is the dreamer being given time to respond after each integrating projecting?
5. Are group members aware that they can offer connections to an image, a scene, or the entire dream?

Closing the Session

1. Has the dreamer been given a chance to offer any final comments?
2. Have you thanked the dreamer for the dream and the work she did with the dream?

Stage 4:
Follow-up

1. Have you remembered to invite any further remarks from the dreamer who presented at the last session?
2. Are there any delayed orchestrating comments from anyone?

The preceding list contains the main check points. A new and inexperienced leader, feeling insecure and struggling to master the process may fall into a number of other errors that can cause difficulty. Depending on the personality of the leader, he may come across as deferring too much to the group or exerting too strong a hold over the group. The former is more common and leads to difficulties along the following lines:

1. Being fearful of taking the initiative in making the shift from one stage to the other
2. Letting the group go on too long at certain points, particularly in Stage 2

3. Failing to control any inappropriate activity by the group—for example, asking inappropriate questions just to satisfy personal curiosity
4. Failing to monitor the time so as to leave enough time for the dialogue
5. Being reticent about confronting the dreamer with the details of the dream in the playback phase of the dialogue

Problems

A leader should be felt as a leader without being intrusive or taking too much on himself at the expense of encouraging group participation. The process has to be carried by the entire group. In contrast to a leader who is too loose about structure, one can be too rigid. A leader's determination to see the process through to its very end may involve a greater concern with the process than with what may be happening to the dreamer. Sensitivity to the feelings of the dreamer takes precedence over any compulsion to complete the process. Remember that a sense of closure can occur at any time in the course of the process. A natural point of closure may be experienced by a dreamer and missed by a leader too preoccupied with going through all the steps in the process.

Initially, inexperienced leaders have difficulties keeping in mind their various responsibilities as leader and at the same time functioning as a participant. Taking their responsibility as leader too seriously, they may fail to realize that the group has responsibilities as well. Everyone shares in the responsibility to see to it that there is a dream to work on and to actively participate in the work that has to be done. I have seen new leaders experience a feeling of desperation over whether or not they will succeed in eliciting a dream. Out of his growing anxiety, a new leader may canvas the group personally to see if anyone has a dream to share. In doing this, he puts pressure on someone who may have a dream but doesn't wish to share it. The leader is responsible only to do his utmost to elicit a dream in the proper manner. When no one is made to feel on the spot, this shared responsibility is soon felt in the group, and there is generally no dearth of dreams. The degree to which each member will respond to the call for a dream will, of course, vary.

An exaggerated sense of responsibility can get a leader into trouble when more than one dreamer volunteers. He may be tempted to intervene too actively instead of leaving it to those who volunteered to arrive at a decision by themselves or to arrive at it by chance. An inappropriate intervention of this kind might be something like this: "I think Mary is more anxious to share her dream than Jane." A leader should make it clear to the group beforehand that when several people do volunteer to share a dream, the one who has not shared a dream as recently as the others has priority. Then the leader should leave it up to that person to decide whether or not to use that priority.

Another situation difficult for inexperienced leaders is reading the signals someone gives when he volunteers a dream. In most instances, a dream is volunteered in a straightforward way, but many situations occur in which a dreamer seems to equivocate in one way or another. These are some examples[1] of how he might qualify his offering:

"I have a dream, but maybe someone else has a more important dream."

"I have a dream that doesn't seem very interesting. Maybe I ought to wait until I have a better one."

"My dream seems clear to me. I don't know whether I should take up the time of the group with it."

"I had a dream several days ago, but maybe it's too old."

"A lot went before the part I remembered, so maybe it isn't suitable."

All of the preceding introductory comments may spring from an ambivalence on the part of the dreamer about sharing the dream. It is important that this ambivalence be recognized and an attempt made to resolve it. None of these reservations justifies not sharing a dream, and the dreamer should be told this. Depending on what question the dreamer raises, one of the following clarifications might be helpful:

"All dreams are to be considered important. Some might be more important than others, but there is no such thing as an unimportant dream. Besides, one cannot make a judgment of the importance of a dream before it is worked on."

"The same applies to the question of how interesting a dream is. So-called dull dreams often have surprising and exciting aspects."

"No matter how clear a dream may seem to the dreamer, group work will add a richer and deeper dimension."

"If a dreamer really wants to share a dream, the time of its occurrence plays a secondary role."

"None of us remembers all that went on during a dream. Any remembered portion of a longer dream is suitable."

It is important, however, for the dreamer to know that he is under no obligation to share a particular dream unless it is clear in his own mind that that is what he really wants to do.

One does not meet all these difficulties at the same time. I have condensed almost two decades of problems of this kind into these few pages. Once the mechanics of the process become automatic, the leader will feel freer and more confident in managing the problems that occasionally arise. She can devote herself more freely to the mission of protecting the dreamer, guiding the group, and making her own contributions.

Rules:
Breakable and Unbreakable

This process offers a structure within which safe dream work can be carried out. A structure is not a rigid container. There can be some "give" to it, providing one has a clear understanding of the purpose of the structure. Clearly stated, that purpose is to provide the dreamer with the help she needs to the extent that she wants help. Within the structure and with this goal in mind, there is the freedom for all to say whatever they wish to say but at the proper time and in the proper way. The only truly unbreakable rule is, "Thou shalt not do harm to the dreamer." That harm can come about whenever the dreamer's authority and control is threatened as it is when leading questions are put to the dreamer. These run the risk of touching on areas the dreamer is not ready to go into or does not wish to go into. Any attempt to push a dreamer beyond the limits she has set will have the same effect. This is also true for orchestrating projections based on speculations or theoretical knowledge not justified by anything forthcoming from the dreamer.

There is enough flexibility in the process to adapt to the constraints of time when a dream is very long. Combining the two substages of Stage 2 (feelings and metaphors) can save time. Even when one engages with both of these substages separately, they can be limited in the interest of time. Combining these substages is also more expedient when a dream is offered that consists of a single image. In that instance, it generally proves easier to develop feelings about the image as one develops its metaphorical possibilities. When one comes to the playback and time is running out, one need not play the entire dream back scene by scene but simply call images to the dreamer's attention that have not yet been sufficiently developed.

At any point in Stage 3, the dreamer may say to the group that she feels in good contact with the dream except for a single image and may express the wish to have the group go back into the game mode (Stage 2) and offer further metaphorical projections around that image. Having had the dreamer's response and perhaps part of the dialogue, these ensuing projections may strike closer to home. Should this be the case, there would be no necessity to go further with the dialogue.

A dreamer may wish to present two dreams from the same night. If time is available, this wish should be respected. By the same token, a dreamer may feel that dreams from two different nights are related and wish to share them. That, too, is acceptable if they are reasonably short and time is available.

Criteria for Leadership

There is a distinction to be made between someone who functions as the leader of a group of peers starting out at the same level in dream work and someone doing it professionally on a fee basis with the group open to the public. With regard to the former, I would encourage lay groups to form, become as familiar as possible with the rationale of the process, and to learn more about it by working together. There is much to learn, but that learning can come out of ongoing experience. Functioning in this way at an amateur level, so to speak, there is no one who carries more authority than anyone else. A sound mastery of the principles of dream work will provide the group with a self-corrective device. Many groups start out this way, and then at some point, one or two will seek specialized leadership training and bring what they learn back to the group. I have seen the successful development of groups come about in this way. The ultimate goal is to help more and more people get in touch with this creative and valuable source of information about themselves.

Any approach to dream work can be misused, and this process is no exception. In its emphasis on the unique situation of the dreamer and his attendant vulnerability when a dream is shared in public, the process considerably lowers whatever risks there may be in dream work. It provides no platform for authoritarian performances of any kind. Working within the guidelines, group members become sensitive very quickly to anyone's stepping out of line in his or her approach to the dreamer. Because of my heavy emphasis on the safety factor, difficulties may arise in the opposite way, by the group's being too timid in their approach to the dreamer.

Let's look at the other side of the story, the person who wants to engage in dream work professionally using this process. What are the criteria for doing so? I have been asked this question and have considerable difficulty in answering it in any way that can provide clear-cut and uniform criteria. I can only describe, as I have done, what is entailed in group dream work and the responsibilities one would face in doing it professionally. Certainly, the basic skills have to be mastered before one is in a position to teach others.

In addition to the basic skills of how to listen to a dreamer and how to help the dreamer transform what is symbolically expressed in a dream into a genuinely felt waking experience, there is also the need to recognize any tensions that may arise in the group and when it's necessary to resolve such tensions through an appropriate group process.

The central question, of course, is whether or not one has to be accredited in one of the mental health disciplines to undertake group dream work professionally. Provided the criteria outlined above are met in good conscience, I do not think that a reliable dream group leader has to come only from the ranks of those with degrees in one of the helping professions. On the other hand, I do believe that if dream work is to reach a significant sector of the public, professionals will have to play a key role. Those who are accredited have, or should have, two things going for them. First, learning the art of therapy involves mastery of the skills noted earlier. Second, by virtue of their professional status, these individuals are more likely to have the opportunity to reach an interested audience, more likely to receive support by working through an umbrella agency of some kind, and more likely to be accepted as credible by the public. A professional is also more apt to, or should be more apt to, know his or her own limits. My own feeling is that anyone, lay or professional, who seeks to offer group dream work to the general public on a fee basis should have specialized leadership training and supervision.

There is also a downside to what I have said about people who come with professional credentials. They may encounter considerable difficulty in moving away from the stance of a therapist and fully accepting the differences between this process and formal psychotherapy. In some instances, there is much unlearning that has to take place. Being a leader in this process means letting go of the therapist role and accepting the limitations in never leading and always following the dreamer (which is good therapy anyway, but not all therapists abide by it). A therapist is used to operating with more knowledge about a patient than we have about a dreamer. Historical data provides her with a broad base for interpretive responses. There is no such base in the dream group.

In short, professionals should, by virtue of their training, be better equipped to deal with the possible complications that may arise and have the skills necessary to facilitate the process. On the other hand, aspects of their training and experience can be counterproductive. A layperson can master the process through adequate leadership training experience, become sufficiently familiar with the things that can go wrong, and get to the point where in good conscience he or she feels knowledgeable and experienced enough to take it on in a professional capacity. I don't issue any certifying statements regardless of how many leadership training sessions someone may have had with me. I think this is a matter of an individual's judgment and conscience. This is the situation as it is now in the United States. I can envisage a time in the future when a more definitive statement may have to be made about certification as a leader.

A Note on Note Taking

No note taking is obligatory, but I would encourage taking at least some notes. Everyone undertaking to lead a group will have to judge for himself or herself just how much writing will be helpful. What follows is my own preference. I try to keep process notes consisting of (a) a verbatim report of the dream and everything the dreamer says in the third stage, briefly noting the questions in the dialogue and getting down the answers as completely as I can, and (b) briefer notes concerning the group's input and my own thoughts. I rely heavily on these notes for both the orchestration and my own efforts at a postsession review. I have found that such a review often provides me with new ideas about the dream that can then be put to the dreamer as a delayed orchestration on the next occasion. I have discovered that I can take a dream down more quickly if I don't write across the entire page but, with less movement of my arm, use a narrow column as I go down the page. This also has the advantage of leaving space for noting remarks by the group and for my own ongoing thoughts.

Some participants, emulating my own style, overdo it. It is certainly not necessary to take down every projection offered in Stage 2. What I concentrate on in my note taking is as much as I can get down of what the dreamer has said. I don't know at any given moment what may trigger a later insight. When an inexperienced leader is too involved in note taking, however, it may be at the expense of not keeping a sharp enough eye on the dreamer as well as on the others in the group. In note taking, do what is comfortable. If you are blessed with a good memory, you may not bother to even write the dream down. This presents no problem if the dream is short. Reliance on one's memory, however, often leads to unnecessary and inappropriate questioning at a later stage in the process.

Nor is it necessary for the dreamer in Stage 2 to write down all the feelings and metaphors the group comes up with. Some have said that they find this useful for later reflection on the dream. What is important, of course, is only what the dreamer feels applies to her. Some dreamers prefer not to take any notes in Stage 2, finding it easy to remember and use whatever affected them.

In summary, the leader's responsibilities are as follows:

WITH REGARD TO THE PROCESS

1. Lead the group through the various stages of the process.
2. Function as a timekeeper, seeing that the time allotted to each stage of the process is commensurate with its importance and that the process is brought to completion in the time allotted.
3. Manage any tensions that may arise in the group.
4. Recognize and respond if the process gets off track.
5. Act as the spokesperson of the group in acknowledging the work of the dreamer.

WITH REGARD TO THE DREAMER

1. Maintain an awareness of how the ongoing work is affecting the dreamer.
2. Be prepared to interrupt the process at any point should the dreamer appear to be in difficulty.
3. Make sure the dreamer is clear about his role, responsibilities, and prerogatives at each stage of the process.
4. Be of help to the dreamer in using the group properly.

WITH REGARD TO THE GROUP

1. Maintain an awareness of how the ongoing work is affecting each group member.
2. Stimulate the group to respond appropriately at each stage of the process.
3. See that group members understand both their responsibilities and their limits.
4. Deal with any breaches of the structure.

WITH REGARD TO ONESELF IN THE ROLE OF LEADER

1. Fulfill the dual role of the leader and participant.
2. Share the responsibility for carrying out the process with the members of the group.
3. Feel prepared to exercise one's option to share a dream.
4. Be responsible for containing one's own reactions as the process unfolds.

ERRORS IN LEADERSHIP ARE MOST APT TO RESULT FROM

1. Not listening to the dreamer
2. Not knowing where the dreamer is
3. Being too mechanical about the process
4. Failure to realize that everyone shares in the carrying out of the process
5. Pushing too hard for a successful outcome
6. Poor timing

7. Not respecting the dreamer's limits
8. Not giving adequate instructions
9. Not protecting the dreamer from interruptions, leading questions, and so on
10. Not recognizing the spontaneous occurrence of closure

Leading a dream group is a skill that requires time and practice. If you try to abide by the principles set down, the mistakes you make won't be serious. The important thing is to recognize mistakes as mistakes and learn from them. There are so many nuances and subtleties to the task of helping a dreamer and the work can take so many unexpected turns and twists that one can expect to encounter new challenges with each new dream.

Note

1. See Chapter 2 for a more inclusive list.

10

Leading a New Group

In addition to all the intricacies of leadership already mentioned, a number of special considerations apply to a new group just beginning dream work. A two-part orientation is required, first to familiarize the participants with what a dream is and wherein lies the healing power and, second, to present a full description of the process, the rationale for each stage, and the role and responsibilities of each participant at each stage.

Teaching the process also involves modeling. In Stage 2, it is up to the leader to take the initiative in responding to the dream as her own and in encouraging others to do so as well. When it comes to the dialogue stage, I explain that not only will I model the dialogue by asking the questions that should be asked but that I will also share aloud the thoughts I have that lead up to the question. I do that with all three steps in the dialogue but not to the exclusion of encouraging participation from the group. The group is invited to help explore the context, to participate in the playback, and to offer any orchestrating ideas they may have. I tell them in advance that if any questions are wrong, inappropriate, or premature, I will point that out and explain my reasons for doing so.

The first few sessions with a new group are to be seen as learning experiences. The best teaching occurs when mistakes are made and the group learns from the mistakes. The leader continues to teach through modeling as she judges the group's readiness to assume responsibility for the process to accept the leader as a participant and not as the one who will do all the work. Until a group is fully at ease with the process, it devolves on her to manage the process and familiarize the participants with what is expected of them. It takes some experience to learn how to fit the process into the time frame, to keep on the alert for any problems that may arise, to see that the dreamer remains in control, and when necessary, to remind the dreamer of this right. Even in a group that has been ongoing for some time, the participants can benefit from seeing the skills of the leader in action, her ability to model the process at critical junctures, her sensitivity to the dreamer in knowing when to pursue a line of questioning, and her awareness as to when the questioner is being "invited out" by the dreamer. What follows pertains specifically to the first dream work session with a new group.

The First Session

The leader explains that she has a twofold goal in this initial orienting session. Her primary goal is to see to it that the dreamer gets as much help as possible through the various interactions that will take place between the dreamer and the group. Her second goal is to get across to the group a clear demonstration of the way the process works. To carry out this teaching aspect, she will modify the question a leader would ordinarily put to the group in two ways. Instead of just asking for a dream, she will ask for a short dream that was dreamed the night before the session. The reason for these qualifications is then explained to the group. A dream from the preceding night will allow the leader to model the kinds of questions put to the dreamer at the dialogue stage of the process that will enable her to reconstruct the emotional atmosphere she took to bed that night. This is more easily done with a recent dream than one that is days or weeks old. There are practical reasons for asking for a short dream. In this first session, the leader is actively engaged in teaching the process. As each stage of the process is encountered, she describes in detail what is to take place, deals with any questions that arise, and makes sure that everyone understands the rationale for what is happening. All of this adds considerably to the time it ordinarily takes to work out a dream. A long dream would, because of the time involved, present too many difficulties in the early learning stages of dream work.

Based on my experience, I would like to offer a word of caution with respect to the request for a short dream. When the leader asks for a short dream in the first session with a new group, he should maintain a kind of silent skepticism and try diplomatically to determine if, indeed, the dream is really short. The reason for caution is that all too often the dream turns out to be anything but short. How can one tell if the dream is truly short? First, explain that a short dream is one that can be told, even speaking slowly, in 2 to 5 minutes. Second, if it is written down and covers more than a half to a whole letter-sized page, it is probably longer than optimum. Sometimes, a dreamer honestly does believe he has a short dream, but in telling it, it turns out to be longer than he thought. There is nothing to do about that. Once we embark on a dream, we go through with it. On occasion, someone is so anxious to share a dream that he really doesn't hear your emphasis on the word *short* and knowingly or unknowingly offers it as a short dream. Again, we will work with it even though soon it becomes apparent that it is too long. I will, however, indicate that the dream was longer than I had anticipated and that we may not be able to do it justice in the time available. At least, that reality has to be communicated and understood.

When someone does, indeed, have a short dream but hesitates to volunteer, giving as his reason that the dream was longer but the rest of it had been forgotten, he should be reassured that this is the case with most dreams. We rarely recapture all that goes on during our periods of dreaming consciousness. For an introductory session, I would prefer to have a dream with more than one image. I would nevertheless stay with the basic maxim that a dream cannot be too short to work with.

With these considerations in mind, the question put to a beginning group is, "Did anyone have a short dream last night that he or she would like to share with the group?" If one person, and one alone, responds positively, the leader's first concern—namely, to have a dream to work with—is set to rest. More often than not when the question is put to a new group, it is greeted with an embarrassed silence, with the participants casting shy glances at teach other to see if anyone else is going to volunteer.

Here are a number of possible scenarios a leader should be prepared to encounter:

No One Volunteers. Silence ensues. How long should one wait and what should one do? I suggest waiting and doing nothing for up to 1 full minute. This allows enough tension to generate and possibly influence someone to share a dream. Then go through the same routine but ask for a dream from the night before last night. Silence continues. Repeat the same routine, but this time just ask for a recent dream. Silence continues. Then, with some air of resignation, the leader asks, "Well, does anyone have any dream he or she would like to share?"

Usually, one doesn't get to this point before someone volunteers. The average dream group consists of six to ten members. It has been my experience that in groups that size, by the time one gets to the second or third question, someone will finally offer a dream from the previous night. It is as if a certain amount of tension is necessary before someone can resolve the dilemma of wanting to share a dream, while at the same time, hoping that someone else will volunteer.

Two or More People Volunteer a Dream. At the opposite extreme, in response to the first time the leader puts the question to the group, two or more people will respond. Then I will say something such as this to the volunteers:

> I'm going to ask you two (or three or more) to try to decide between (among) yourselves who will share the dream. I don't know what your feelings are about how important the dream is to you and how eager you are to present it. Only you do. Can each of you share with the other(s) how strongly you feel about wanting to work with the dream? Try to be as frank and honest with each other as you can. If both of you (or all three or more) feel the same way, we can decide by chance (toss a coin if there are two; draw lots if there are more). The thing you should not do is ignore your own feelings and withdraw out of politeness. You will regret it later on. Simply be guided by your feelings and whether or not you really do wish to withdraw as you listen to the feelings of the other(s).

When more than one member of the group volunteers, it is important to urge them all to share their feelings as frankly as possible about why they want to present a dream. I have seen people who surrender their option for misguided reasons (politeness, shyness, not wanting to seem aggressive). They then feel so upset about what they did that they have difficulty concentrating on the ensuing process.

It is important for the leader not to allow anyone else in the group to intercede while those who have volunteered are sharing their feelings with each other. Others in the group often try to offer suggestions they think will be helpful but that generally are not. As an example, someone might suggest we do both dreams. This springs from ignorance of the fact that in an ordinary session (1.5 to 2 hours), there is generally time for only one dream. Even if there is more time available, when it comes time to ask for another dream, one of the people who volunteered earlier but didn't have the opportunity to share a dream, might change his or her mind. Furthermore, others who didn't volunteer earlier may do so at this second occasion. It must be clear that when a choice is surrendered or lost on the first go-around, there is no special option on the next go-around.

In a new group in which all the participants are unknown to me and two or more members volunteer to share their dream, I will further modify my instructions to the group about coming to a decision among themselves as to which dream is presented. Let us say that two people volunteered. I tell them that on this first occasion, I will reserve the right to make the decision and then explain the reason—namely, that it gives me the freedom to make a choice based on which dream I think is most suitable for demonstrating the process. I emphasize that, after this initial session, I will no longer make such a decision and that, furthermore, my choice is not in any way a value judgment on the significance or importance of the dream. Generally, I try to avoid exercising this option if I can, because I do not like to put anyone in the position of telling a dream and then not working on it. Whenever possible, I prefer to leave it up to those who volunteered to make the decision.

There are a few reasons why the dream might not be suitable for demonstration purposes. Based on my experience, it is best to start with a dream that is short but not too short. A dream with very little detail or only a single image does not provide enough opportunity for the group to exercise the full range of strategies in the later stages of the process—for example, the importance of exploring the sequential changes in a dream, the symbolic significance of unknown characters that appear in a dream, references to earlier stages of one's life, and so on. Another reason influencing the choice is that when the group is not known to the leader, there is always the risk that there is someone in the group who should not be there, someone who is disturbed and needs more than what a dream group has to offer. This has not occurred often in my experience, but when it does and is recognized, in the behavior of the individual or in the content of the dream, it is a justifiable reason for the leader to make the choice. In general, one is on very uncertain grounds in inferring pathology from any one dream, but for a first go-around, I would prefer a dream without too much disturbingly bizarre imagery. In the first session, there is also very little behavior to go by. Still, there may be telltale signs that would warrant caution—the general appearance, tone, and behavior in connection with the act of volunteering a dream; extraneous comments; and so on. In regard to the question of choice when several volunteer, at times, my own intuition has failed me, and when I thought I had made the right choice, the dreamer turned out to be either highly defended or unable to work within the structure. This, of course, creates problems for the leader, making it difficult, if not impossible, to adequately and in a gratifying way demonstrate each stage of the process.

The first session with a new group is always somewhat risky. A frightened, defensive person is apt to stop the process at the end of the second stage or early in the dialogue. Someone beset by personal problems may use the dream as a point of departure in seeking support from the group or may use the group as a sounding board, getting further and further away from the dream as if it were only incidental to his real purpose in being there. The only reassurance I can offer the leader is to persist, in the hope that the next time things will be better and the needed demonstration will ultimately get across.

Even when the dreamer and the dream seem ideal for demonstration purposes, it has been my experience that it sometimes doesn't work out that well. It is very hard to predict in advance where a dream will take one, what depths of personality will be tapped, what long dormant conflicts will be exposed, what powerful reactions will ensue, and what defenses will be mobilized. When the demonstration works out, the group is off to a good start. When it doesn't, there is always a second chance.

I have mentioned that teaching is a very important part of this initial session. The leader instructs the group members in their roles at each stage of the process and in the rationale for each stage as it is encountered in the course of the process. They have been told all that before in the orienting session, but now as they engage in the process it becomes more meaningful.

The leader should not share a dream in the first session. Although she is free to volunteer her own dream at any subsequent session, in general, it should not be done until the group is familiar enough with the process. The group has to develop trust in the process. This comes about as they witness, firsthand, how the dreamer and not the leader controls the process. That trust is consolidated as each member of the group has the opportunity to work on his or her own dream. What follows are some of the concerns, stage by stage, that a leader needs to consider.

Stage 1A Concerns

1. Often, a new leader with a new group is so relieved when someone does volunteer to share a dream that she neglects to be sure that the date of the dream is known in advance. This information is particularly important in the early stages of dream work when, not infrequently, dreams have a reference to the dreamer's concerns about sharing a dream.

2. A dreamer who is new to the process may start giving associations immediately unless stopped by the leader.

3. Members in a new group sometimes look at each other as if to ask, "Did you have a dream?" or sometimes ask it explicitly. It bears repeated emphasis that each person must be left to make that decision by himself or herself.

Stage 1B Concerns

Asking too many questions can be a stalling tactic out of some hesitation and uncertainty about moving on.

Stage 2A Concerns

1. Almost always, someone in the group will not have heard the leader's directions to focus on feelings only and will talk about the symbolic meaning the dream has for him or her. The leader then can inquire about the feelings that that person connects to the meaning he or she gives the images, and urge the group member to try to stay with the feelings the dream evokes.

2. The group members must clearly understand that they are free to talk about any feelings the dream stimulates in them but that they are not limited to any feelings they actually have at the moment. They may talk of any feelings that they imagine they might have as they continue to work with the dream as their own. They are free to bring in feelings they think the actual dreamer may have had as long as they do it as their own projections into the dream.

Stage 2B Concerns

1. As already mentioned, questions arise here about the use of words such as *metaphor, symbol,* and *interpretation.* The leader must be clear in her own mind about these terms. A symbol can be understood in contrast to a sign. The latter is an arbitrarily agreed on indicator with a specific meaning—for example, a road sign calling attention to curves ahead. A symbol conveys a more abstract and less circumscribed reference. A country's flag, for example, is a symbol that conjures up feelings of different levels of intensity reverberating around the general idea of patriotism. Metaphor can

be considered a subclass of symbolism. Metaphor is the essence of poetry. A definition of poetic metaphor from Briggs and Monaco (1990) applies with equal meaning to the visual metaphor of the dream: "Put simply, a poetic metaphor is the union of unlike things (pictures to ideas, ideas to feelings, feelings to objects, objects to pictures, and so on) such that the mind discovers unexpected relationships and comes upon new insight" (p. 3). In a dream, for example, a house may be a self-image in which the attic represents stored memories and the basement, the unconscious, or it might allude to a definite house, evoking feelings from an earlier time. Interpretation, as described earlier, is a term best reserved for its technical meaning in therapy where it is used in a more generalized way to highlight an aspect of behavior as observed by the interpreter over time, behavior that goes beyond any immediate connection to the dream. The therapist, being privy to more of the dreamer's history than we are, can draw more far-reaching implications with regard to what light the dream can shed on the dreamer's personality and problems.

2. It may require repeated emphasis to get across the idea that there are no constraints as far as what group members can say about the dream as long as they talk about it as their own and do so in the spirit of sharing their own projections with each other.

Stage 3A Concerns

1. Some dreamers respond enthusiastically and vociferously from the beginning once the dream is returned to them. Some are shy, hesitant, and more defensive. It can be helpful to those in this latter group for the leader to reassure them as often as necessary about their rights and privileges with regard to self-disclosure. The dreamer has to be clear about the fact that she can say as much or as little as she wishes. She is free to give whatever associations occur to her and to link any aspect of her life, recent or remote, to the dream. She is free to say whatever she can about the meaning the dream has for her. Sometimes, the dreamer is under one or more misimpressions of what is expected of her—for example, that she is to focus only on her response to the projections of the group or that she is not to talk about the current context but to leave that for the group to ask questions about.

2. If the dreamer feels apologetic about having very little to say, she should be reassured by the leader that more will probably occur to her in the course of the dialogue.

Stage 3B Concerns

1. Most issues that arise at this stage have already been discussed. One must discover the middle road between questioning that is too insistent and questioning that is not persistent enough. It is incumbent on the leader to model the more difficult technical points, such as how to put the question in the most simple and open way possible, how to recognize the indications for follow-up questions, how to sense whether one is being "invited in" by the dreamer or "invited out," and most important, how to be aware of a point of closure if it has been reached.

2. Problems can arise when a dreamer new to the process has difficulty deciding whether or not to go on to the orchestrating phase. Having no experience with what an orchestration can do, he may feel uncertain about what to do. A leader can always intervene and indicate whether or not he feels an orchestration might be helpful. The ultimate decision is then left up to the dreamer.

3. Generally, in a beginning group, the leader takes the initiative in offering an orchestration. Although there is much to learn about how to do it correctly, group members are usually not shy about making the attempt. We all seem too eager to be given the opportunity to "interpret" someone else's dream. Sometimes, I think it is a built-in drive that is almost impossible to control!

11
■

The Dreamer

We are now ready to consider in greater detail the special features of the dreamer's situation as he begins the exploration of his dream in the group. We will follow the dreamer from the time the decision is made to join the dream group to the final stage of the process once a dream is shared. We will note the range of subjective responses that dreamers encounter at each stage as they learn how to use the process to their advantage.

The Decision to
Engage in Group Dream Work

People come to dream groups for a variety of reasons. Because there are many different kinds of groups engaged in dream work, the observations that follow pertain to the groups I have led or groups led by people who have had their training with me. Although in some instances, people come under the influence of a friend who has responded enthusiastically to the experience, in most instances, the motivation to do dream work arises from within. In recent years when all of my professional activity has focused on dreams, I keep meeting people who have been tracking their dreams on their own, recording them, working on them, and relying on them to provide important insights. The group experience adds an enriching note to their ongoing personal dream work. They are the true oneirophiles.

Then there are those who discover their oneirophilia only when they encounter their dreams in the course of therapy. Some seek further dream work after completion of therapy. Many engage in the group concomitant with therapy. Some have found it helpful during the terminal phase of therapy as a bridge between the support of a therapist and being on their own.

Then there are the latent oneirophiles and the closet oneirophiles. In the first instance, there is no awareness of interest until it is sparked through chance reading or an encounter with a friend interested in dreams. The closet oneirophiles have a different kind of problem. They are aware of their interest in dreams, but for one reason or another hesitate to make that interest known publicly. They may be inhibited by feelings of shyness, shame, or self-indulgence, or they may anticipate a critical or negative response from their peers. Here in the United States, cultural pressures, particularly in urban areas, would be more apt to support rather than inhibit such an interest. In Sweden, however, where I have done dream work in many remote areas, it is not at all uncommon to meet someone who is secretive about actively pursuing dream work for fear of a negative reaction from peers.

The true oneirophiles are the ones who form the backbone of a dream group. They are the ones prepared to make a firm commitment and to stay with it. There is another group of those who may or may not turn out to be oneirophiles. They generally have had little prior experience with dreams and come at the behest of a friend, a mate, or in some instances, a child or a parent. A real interest may or may not develop after the initial trial period of 4 weeks.[1]

Occasionally, someone finds her way into a dream group for the wrong reason. Someone in need of therapy but hesitant to start it may see the dream group as a less threatening alternative. The motivation for coming into a dream group may stem from neurotic needs of one sort or another and not from a genuine interest in one's dream life. That person may, for example, seek a group setting as an outlet for exhibitionistic needs. When this happens, the dream work is secondary to the manipulation of the group in the interest of meeting these needs.[2]

An unusual problem I met up with on one occasion was a situation in which a preexisting group, studying together in an area unrelated to dreams, decided to transform themselves into a dream group. Two participants then found themselves joining in somewhat reluctantly. Their latent resentment soon became manifest in their dreams.

Therapists have been drawn to my group ostensibly to increase their professional skills in working with the dreams of their clients. The majority of them turn out to be true oneirophiles and welcome the opportunity to work on their own dreams. A few have shied away from sharing their own dreams and limited their participation to the work being done with the dreams of others. Problems become manifest when they cling to their role as therapists, going into areas the dreamer has not yet opened up but that the therapist feels may be relevant or using theoretical terms derived from Freudian or Jungian systems that go beyond the specific meaning or associations related by the dreamer. For our purpose—namely, to help a dreamer find a place for the imagery in the framework of his concrete life experience—it is best not to work with terms such as *oedipal conflict, anima,* or *animus* unless introduced by the dreamer himself. Otherwise, you run the risk of casting the dream into an unwarranted frame of reference.

In summary, people seek out dream groups out of interest or out of need, healthy or otherwise. In most instances, their goal is to learn how to work more effectively with dreams on their own. Some are content to simply enjoy the benefits of group dream work. Some may become intrigued with the process and go on to leadership training with the purpose of ultimately leading groups. Therapists come to sharpen their ability to use dreams more effectively with clients. People in therapy come to work more leisurely with dreams than they are able to do in a therapy session. Finally, there are those who come to dream work out of a religious motivation, drawn by what they sense is a spiritual dimension to their dream lives.

Beginning Attitudes Toward Dream Work

Along with the different motivations that bring dreamers into dream groups, there are also different states of preparedness. People come with different conceptions about dreams and their importance. They come with differing levels of sophistication. They may come with entrenched allegiance to one or another school of dream interpretation. They differ in their readiness to surrender some of their ideas. They come with differing kinds of prior group experience that in turn shape their expectations of what is to happen. They come with differing ranges of dream recall. Some barely eke out an occasional fragment. Some tend to have short, clear vignettes; others favor many-scened, epic-length dreams. Most important of all, they come with differing capacities to be sufficiently open to the process.

The success of the process depends on the development of trust: trust in the honesty and reliability of dream imagery, in the process, in the group, in the leader, and in oneself. All of the motivational factors alluded to influence the ease and depth of that trust. They also influence the beginning attitudes people have toward group dream work. Some approach it with confidence and eagerness; some with anxiety. Some are bold, jumping right in, feeling relaxed, and trusting from the start. Out of anxiety, some volunteer early to share a dream, eager to get the initial experience over with. Some are cautious and hold back, preferring to test the waters first.

Attitudes toward authority play an important role in our culture and quickly become manifest in a dream group. Greater or lesser difficulty is encountered as each participant learns to come to terms with the reality that he or she, and not the leader, is the final and only authority on the meaning of the dream.

Those who come to the process from an experience in group therapy sometimes find the structure a bit difficult to get used to, differing as it does from the more free-wheeling reciprocal style that characterizes exchanges in group therapy. It takes time for them to get accustomed to the idea that the leader is not the therapist and that the process is oriented to meeting the needs of the dreamer and not to the working through of whatever others in the group may be experiencing in the course of helping the dreamer.

Deciding to Share a Dream

In response to the leader's request for a dream, each person who has a dream is faced with the decision of whether or not to share it with the group. The ease with which that decision is made and the way in which that decision is acted on will vary. How comfortable does the dreamer feel in the group? Does she fear that too intimate an aspect of her life will be brought out into the open? How important does the dream seem? Other factors that influence the decision are clarity of recall, recency of the dream, whether the dream is a repetitive one, and whether it is an old dream that has never been set to rest or one that has striking or unusual features that pique the curiosity of the dreamer. Particularly in the case of presenting a first dream to the group, the dreamer may wait until she has what she regards as a "safe" dream. Sometimes, a dreamer feels she has satisfactorily worked through the meaning of a dream on her own and is just curious to see if the group can do more with it.

In trying to decide about sharing a dream, a dreamer may be puzzled as to which of a series of dreams the same night should be chosen and whether or not to include others of the same night if they seem related to the preferred dream. This is a decision to be made in consultation with the leader. It will usually depend on the length of the various dreams and the amount of time available.

The decision point for the dreamer is somewhat analogous to standing on a precipice poised to jump, knowing there is water below but not knowing how far below it is or how deep it is. How safe will it be to jump off and find out? What will she find? A new and interesting world to explore or monsters ready to devour her? If she finds herself in water that is too deep, will there be enough help to get her back to shore?

Given these starting conditions, it is no wonder that there is hesitation on the part of some to share a dream, at least in the beginning. As we have noted, the hesitation, arising out of anxiety, can be rationalized in any number of ways. The dream is too short, too dull, or too unimportant. Others are sure to have more urgent or interesting dreams. When a dreamer does decide to share a dream, difficulties may arise when others also volunteer. The first dreamer may take the "altruistic" way out, deferring in favor of the others but in reality responding with relief at getting off the hook. Conversely, he may feel upset at the possibility of losing the opportunity to share his dream. The dreamer has to avoid either underestimating or overestimating his own need and desire. It is a moment that calls for frankness and self-assertion rather than polite yielding. The volunteers have to be reminded that when everyone involved seems equally eager to share a dream, the decision can be made by chance.

Having decided to share a dream, dreamers go about it differently and in ways that can be quite revealing. One may welcome the opportunity and be obviously eager to tell the dream. With others, some of the antecedent hesitation may make itself apparent. The dreamer may engage in a "giving out-taking back" maneuver with the group—on the one hand wanting to be recognized as someone willing to share and, on the other, hoping someone else will volunteer and rescue him from the ordeal. Ambivalence and self-deprecatory attitudes are projected onto the dream, which is then offered somewhat apologetically.

Sharing the Dream:
Stage 1A

Once these preliminary rumblings are dissipated, the task of the dreamer is to give an account of the dream as *dreamed* in as complete and detailed a manner as possible. That means resisting the temptation to censor, prejudge, omit, edit, or in anyway tamper with the memory of the dream. The remembrance itself is already one step removed from the actual experience of dreaming. To transform it further in the telling is to risk tampering with its essence. There is usually no difficulty in sharing the highlights of the dream, the action and course of events as recalled by the dreamer. What requires a degree of conscious effort is to include as much as possible of the background setting, mood, feelings experienced while dreaming, awareness of color, the sense of one's age in the dream, and the topographical arrangements when relevant.

The telling of the dream may also raise questions of confidentiality. When a person known to the dreamer appears in the dream, it may be someone whose identity the dreamer wishes to protect, either because that person may be known to other members of the group or for personal reasons. Before making the decision to withhold a name that appears in the dream, it is important to consider the possibility that the name itself, rather than the person, may be the important element, either because it lends itself to a meaningful pun or has some other relevant meaning for the dreamer. It is up to the dreamer to decide which choice has to be sacrificed.

The decision to read the written account of the dream or to rely on spontaneous recall is up to the dreamer. One can tell the dream from memory and then check one's notes to see if anything was omitted. The important point is that the rendering be as complete as possible and that it be told slowly enough so that those who wish to write it down have the time to do so. In the case of a short dream, one may prefer to relate it in a natural and spontaneous way and then repeat it slowly so that it can be written down. In the case of a dream of some length, it may be too time-consuming to have the dream repeated in this manner. I have found it most expeditious if the dreamer tells the dream only once but slowly enough for others to write it down regardless of whether it is being read or offered spontaneously.

The actual dream work begins with the sharing of the dream. Making the dream public, and in so doing surrendering to some extent one's own privacy, initiates the "opening-up" process. The simple act of sharing the dream with others may result in a sudden insight. When this does occur, it registers quite visibly in the countenance of the dreamer. On occasion, at the conclusion of telling a dream, I have heard a dreamer remark, "I think I now know what the dream means." Even apart from such dramatic effects, the dreamer, by refocusing on the dream, begins the process of the inward journey toward the dream's origins.

An inexperienced dreamer may feel some anxiety at this point and even regret the decision to tell the dream. The latter usually dissipates as the process develops. Suffice it to say that, in my experience, it has been a very rare occurrence for anyone to regret sharing a dream.

Clarifying the Dream:
Stage 1B

There are two things to consider here: Is everyone clear about the dream as reported? Do the group members know everything about the dream that they are entitled to know? The questions should be limited to these two objectives. In questions relating to clarity, the dreamer may be asked to repeat certain portions of the dream. When something is alluded to in the dream but is not clear, the dreamer may be asked if there is more she can say about it. If spatial arrangements referred to in the dream are unclear, the dreamer may be encouraged to make a rough sketch.

I like to direct the initial questions to ascertaining whether any of the characters in the dream are real and known to the dreamer in waking life and, if they are, finding out, very briefly, what their connections are to the dreamer. This should be a limited response and not taken as an opportunity by the dreamer to associate freely about the character and the reason he or she appears in the dream. One might inquire about the age of a character if in the dream this is not clear from the context. If older people are mentioned, are they alive or dead? The group should be clear about the age of the dreamer in the dream if this is not clear from the context. The group may inquire about feelings in the dream if none have been noted spontaneously by the dreamer. This also applies to the appearance of color in the dream.

In responding to the questions, the dreamer has to use caution in limiting herself to the remembered dream and checking any impulse to include associative data. It sometimes requires a good deal of self-control to contain the impulse to share associations that she feels will be helpful to the group. Undoubtedly, some associations would be helpful, but along with them might come others that are misleading. In any event, they would serve to track the thinking of the group members along certain lines at the expense of not pursuing other possibilities once they make the dream their own in Stage 2.

The dreamer should not be pressed to make vague, confusing, or ambiguous events in the dream any clearer than the way they were actually experienced in the dream. Any incongruities, which often characterize images and events in a dream, have to be accepted as such. It is important that the dreamer be aware of these guidelines and not feel called on to respond to questions that are inappropriate or too insistent and aimed at establishing a clear and logical understanding of aspects of the dream that are neither clear nor logical.

With inexperienced group members, it may take a good deal of repetition before they learn how to work with the guidelines and to limit their questions to clarification and the addition, if possible, of greater detail. It may take some time before a dreamer new to the process learns how to draw a sharp line between what was actually in the dream and what occurred to her in connection to the dream subsequent to waking up. Proper questions will not only enrich one's detailed grasp of the dream by stimulating a more detailed recall by the dreamer but may also result in the recall of additional dream fragments.

Playing With a Dream:
Stage 2

The game is now ready to start. I use the word *game* advisedly to refer to the serious yet playful and respectful way in which the group members make the dream their own and draw on their feelings and imaginations in an effort to come up with responses that may be of help to the dreamer. The dreamer's stance in the course of the game is outwardly passive and inwardly active. The dreamer does not engage actively with the group while the game is going on except to correct any misimpressions about the dream, to share any additional information about the dream that is suddenly recalled, or to ask a group member to repeat something he may not have grasped. In terms of inner events, however, the dreamer is engaged in an active process that proceeds along several fronts at the same time.

What follows is an amplification of the instructions to the dreamer noted in Chapter 2 concerning the nature and impact of the work of the group in Stage 2.

Instructions to the Dreamer

You are noting all that is emerging from the way the group members play with your dream. Every now and then, something they come up with may resonate with you at a gut level. A lot of what they come up with may strike you as wide of the mark. One of their projections may touch you but leave you unclear about its relation to the dream. You may find yourself responding at many different levels of your psyche to what you are hearing. Sometimes, you are left with the feeling that practically all that the group comes up with is relevant to you. You may feel amazed at how productive the group has been with a dream you thought was hardly worth sharing.

You are free to accept or reject whatever you hear. Your task is to sort out what you feel to be true from what you may intellectually respond to as possible or logical. You are the sole judge in this matter. You are being left alone to feel your way into your own dream with the help of the group and without any outside interference or sense of obligation to the group. Just as you have the freedom to accept or reject anything you hear, you have to allow the group to work freely with their own projections on your dream. In practice, this means not taking personally anything a group member offers. If it produces a reaction in you, you have to accept responsibility for that reaction. The projection may have touched on a truth about yourself. The group members are responsible for their projections, and you are responsible for your reactions. As the game progresses, you may find yourself feeling anxious, threatened, or angry, but when that happens, it is generally because of two things: (a) You have taken a group member's projections as an interpretation of your dream, and (b) you are feeling something is true, have become anxious about its becoming known, and fail to realize that it is you who determines whether it will become known or not. More generally, one feels quite safe during the game playing and good about being in control of the situation and able to manage one's responses. Usually, there is a growing appreciation about the help one gets and a deeply felt response to the seriousness with which the group members work with your dream, the interest they take in it, and the degree of caring and concern it has evoked.

Another interesting event is taking place on a parallel track. You will find that as the group works on your dream, you begin to make your own connections to the imagery. The fact that there is help being offered to you in a nonthreatening way seems to have the effect of lowering your own defenses and opening up your risk-taking potential. In other words, working on a dream in a social context in which you feel safe exerts a nonspecific effect in helping you move closer to the dream. This effect is enhanced by whatever on-target responses are forthcoming from the group. Interestingly enough, even wrong responses from the group are helpful. By helping define what the image is not, they move you closer to what it is. The process of flowing into the dream is initiated, powered both from within and without.

The dreamer is listening to the group and working on the dream at the same time. The group members are free to tackle the dream in any manner they choose, so their contributions come at the dreamer in a somewhat random fashion. The dreamer is faced with the task of sifting out these contributions, testing them against the direction his own thoughts take, accepting some, and rejecting others. Even though cautioned against it, dreamers sometimes react personally to a projection that was offered, losing sight of the fact that the group members have the privilege of shaping their projections in a manner of their own choosing without being challenged. The dreamer's only concern should be to give meaning to the imagery and to seek the answer to the question, Why did I have this dream at the time I did?

The dreamer does not have to keep a poker face through all this. He may unwittingly and quite naturally have nonverbal reactions that offer clues to the group that a hit has registered. There are times when he may be overcome by his own feelings and needs the help of the group in dealing with them. Stopping the process for a few moments and offering quiet support is generally all that is needed.

As the game progresses, the dreamer can experience a wide range of responses, from astonishment at how much has been given to him and how helpful it has been to any feelings of disappointment at still being in the dark. More often than not, there is the feeling of having gotten something from the group. There are times when he feels so overwhelmed by the input that he feels he can't be open to any more and wishes the game would end. He should feel free to act on this feeling. There are times when the game generates so much excitement that the dreamer has difficulty checking the impulse to interrupt and share his discoveries with the group.

How the dreamer reacts to what is coming from the group depends both on his attitude and experience with the process. His attitude can vary from one of interest and curiosity (which it usually is) to one that is defensively closed to the projections of the group. With practice, he learns how to listen effectively to the group and to discriminate between what resonates, what does not resonate, and what he resists allowing to resonate. He comes to realize that the projections can touch him at many different levels. At the same time, he is concerned with what he will later on share with the group and what he won't.

The criterion for acceptance or rejection is not who offered the projection, but does it or does it not help the images fall into place in a natural and felt way? The dreamer is in charge of whatever reactions, good or bad, these projections evoke. He has the freedom to do with them as he wishes and is not under any constraint at any subsequent point in the process to do anything other than what he wishes.

Sometimes, the dreamer finds himself in a tension resulting from a conflict between the logic of much of the group's input, particularly when there appears to be a consensus about a certain point, and what he himself actually does feel. It is as if it's hard for him to say to himself, "But that's not the way I feel about it."

When a contribution from the group is not accepted, usually it is for one of three reasons:

1. It doesn't fit.
2. It fits but evokes too much anxiety.
3. It fits, but the dreamer does not yet see the fit.

Although it is not uncommon for a dreamer to experience some anxiety during the game playing, it is rare for this to be sufficiently bothersome to cause a termination of the process. The more characteristic response is for the dreamer to feel that the group has given him the push needed to begin to get closer to the dream. It leaves him eager to get still closer.

The Dreamer Responds:
Stage 3A

When the game ends, the dreamer has to change her mind-set from one of looking inward to one of sharing outwardly. For a dreamer new to the process, there may be anxiety about taking the center of the stage, concern about performance, uncertainty about how to organize her response, confusion as to where to begin, and hesitation as to what to share and what not to. She may feel at a loss as to just what is expected of her at this point. Should she present her own ideas about the dream or respond to what the group offered? A simple reassurance that she can proceed as she wishes generally suffices.

Dreamers may need some time alone with their thoughts before they feel able to respond. There are times when the dreamer is so suffused with feelings that it is difficult to begin talking. Providing a brief interval of time is helpful to the dreamer in making the transition. It gives her the opportunity to organize her thoughts and ready herself to take over and respond. She is now the focus of attention. All eyes are on her. She is confronted with her own expectations of herself and the expectations she attributes to the group. Let us look more closely at the tensions that beset the dreamer at this point.

The expectations she has of herself in shaping her response will depend on a number of factors. It will be determined mainly by (a) how safe she feels, (b) how much she has gotten from the others, (c) how private is the dream's content, and (d) how important the dream is to her. It will also depend on how experienced she is in the group work, how well she knows the others in the group, and how well they know her. She may have an unreal sense of what the group expects of her in terms of performance. A false sense of obligation to the group may result in self-critical feelings, especially if much of the meaning of the dream still eludes her.

Generally, the dreamer is both surprised and grateful for the help and stimulation she has been given. It is often explicitly acknowledged as a gift. More important, it moves the dreamer to share freely, openly, and honestly. Often, there is a sense of amazement at how much of what the group came up with is relevant to her life generally and to the dream specifically.

There are, however, many variations in the way the dreamer will respond to the thoughts and feelings expressed by the group. Dreamers who are new to the process tend to orient their responses to general issues that have been on their minds for some time and that have been touched on by some of the comments of the group. This is a very natural tendency, because the group's responses do tend to strike the dreamer as pertinent to her life at many different levels, opening up old as well as recent issues. All this may be quite relevant to an understanding of the dream, providing that the dreamer does not fail to take into account, to the extent that she can, the specific recent context occurring around the time of the dream. With greater experience, there is a more conscious effort to locate the dream in time by searching for events that could relate to the timing of the dream.

The inexperienced dreamer will tend to focus responses on the outstanding or most striking elements in a dream. With further experience, there is more of an effort to say something about each element in the dream, regardless of how seemingly insignificant it may appear. What appears trivial from the point of view of the waking state may have deeper ramifications.

There are almost as many different kinds of responses as there are dreamers. Not all are equally productive. Individual personality styles become apparent at this point in the process. Some dreamers try obsessively to fit everything they heard into the fabric of the dream, operating on the assumption that the others are wiser or more perceptive than they are. Or they may feel under obligation to respond to each and every comment when, in reality, their only obligation is to themselves and to concern themselves with what they found to be helpful. Some feel obligated to note projections that were wrong as well as those that were helpful. Some dreamers are very free. Some remain guarded. Although most emphasize what they did get, some show more concern with what they didn't get from the group. Some misuse the group and launch into a theatrical or attention-getting response, showing little concern for the imagery of the dream. Some act out judgmental needs to criticize the contributions of the group by expressing disappointment at the group's performance. Others may be seeking reassurance or make their dependency needs apparent. Some are so withholding that they are reluctant to share very much with the group. There may be extreme variations from an overly compliant acceptance of all the group's comments to an obstinate refusal to allow any of the group's comments to influence the prior ideas the dreamer had about the dream. Some unconsciously distract the group by associating away from the dream so that what they share has little connection to the dream. Usually, when there is a "Eureka!" response, the dreamer is eager to share it with the group. Sometimes, the dreamer can feel indecisive about whether to share it or not and feels uncomfortable or guilty if she decides not to. This last reaction is no longer a problem once the dreamer is reassured that it is her legitimate responsibility to withhold anything she has any qualms about sharing. A dreamer may express surprise that something that was obvious to her was not picked up by the group.

In her response, the dreamer may note that the group members overlooked a specific image in the dream as they made the dream their own. If the dreamer so wishes, she may ask the group to go back to the game for a few moments, focusing on that image.

Sometimes, the dreamer will be curious as to why a group member offered a specific projection. There is no objection to raising this question and getting a response.

Not infrequently, when the time comes for her response, the dreamer has a clearer idea about the dream or remembers an additional fragment she has not yet shared with the group. She may take this opportunity to do so and also to correct any misimpressions she now sees the group had about the dream.

We have referred to the situation in which the dreamer has gotten so much from the group that by the time she has finished integrating all of it into her response, it seems as if the dream has been worked through in a satisfactory way. The elements of the dream have been connected to the issues stimulated by recent events and arising out of past emotional residues. The dreamer is in close enough touch with the dream so that no further input from the group is necessary. It is important for the dreamer to be aware of this and not feel obligated to go any further to complete the other stages of the process either because she thinks it is expected of her or that the group expects it of her. It is perfectly all right to stop at this point if the dreamer feels she can go the rest of the way by herself. There is always more that can be done with a dream, and there is a limit to what the group can do with someone else's dream. There will always be areas that are best pursued in private. When there is this sense of closure at the termination of the response, all that the dreamer may need is validation from the leader that others also feel that same sense of closure.

There are instances, particularly with a dreamer new to the process and still feeling her way, when the dreamer acknowledges that she has gotten some help but does not wish to go further. Her decision to stop at this point should be reinforced by the leader even though the likelihood is that the dialogue could be helpful and despite the sensed eagerness of the group to continue.

In most instances, the dialogue follows and is welcomed by the dreamer as a way of getting deeper into the dream. Despite the partial gains she has made, she is still puzzled either about some of the specific elements of the dream or about the meaning of the dream as a whole.

Questions and Answers:
Stage 3B

The dreamer has done what he could with the dream and now turns to the group for the initiation of the dialogue. It is most important for the ground rules to be understood, particularly with regard to the dreamer's rights and responsibilities. He has the right not to answer a question, and he has the responsibility to set the limits on what is to remain private. If a dreamer decides to respond to a question, his obligation is to answer it in as honest a way as possible within the limits of whatever level of self-disclosure he feels comfortable with. The principle must prevail that the dreamer remains in charge of the dialogue, deals with the questions as he wishes, and has the freedom to terminate the proceedings at will. Because the questions are to be used as exploratory instruments, the dreamer may need time, sometimes considerable time, to use them as such even if it involves extended periods of silence.

The first two phases of the dialogue—namely, the amplification of the recent context and the playback—are devoted exclusively to helping the dreamer develop as completely as possible the associative matrix of the dream. The dreamer has the freedom, of course, to share whatever new insights occur as more and more associations are made to the dream. Only in the final phase of the dialogue are the group members free to offer, in the form of orchestrating projections, the connections they have made.

As with every other stage of the process, things may or may not run smoothly. What happens is always contingent on the motivation and experience of the dreamer and the skill with which the group formulates the questions and stays within the guidelines.

Let us look more closely at some of what the dreamer may be experiencing as questions are put to him. In the first phase of the dialogue, he is being called on to reconstruct the emotional tone of his life for the immediate period preceding the dream along with the thoughts that occupied his mind. The biggest problem is the tendency to overlook or minimize recent events that were associated with residual feelings of one sort or another. Until one has had some experience in dream work and has seen how such residual feelings and thoughts play so important a part in giving direction to the dream, there is a tendency to discount much of what later turns out to have been of significance. The inexperienced dream worker often screens out some of these recent events, as if consciously or unconsciously he has made a judgment that they are unrelated to the dream. The way these recent residues become manifest in the dream is something that has to be learned. Sometimes, a good deal of persistence is needed to gently lead the dreamer back to his own life and to take seriously thoughts and feelings connected to recent experience. In most instances, day residues do not boldly announce themselves. They have to be exposed. It takes time to become aware of their importance and the role they play in dream formation.

In the next phase of the dialogue, when the dreamer is confronted by the dream as it is played back to him by a group member, further associations are generally elicited. When they aren't, it can be helpful to remind the dreamer of some of his earlier associations to the imagery in the hope of stimulating more. When this also fails, the dreamer may feel chagrined at his inability to come up with further associations. It is important that he be reassured that the intent of the procedure is to see if there are more associations and not to imply that there are. Furthermore, as the playback continues, it often happens that more associations occur for images that earlier drew a blank.

When a dreamer is hesitant about responding to a question, he should be reassured of his right not to do so. He may relate to the group as if it had power over him and find it difficult to express his wish not to answer. Or he may not wish to hurt or antagonize the questioner by not answering. The dreamer needs the help of the leader to see that these feelings are irrelevant. The dreamer may feel like initiating closure at some point in the playback and again find it difficult to do so out of a false sense of obligation to the group.

Occasionally, there are dreamers whose guardedness and resistance spill over into the dialogue. Here, even the most carefully phrased question may evoke defensiveness and a determination to say as little as possible. For the most part, dreamers respond positively to the first two phases of the dialogue and the questions necessary to carry them out. They learn to use the questions as instruments and search out the answers. As they see the way their associations enable them to build the bridge between dream imagery and waking life, they become freer and freer in their responses. When the playback is done well, it often leaves the dreamer feeling much more in touch with the dream and feeling that he can go the rest of the way himself.

Up to this point, every aspect of the process has been oriented to bringing to the surface information hidden somewhere in the dreamer's psyche in the hope that he himself can spark across the metaphorical gap to link image and meaning. There are times, however, when the potential insights of others, offered in the form of their orchestrating projections, are needed for this to happen. Although in greater contact with the dream at the completion of the playback, the dreamer may still feel puzzled as to what it all means or feel so immersed in the data that he has difficulty in organizing them in any coherent way.

In the last stage of the dialogue when an orchestration is offered, it is to be regarded by the dreamer as a question and dealt with in the same way as the explicit questions in the earlier phases of the dialogue. The dreamer is free to respond or not. When a projection is on target, it results in a felt response by the dreamer and usually releases further validating associations. When done well, the orchestration can provide the dreamer with a more coherent view of the dream's meaning and a clearer sense of how the metaphorical sequences of the dream interrelate around a particular issue.

When the outcome of this third phase of the dialogue is successful, there is usually a clear indication from the dreamer that closure is at hand. This may vary from a subtle insightful look at the dreamer's eyes to a more dramatically apparent gesture of relief.

There are times when that kind of felt sense of closure has not been reached by the end of the session. Perhaps time and the complexity of the material has made it difficult for the group to come up with helpful enough orchestrations.

On One's Own:
Stage 4

There are still two ways the process can continue to move toward closure. The first involves further work done by the dreamer in the interim between the time the dream was presented and the next time the group meets. Alone and with the passage of a little time, the dreamer may be able to make freer use of the data that have been made available to her and may capture a bit more of the dream's meaning. The work of the group can have a long-lasting impact, and the dreamer may find herself ruminating on the dream over a period of several days with more and more hidden meanings coming to light. Scattered data may come together in a way that results in a more integrated sense of the dream's meaning. In effect, the dreamer is learning how to orchestrate her own dream.

The second approach that can be helpful is for the leader or anyone else in the group so motivated to engage in a delayed orchestration (see Chapter 7). Here, the dream and the data elicited are reviewed in the interim between the two successive sessions. Without the pressure of time and with the materials fresh in mind or reconstructed from notes, new insights may occur or result in an entirely new way of looking at the dream.

At the session following the presentation of the dream, the dreamer is invited to share any additional thoughts with the group. This is the time when the leader or anyone else may offer a delayed orchestration. When this occurs, the dreamer is once again in the position of trying on someone else's projection. If it fits, fine! If it doesn't, don't bother with it. A delayed orchestration, carefully done, can dramatically relieve the frustrated sense of not having achieved closure in the prior session.

Problem Areas

Most of these have already been alluded to. In dream work, however, there is no end to the kinds of problems that can arise. Here are a few additional ones to anticipate.

A dreamer may have unreal expectations of what group work can do. It is not a substitute for therapy, and those who regard it as such are soon aware of the difference. Someone in need of therapy requires far more personal attention and professional management than can be given within the structure of the process as I have described it. That is not to say that such a person cannot benefit from the dream work, but it alone will not be sufficient.

Another kind of unreal expectation derives from the dreamer's notion that every dream should go "deep,"—that is, carry one deep into the heart of long-buried complexes, exposing something completely new and resulting in an earthshaking response. Although dream work often touches on the deepest realms of our psyches, this is not the sine qua non of dream work. Our dream lives mirror the range and depth of the issues that confront us in daily life.

In most instances, they simply confront us with truths about ourselves that we have always had some dim awareness of. We are helped to see that truth in a clearer and more felt way and in relation to a specific context. What is characteristic about dreaming is the way it links something problematic about ourselves, something that we are aware of in greater or lesser measure, to the specific events in our current life that exposed it and to happenings in our past that touch on it. There is often the feeling at the end of a session with a dream that "I've known it all along, but I feel it differently now."

Despite the best of intentions, a dreamer's defensiveness may work in a way that leads to the misuse of the process. When defenses are evoked, there is usually some accompanying discomfort. To offset this feeling, a dreamer may resort to a number of self-defeating maneuvers. He may do this by creating the appearance of sharing but making a very biased selection of what is shared, coloring what is shared so that it appears in a better light, or manipulating his responses so as to seek reassurance. In extreme instances, he may so thoroughly identify with his a priori notions about the dream that he is closed to whatever the group has to offer.

Another difficulty that seems to be characterological may or may not be defensive in nature. I refer to what Jon Tolaas[3] (1978) refers to as "metaphor-blindness." The dreamer may seem to have an inability to do anything with the imagery except deal with it in a literal fashion. The ability to see beyond the literal to the abstract and metaphoric possibility of the image may seem to be beyond him. He is so blocked in his ability to see the true connections of the imagery to his life that he soon becomes discouraged and discontinues his efforts. For others who stay with it, gradual learning may take place, leading them away from literalness to a growing appreciation of the nature of metaphor.

Notes

1. The arrangement I make with those entering a group is that they attend for four successive weeks. They are free to renew or not after each four-week period.

2. If someone is too disturbed to be in a dream group and is in need of professional help, that fact is generally recognized by the person involved and acted on by the time the initial four-week period ends. When over a longer period of time the need for formal therapy becomes obvious, I will approach that person about it privately, leaving it up to him or her about continuing in the dream group at the same time.

3. A Norwegian colleague who has written extensively on dreams.

12
■

The Group

My intent in this chapter is to scrutinize in greater detail the part played by members of the group at each stage of the process. Some repetition is inevitable. Long experience has convinced me that some points require repeated emphasis.

The needs of the dreamer have been described. They can best be met in a social setting that is both safe and stimulating at the same time. For the group to respond to those needs, there must be a clear understanding of its role and function in the working through of each stage. The strategy remains the same from beginning to end—namely, maintaining the dreamer's feeling of safety and, in a nonintrusive manner, furnishing the instruments needed for the kind of inner probing essential to dream work. The tactics employed by the group differ, however, with each successive stage of the process. The group's job is to help uncover information. The dreamer's job is to use that information. The group can get on with its job only to the extent the dreamer is motivated to do her job. The recognition of this interdependency is paramount. For a dreamer new to the process, there may be an undercurrent of the dreamer versus the group. With experience, this gives way to the acceptance and appreciation of this underlying unity. The meshing of the dreamer and the group is the precondition for the emergence of the dream as an event of singular importance in the life of the dreamer.

The group is there at the behest of the dreamer. The fact that group members follow rather than lead the dreamer and never usurp the dreamer's control of the process does not mean that they do not have active and clearly defined responsibilities. These will be specifically delineated for each stage. Through the feeling responses they generate, the imaginative projections they offer, and the way they raise questions, the members of the group create an environment that is optimal for dream work. They provide the dreamer with the space, time, and privacy needed to engage in the honest self-scrutiny that is required. By its very nature, the process exposes and contains the anxieties that arise. The level of sharing that takes place in the course of the work with a dream and the mutual sharing of dreams in an ongoing group results in everyone's feeling closer to the ground of their common humanity. It does not take long for this sense of deeply felt communion to take place. Those who come to dream work with a variety of experiences in other kinds of groups express amazement at how quickly feelings of trust and profound intimacy are generated. I have often wondered why the psychiatric community is not more aware of the unique ability of group dream work to mitigate defensive structures and to evoke authentic contact.

Listening to the Dream:
Stage 1A

Everything the dreamer says should be regarded as potentially significant by the members of the group. This involves an active listening process that begins with listening to the way that people make known their wish to share a dream. What qualifying comments accompany this initiative? Are they eager, hesitant, apologetic, regretful, or ambivalent, hoping that someone else will volunteer? Do they offer value judgments as to how important or unimportant a dream is? Are they concerned with how their dreams compare with others'? These observations may be reinforced later by what you pick up in the dream images.

Once the dreamer starts to tell the dream, one's mind-set is important. Remember that the dreamer, in relating the dream, is at the same time translating it from a pictorial to a verbal mode. The pictorial elements of the dream do not follow the ordinary rules of logic and may therefore be difficult to convey in words. Further difficulty with the verbal rendering arises from the elusiveness, bizarreness, or other unfamiliar features of the images. Although your goal is to be as clear as you can about the actual dreaming experience, you must be prepared to settle for a certain level of vagueness or lack of clarity and contain for the time being any feelings of puzzlement.

If you take the trouble to write the dream down, and I strongly advise you to do so, you will have a ready reference to it in the later stages of the process. I emphasize this because I have had the experience in which people who rely on their memories alone find they have to refresh their memories later with questions to the dreamer. In doing so, they take time away from the ongoing process. Try not to interrupt the dreamer's account unless you didn't hear what was said. If you are not clear about something the dreamer says, it is best to wait until he finishes when there is an opportunity to put questions to him.

There is a playful quality to dream work regardless of what the dream may be conveying. The work itself is challenging and stimulating and maintains a creative tension seeking to be resolved. That playful quality should be preserved but not misused. For that to happen, one has to be very much in tune with the dreamer and aware of the fact that, in sharing a dream, a dreamer may be exposing many different levels of his psyche, levels that are not immediately apparent on the surface. That kind of sensitivity will check any glib or impulsive responses.

Clarifying the Dream:
Stage 1B

Certain information the group should have about the dream may not come through in the telling of it. The general guideline is that whatever was in the actual dreaming experience should be shared with as much detail as possible. To repeat for the purpose of emphasis, this includes the following:

- Are there any feelings the dreamer may recall having had?
- When characters appear in the dream who are known to the dreamer in waking life, what is their relationship to the dreamer (spouse, friend, relative, coworker, etc.)?
- What is the age of the dreamer in the dream (if not clear from the context) and any other character, named or otherwise (as close as the dreamer can say)?
- Were any colors specified in the dream? If not, were there any?
- Are the spatial relations in the dream clear? If not, invite the dreamer to make a rough sketch.

In practice, certain considerations should be kept in mind in following these guidelines. There are limits to the information to be sought at this time. To take an obvious example, if a spouse appears in a dream, the dreamer may be aware of a great many background ideas and feelings connected with the image. He should not be pressed beyond stating the relationship and any specific feeling evoked by that image at the time of dreaming. Also to be avoided is questioning aimed at trying to get clarity about certain elements in the dream when no clarity exists in the dreamer's mind. In such instances, ambiguities and incongruities simply have to be accepted as such. It may even turn out that these very features of the image have informational value. The most frequent error made at this time is to attempt to elicit the waking associations of the dreamer to the imagery. They are of prime importance but not at this time, for reasons already noted.

A good general rule is to make the questions as brief and few as possible and limited strictly to the essentials noted earlier. Dream work takes considerable time, and that time is more profitably spent in the later stages. In the case of a group new to the process, it is easier for members to keep asking questions of the dreamer rather than to move into the more active role of working with the dream as their own. The fact that we avoid going after the dreamer's associations at this point in the process is particularly difficult for some therapists before they fully appreciate the rationale for doing it this way. Their frustration is understandable because in formal therapy one always starts with the spontaneous associations of the dreamer. In this process, however, in the succeeding second stage, when the group members make the dream their own, it works out better if the members have free reign to go wherever the images take them, including events and tensions in their own lives. The dreamer stands to gain by this. He will always have his own associations, and he will be allowed all the time needed to develop them. When given after the group has offered its input, these associations are invariably enriched, often to the surprise of the dreamer.

Borrowing the Dream:
Stage 2

For easy reference, here is a summary statement of the general guidelines for the work of the group in the second stage. There are two aspects to the freedom the members of the group have in developing their projections. They may identify with the dreamer and orient their projections to what they know or think they know based on their past knowledge of the dreamer's participation in the group. This would include issues that surfaced in earlier dreams shared by the dreamer as well as the general life context of the dreamer already known to the group. Here, one takes cues more from the dreamer than from the dream and allows one's feelings and metaphorical soundings to be shaped by them. This can be effective, but bear in mind that these clues may turn out to be irrelevant to the current context and certainly are incomplete.

The other aspect is the freedom to use the dream as a template over one's life to see what specific feelings, experiences, and issues it brings back from one's own past. In doing this, it should be made clear that one is not changing the dream but, rather, recalling memories touched on by the dream. This can often be quite helpful because of the sharing taking place and the more authentic quality to the feelings being expressed. The soundings are coming from one's own being. The problem is that one can go too far astray in sharing one's past.

These are not mutually exclusive approaches, and it works best when one feels free to use both.

The challenge posed at this stage to each group member is simply this: Through the use of your creative imagination can you match the creativity the dreamer displayed in putting these images together in the first place? Make use of the one important advantage you have over the dreamer. Because the dream is not yours in a real sense and you don't have to live with the consequences of whatever it is you say about it, you may be freer to see things that hold true for the dreamer but are not yet visible to her. Your projections may remove the veil from her eyes. She is free, of course, to replace the veil immediately, but she is more apt to take a healthy interest in what is unveiled.

The group's ability to be free-wheeling in the exploration of feelings and images results in a number of benefits for the dreamer. It is an exercise that develops a range of feelings and metaphorical meanings that radiate from the image and in doing so may strike a responsive note in the dreamer. It provides a unique opportunity for the dreamer to try on various meanings privately and to assess their emotional fit without being under any constraint to acknowledge publicly any of the reactions she may be experiencing. As the group works with the dream, the dream assumes a greater and more interesting reality for the dreamer. It is as if Jung's concept of the collective unconscious comes into play as the group exposes a common unconscious domain. There is a feeling of tapping into this domain as the group responds to the gift of the dream with its own reciprocal act of self-disclosure through the projections offered the dreamer.

Group members will vary in their abilities to get into the spirit of the game. They are dealing with a "borrowed" dream and may have difficulty in the

beginning remembering to use the personal pronoun *I* in relating their projections. Occasionally, one comes across someone who has a hard time with
this and who tries in subtle ways to depersonalize what he or she has to say.
Instead of, "This scene makes me feel . . .," what comes out is, "In that kind
of situation, one could feel . . ."

The interaction among group members in this stage should be of mutual
stimulation rather than one of competition or challenge. We can build on each
other's projections, but it is not our place to take issue with any that are
offered. Nor are we free to change the text of the dream to better suit the
projection we have in mind. We are shooting arrows in all directions, but
they should all come from the same bow and be within the limited firing
range of that bow. We don't know where the target is, but working within
that range, we may end up with some arrows close to the mark.

Another apropos analogy is one in which the dreamer is faced with a
mystery she has to solve but needs help in finding the clues. The members
of the group are blind detectives and therefore do not have direct access to
the scene of the mystery. They do have, however, their collective experience,
and guided by the intimation of the mystery as given in the dream, they
exchange thoughts about possible clues in the hope of helping the dreamer
shed some light on the mystery. In the end, the dreamer may remain in the
dark, suddenly solve the mystery, or find herself somewhere in between.

The most frequent infraction of the rules of the game occurs when a group
member directs his projections at the dreamer, forgets that the dream is his
for now, and talks of it as the dreamer's dream or dodges responsibility for
his own projection by talking about it in an impersonal way as if it belonged
to an anonymous third person.

Images and Feelings:
Stage 2A

The feelings we talk about in this stage are either the abstract product of
our imaginations or something genuinely felt. Both are appropriate for the
goal we have in mind—stimulating the dreamer. In the former, we are talking
about feelings that one might associate with the dream images or what one
imagines the dreamer might have felt rather than actual feelings in response
to the images. The simple conceptualization of a possible feeling is what can
be of help to a dreamer. More spontaneous feelings are evoked when the
respondent is able to so identify with the dream that real feelings are released.
Even without that sense of identification, the dream may still trigger feelings

associated with childhood recollections or current preoccupations. When feelings evolve out of one's own life experience, they are often more meaningful to the dreamer than when they don't seem so rooted but are more the product of the imaginative play with images.

Dream images can evoke feelings in several ways. The context may evoke a particular feeling—for example, a feeling of dread at being alone in a dark alley at night. A specific image may evoke a specific feeling of power and force. In both instances, one is responding literally to either the context or the image. One can get to feelings more indirectly by letting the metaphorical response develop and capturing the feelings associated with it. A locomotive, for example, can be experienced as a powerful force, capable of moving a big load on a track. The feeling might then be one of being strong-willed and determined.

One can be very inventive in describing feelings:

"I have the feeling of being in the middle of an Ingmar Bergman scenario."
"I feel like Alice in Wonderland."
"There is a fairy tale feeling in my dream."
"I feel like an actor in a Grade B movie."

Or more directly,

"I feel panic."
"I feel blissful."
"I feel angry."

In giving these shorter responses, it is best to avoid one-word answers such as *anxiety* and to tie the feeling to its source in the dream. For example, "When I turned and saw that threatening figure I felt anxious."

Beginners sometimes have difficulty in responding to the request that they draw an imaginary and temporary line between feelings and meanings. They begin to develop the metaphorical quality of the image without reference to any associated feelings. When this happens, the respondent can be asked to try to identify more explicitly any feeling tones behind the thoughts he is expressing.

Sometimes, even experienced group members get so fascinated by the metaphorical possibilities of the image that they engage in what I refer to as "sneaking in a metaphor under the guise of feeling." In a dream presented by a photographer, he was disturbed by the light of the early dawn seeping into the dark room where he was working. As the group began to work with their feelings, one member responded with, "I feel like I'm beginning to see the light." This is a perfectly fine metaphor, but its meaning can range over a variety of feelings—relief, excitement, a feeling of things suddenly coming together, a feeling of clarity, and so on. When asked to try to get at the feelings she was trying to express, she responded with, "Lately, life has felt too diffuse and getting beyond my grasp. Now things are becoming clearer and *I feel relieved.*" This was not what the light meant for the dreamer, but the group member was able to express her feelings about the image.

As a member of the group, here are some questions you might ask yourself that can be helpful in getting at your feelings:

- What immediate reaction did you have on listening to the dream?
- Does the dream seem to connect with your own life, and if so, do the images evoke any specific feelings?
- Do the context and changes in context in the dream evoke any specific feeling?
- Consider each image in the dream. Are any specific feelings evoked?
- Are you aware of any aspect of the dreamer's life context known to everyone in the group that can clue you into any feelings—for example, the anxiety of a dreamer's sharing a dream in the group for the first time?
- Are there any impersonal outside events (e.g., a dream occurring during Christmas) that might seem related to the dream and evoke a feeling?
- Is there any information from past dreams shared by the dreamer that provides a clue as to the feelings connected with the current dream?
- How might I feel were I in the role of the dreamer and having the dream on that particular night?
- Supposing I were to identify with one or more of the characters in the dream, would that result in any particular feeling?
- Can I capture an overall mood of the dream?

In sum, one may react to the feeling qualities of the image in several ways. In the image of a cat, for example, one may respond at a sensory level to the warm, soft feel of its fur or to the idea that cats, having nine lives, are survivors or to what feelings the appearance of the cat triggers about encounters with cats in the life of the respondent.

Images and Meaning:
Stage 2B

The group should be reminded that in turning to their work on the metaphorical possibilities of the imagery, they are free to continue working at the feeling level of the dream. There is a free-wheeling, gamelike quality to the process at this point. Meanings are developed and changed through the interchange. Individual ideas are enriched through the process of building on each other's projections. Here, the group really comes into its own. With no holds barred except to assume temporary ownership of the dream and to work with the images as given, the imaginative input can take many different paths and wander freely over a broad metaphorical field. It is easy to get into the spirit of it and difficult to call an end to it when the time comes to move on.

Again, one can take either or both of two roads. You can put yourself in the role of the dreamer and ask what kind of a situation you think she might be experiencing the night of the dream, or as you apply it to your own life, you can ask yourself what kind of a life situation might you have been in that led to your selection of these particular images. More can be done with the first approach the more one learns about the dreamer through shared dream work over time. Regardless of how much one thinks one knows about the dreamer, however, the second approach should always come into play.

Even experienced groups have to be reminded to work with every detail in the dream; to be on the alert for the metaphorical possibilities of color, puns, and double entendres; and to pay special attention to unusual images and incongruities, such as the absence of appropriate feelings or the appearance of inappropriate ones, and images around which much detail is offered. Images can be played with in isolation, in the context of a particular scene, or in the movement of one scene to another. One can sometimes note the same theme being expressed by different images in successive scenes. Later scenes may be seen as responses or solutions to conflicts or tensions posed in the opening scene. Comparing or contrasting opening and closing scenes may suggest new ideas. Directions—up or down, right or left—may offer significant clues to possible meanings. The arrangement of spatial structures may express analogies to the body or to the different levels of the psyche. References to the unconscious domain often take the form of a cellar or other underground structure, an expanse of water, a dark area, and so on. References to the self may take the form of animals or objects, a close friend, a child, or a sibling. Unidentified characters may be symbolic references to aspects of oneself. The various organs of the body can be expressed as structures—most notably, receptacles of one kind or another as the female genitalia and weapons or intrusive objects as the male genital organ. In short, the more one engages in dream work, the more one learns the syntax and grammar of this nighttime language, a language so elegantly suited to transforming our feelings and concerns into a pictorial mode. The more we master the language, the bolder and more expert we become in our ability to translate it.

Anticipation of and participation in a dream group may create a tension that finds its way into the dream. Suggestive of such a possibility are references to taking a course, trip, or journey; being in a classroom; performing in public; or having transitory sleeping arrangements, such as being in a hotel, as well as references to dream imagery in the form of pictures on television or in a newspaper. Other possible images may refer to the transformation from a private domain to a public one, such as the appearance of others in one's bedroom or bathroom or unexpected guests at one's house.

References to the dream group are more apt to occur in the early stages of dream sharing, or even later, in connection with dreams that occur the night before the group meets (although not necessarily limited to the night before). The dream group provides a common context and can be a powerful one at times when it touches on issues of exposure, fear of intrusion, concern with self-esteem, and so on. Generally, anxieties connected with participation in the group are only the surface manifestations of deeper issues.

References to the leader are not uncommon and are varied, depending on the personality of the leader and the impact he has made. General possibilities include the appearance in the dream of a teacher, conductor on a train, policeman, judge, pilot, or political leader. As I have encountered images of myself in the dreams of others, I have been everything from a wise old man to a lecherous old fool. In between, there have been a variety of representations, from an airplane pilot or train conductor to someone teaching or demonstrating something.

Whether the tensions that shape the dream arise in connection with one's work or one's personal life may often be deduced from the characters and scenes that appear in the dream. All dreams in the end come down to personal issues, but here, we are talking about the instigating factors for the dream. Family references, for example, often include older persons, babies, children, spouses or other family members, friends, and so on. By the same token, references to offices or office buildings, colleagues at work, supervisors or bosses, and so on, may point to issues arising at work.

A dream may be seen as a story told through a succession of pictorial scenes. The scenes do not succeed each other in any obvious way. There is, however, an intrinsic continuity based on the theme that the dreamer is concerned with and the succession of feelings evoked by that theme. In light of this, if in forming one's projections, one gets a glimmer of a possible theme, further ideas can be generated by examining the sequential order of the scenes and looking for the emotional contiguity that can give meaning to the way one scene succeeds another. There may be a sense of movement in the dream from the initial presentation of the particular tension to its working through and final resolution.

A group member sometimes hesitates to offer a projection because he feels it might apply in too disturbing a way to the dreamer. Two factors militate against the possibility of this happening. One of the principles I have stressed is that if we recall a dream, we are ready to deal with the information it contains, irrespective of whether we wish to or not. Second, if we do not wish to deal with that information in the context of a dream group, we are free, consciously or unconsciously, to maintain our defensive structure. In the group situation, we can always cast something aside as someone else's projection and resist applying it to ourselves. People generally come to dream work to search out the truth about themselves. They soon become sensitive to the feeling cues that, if attended to, can alert them to the choice they are making. Are they rejecting a projection because it is really true for them but they don't want to deal with the anxiety or discomfort it makes them feel in the group context, or is it simply wrong and does not apply? Experienced group workers know that the most benefit can be obtained if they choose to stay with the discomfort and either continue to explore it on their own or with the help of the group.

Keep the following pointers in mind as you work with the meaning of the images:

- Examine the setting carefully. Can you pick up any theme, tension, or contradiction?
- Examine each element in the dream for its metaphorical potential.
- Are there suggestive childhood references?
- Are there conspicuous absences that are suggestive?
- Is there an identifiable life context known to all that could connect with the imagery?
- Are there any identifiable social stereotypes suggested by the imagery—for example, depicting a young black male in an aggressive or negative light?
- Does the succession of scenes suggest any story line?
- Have you checked for puns or double entendres?
- Have you tested the possibility that characters in the dream may be a self-reference?
- Have you tried to work with every detail of the dreamer?

To sum up, these guidelines are important for managing one's projections in Stage 2:

- Every utterance of the group members is to be considered as referring to themselves—that is, what the group members have to say is to be regarded as their way of projecting themselves into the dream.
- To implement this, they talk of the dream as their own, using the first person.
- They share their projections with each other.
- They avoid talking to or looking at the dreamer while offering their projections.
- They are urged not to suppress or inhibit any projection for fear of its being too unlikely to be relevant or that it is too idiosyncratically linked to their own lives. There is no way of telling in advance what the dreamer will respond to.
- The goal is to make the widest possible use of group members' imaginations in mobilizing feelings and coming up with meanings without any concern as to whether what they have to say is true for the dreamer.
- There is a fun element to the game even if it is played out with a so-called heavy dream. The game takes place in an atmosphere of play and challenge.
- Some dreams are more or less gender specific (e.g., focusing on the dreamer's relationship with a member of the opposite sex). When such is the case, group members are free to identify with the sex of the dreamer if that is different from their own and generate their feelings and thoughts from that point of view.

Listening to the Dreamer:
Stage 3A

From the point of view of the group, this stage is preparatory to the actual dialogue with the dreamer. In the previous stage, when we made the dream our own, our stance was an active one, and there, we had to learn to sensitize ourselves to the mood and feelings evoked by the images as well as learn how to guide our imaginations along metaphorical lines. To the extent possible, we put ourselves into the dream and, often, develop some measure of conviction about the relevance of the feelings and ideas we generate. Now, as the dreamer begins her response, we have to assume a receptive stance, one that requires a different set of skills—namely, skills involved in the act of listening. This means disengaging from one's own view of the dream and being open to what is coming from the dreamer in a nonevaluative, nonjudgmental way. From here on, you work with the basic assumption that the answer to the dream lies in the dreamer and that your ability to help the dreamer is contingent on your ability to hear what the dreamer has to say.

This change in mind-set is necessary if we are to allow ourselves to take a fresh new look at the dream through the eyes of the dreamer. Becoming receptive in this total way is often more difficult than it seems. It means thoroughly shedding any earlier preconceptions as to what the dream might mean. Our own views tend to be rather sticky and often stand in the way as we try to reorient ourselves to the point of view being presented by the dreamer. We have to try to relate our thoughts about the dream to the specific life events of the dreamer as they unfold. This transformation, which amounts to a 180° change in perspective compared to the second stage, is essential if the dialogue is to be most productive.

These are the points to keep in mind as you listen to the dreamer's response:

1. Listen carefully to the opening comments of the dreamer as she begins her response. They register not only the impact of the work of the group in the second stage but also very often clue us in to the feelings or issues that preoccupied the dreamer the night of the dream.

2. Note to what extent the dreamer has identified immediate antecedent events to the dream. Sometimes, these are readily available and given in considerable detail. Sometimes, they are bypassed completely. In any event, earmark any clues to the recent emotional context for later exploration in the opening phase of the dialogue.

3. Note whatever seems important to the dreamer as indicated by emphasis, the feeling tone conveyed, or the repetitive way the dreamer comes back to it.

4. Has the dreamer made any connection between the feelings being expressed and analogous feelings in the dream? If not, and if you suspect there may be such connections, note this for future exploration in the dialogue.

5. Has the dreamer seen metaphorical connections between a life event and the situation depicted in the dream? If not, and you sense some such connections, note this for further exploration in the dialogue.

6. Note any elements in the dream that are not touched on by the dreamer. They may be too loaded, too puzzling, or simply overlooked. In any event, they are to be noted and considered later in the dialogue.

Some dreamers are very forthcoming in their response; some are withholding, at least until they have learned to trust the process and trust the group. Careful listening will cue you into areas the dreamer prefers to keep private and give you some idea of the freedom with which the dialogue will unfold. It is not up to the group to attempt to transform a withholding dreamer into a forthcoming one. We accept the dreamer for whatever degree of openness she is capable of. This is part of the principle of following rather than leading the dreamer.

The Dialogue:
Stage 3B

From here on, all that occurs is at the invitation of the dreamer with regard to the various substages of the dialogue. Each step in the process is designed to create openings for the dreamer to move closer to the dream. There is no way of knowing in advance which of any of the steps preceding the dialogue will be of help to the dreamer or to what extent. In the second stage, we are dealing with a random process and one that can fail to be very productive for the dreamer. In that instance, everything depends on the skill and thoroughness with which the dialogue is developed. The dialogue, therefore, varies in importance from being expendable to being the group's critical last ditch effort to be of help to the dreamer.

The mission of the group at this stage is to do what it can to help the dreamer retrieve sufficient information to establish connections to his waking life and come to a felt sense of the meaning of the dream. This is not an intellectual exercise but, rather, a process that is modulated at every step by the feelings of the dreamer. The task of the group is to work with those feelings and to facilitate their emergence. This stage provides the necessary setting for this to occur. The first phase of this stage is the preparation for this task.

The Search for Context:
Stage 3B.1

By the time the dreamer completes her response, we should have a good idea of the ground to be covered in the dialogue. A dreamer's response often provides us with cues as to the role of recent events, the issue that preoccupied the dreamer, the extent to which the dreamer addressed all the elements of the dream, the ease or difficulty the dreamer has with engaging in self-disclosure, and her aptitude for recognizing the metaphorical potential of the imagery.

The opening phase of the dialogue is concerned with amplifying the recent feeling residues that shaped the imagery and feelings in the dream. Through their initial questions in the dialogue, group members teach the dreamer how to search out and identify the recent events that triggered the dream. Even when the dreamer has provided a good deal of information about recent events in her life that she feels may be connected to the dream, there is always room for further explanation. The questions serve to aid the dreamer's recall of the emotional fabric of her life the night of the dream. Our concern is to help the dreamer recall, to the extent possible, the feelings and preoccupations she took to bed with her that night. Often, the dreamer mistakenly assumes that she is expected to talk only about those aspects of her life that she can connect readily with the dream. She should be disabused of this because there is no way of knowing at this point just what may ultimately shed light on the dream.

Whether a dreamer has said a good deal or nothing about the recent context of her life, a good first question (appropriate only for a fairly recent dream) is, "Can you recall any thoughts or feelings you experienced just before falling asleep or anything you might have been preoccupied with at the time you went to bed?" (adding "other than what you have already said" in the event the dreamer has touched on this). Very often, these last remembered residues that stay with us out of the mix of the day's events and that resurface while dreaming shape the course of the dream. A dreamer may have described many emotionally tinged happenings during the period leading up to the dream. Asking this question, however, helps the dreamer focus on those that were most insistent. When this question draws a blank, there are others that can prod the dreamer's memory.

"Was there anything you read that night or saw on television that left you with any residual feelings?" A simple, direct question such as this might help a dreamer recapture a wisp of a feeling tone that otherwise would have escaped her notice. One can pursue this line of questioning to include other events in the dreamer's personal life or at work. As she reviews her recent experiences in this way, there may be a sudden realization of how a family situation, a visit from a friend, or a telephone call might come to life in a new way in its connection to the dream. Sometimes, the yield is small, and the detective work has to be expanded to encompass a longer time span—several days to a week.

"Can you review the events of the last few days in your mind (the weekend if it's Monday) and see if anything stands out as having left you with any particular feelings?" It is surprising how often a review, begun perhaps in not too hopeful a way, evokes a memory of a particular event that, in the light of the dream, now assumes significance. Detailed questions of this kind are possible with a recent dream. A dreamer may be able to respond only in a more general way with a dream that is weeks, months, or years old. The further back in time the dream occurred, the more difficult it is to ferret out the specific, relevant antecedent events in the life of the dreamer.

There are other avenues to explore for possible recent residues. The group can inquire about a context known to all—namely, that the dreamer is in a dream group and is sharing a dream. As has been noted, many anxieties are involved in dream sharing, particularly when one is new to the experience. We have not been brought up to share our dreams in public or to pursue their private meaning with people we don't know. The pressure one may feel to have a dream to share may be a powerful anticipatory day residue. The thought of working a dream out in public may touch hidden anxieties about private aspects of one's life becoming known. Dreams do touch on secrets that we don't want others to be privy to. What will others think of us if we risk exposing vulnerable areas? Will they think less of us or take unfair advantage? Coming from another direction, dream work may feed into our need for attention, our wish to perform well, or our desire to make ourselves known to the group. In either event, our expectation of participating in the dream group may stir up a range of feelings. Questions can be put to ascertain whether this is so or not.

"Were you thinking of the dream group at any time prior to falling asleep? How do you feel about being in the group and sharing a dream?" A dreamer new to the group may experience a conflict between the desire to participate and the anxiety about what a dream might reveal. If she has been in the group for some time and has not yet shared a dream, she may go to sleep determined to have a dream and share it. In response to this line of questioning, she may come to see how her dreaming self handles the anxieties stirred up by these expectations.

Finally, a group member may have special knowledge of events in the life of the dreamer that are not known to the others and wish to use it to help the dreamer explore a possible context. If he feels that to do so might be a breach of the dreamer's confidentiality, he should seek the dreamer's permission privately (e.g., by passing a note) before going ahead with it.

Objectifying the Dream:
Stage 3B.2

In the playback, the group removes the dream from its cozy subjective resting place and transforms it into a highly visible external object seen in new and stimulating light. The dream images are given a life of their own. They now seem to leap out at the dreamer in a way that often takes him by surprise and opens up fresh associative paths.

At this point, the group members become the advocates for the dream. Their job is to confront the dreamer with the dream as an objective entity created out of the fabric of his life. This means not only listening to his responses but also helping the dreamer to focus his associations on each element in the dream, on the way the images relate to each other, and on the story that is being told. In a sense, the dream becomes the instrument of the group to be used as a probe into the associative matrix of the dreamer. Unlike a probe controlled by a surgeon, it is a probe turned over to the dreamer to use to the extent he can and wishes to. Reading the dream back to the dreamer objectifies it in a way that creates a fresh perspective for the dreamer. This, in combination with the information already elicited, usually stimulates further responses from the dreamer.

It is important to avoid reading a scene back in a perfunctory way. To dramatize it effectively, one has to sense its intrinsic mystery, point up the appropriateness or inappropriateness of the feelings the dreamer noted in the dream, call attention to images not yet responded to by the dreamer, and note how in the dream the dreamer is responding to the story that is unfolding.

It is not too difficult to determine what constitutes a scene. In relating the dream, the dreamer often says, "Then the scene changes." Such changes are characterized by a change in milieu, the introduction of new characters, or the introduction of some new activity. In the case of a long dream with many scenes and in a situation in which time is running out, one may be forced to take in several scenes at once to cover the entire dream.

As you listen to the dreamer, it will become apparent whether these further associations relate to the images as they appear in the dream or whether they seem to contradict what the dream is saying. In your role as advocates for the dream, you can point this out to the dreamer. Bringing the dreamer back to a discrepancy of this sort can often open up more relevant associations. Keep in mind the fact that much as the dreamer wishes to pursue the truth of the dream, there may be unconscious disowning tendencies at work. Your only instrument to counter such tendencies is to consistently invite the dreamer's attention to what the dream is saying. That is one reality that cannot be denied or disowned. Pointing up a discrepancy is never a challenge to the dreamer but an invitation to look further. In the event that this is not successful, simply go on with the playback in the hope that later associations may shed more light.

Before saying more about the art of the playback, I want to call attention to a basic assumption that, if adhered to, will help prevent the questions from going astray. At some level, the dreamer is in touch with the source of his own imagery and is the only one so in touch. Keeping this in mind will counteract any tendency of the questioner to try to move the dreamer closer to the questioner's own view of the dream. It can be likened to the difference between tapping into a full barrel to get some of the contents out or assuming that the barrel is empty and that contents have to be poured into it from the outside. The task of the group is to know where to put the tap. The task of the dreamer is to become more aware of the contents of the barrel and control its outward flow.

It may sound paradoxical to say that, at some level, the dreamer is in touch with an aspect of himself that he is unconscious of. Nevertheless, it is true that he was in touch with it while asleep but lacks the ability to deal with it other than in representational form. It exists as potential knowledge that, in the light of full consciousness, can be restored to its proper place in the waking life of the dreamer. The assumption behind every question put to the dreamer about the reference points of each element of the dream is that the answer is known to the dreamer but known at a level of his psyche not easily or immediately available to him. Awake, he is not aware of the extent of his knowledge about the dream. It is our task to tap into that knowledge through our questions, expose it, and help it rise to the surface. That knowledge becomes available to the dreamer only through the slow buildup of the associative matrix represented in so condensed a form as imagery. Questions are never used as an indirect way of suggesting to the dreamer what the dream means. Leading questions do just that and are to be avoided. Open-ended questions pave the way for the dreamer to get closer to this internal source of information at a rate that suits him. Our goal is to bring him to the same state of honest relatedness to his life that he was in while dreaming.

We recognize, of course, that this task is more or less difficult to accomplish in the waking state and that the dreamer needs help. This in no way lessens the dreamer's authority over the dream. The members of the group should never allow themselves the luxury of feeling more knowledgeable about a dreamer's dream than the dreamer himself. We may, of course, come to an insight that we feel is valid, but unless the dreamer ultimately validates it, it is not helpful to a dreamer, and we cannot be sure how valid it really is. We are always dealing with hypotheses for the dreamer to test out on himself.

For the best results with the playback, keep the following in mind:

1. Always read a scene through in its entirety before focusing on specific images that have not yet been developed.

2. When more needs to be said about an image to account for its appearance in the dream, invite the dreamer to say more: "You haven't said anything yet (or can you say more) about the image of the car, house, dog (etc.). Do any further associations occur to you about that image or why it should appear in your dream that night?" If this is unproductive, you can try the following:

a. Recall for the dreamer all that he has already said about the image.

b. Emphasize for the dreamer all the details in the dream connected with the image as well as the context in which the image occurs.

c. If the image is a person known to the dreamer, invite him to look at it objectively in terms of his relationship to that person. The dream may be registering the beginning awareness of a new aspect of that relationship or the discovery of a new facet of that person's personality. Powerful unresolved feelings from the past may have been stirred up.

d. Consider the possibility that the other person is a reflection of some aspect of the dreamer and is being used to express a trait, need, or feeling the dreamer has about himself.

e. Very often, the characters appearing in a dream are not identifiable as real persons. Here, too, there are several possibilities. Unknown characters may be there to express an aspect of the dreamer. They may reflect moods, feelings, or impulses not yet clearly recognized as such when awake. Their very anonymity is an indication of the distance the waking ego is from whatever they represent. They are there as actors created by the dreamer to express by their appearance and actions the interplay of different sides of the dreamer's personality. An unknown character may be vaguely reminiscent of someone once known. In this instance, the feelings connected with that relationship are surfacing in some current context.

f. When the image is an animal or inanimate object, suggest that the dreamer explore what there is about that image in terms of its physical characteristics, its general qualities, and his past experiences with it and, in the case of inanimate objects, about its function or usefulness that may seem relevant.

3. Sometimes a dreamer gets stuck because he is dealing with the image in too literal a fashion. Help him look at it in its possible symbolic meaning.

4. Suggest that the dreamer examine any feelings noted in the dream in their possible connection to the recent events in his life. He might be asked something like this: "You described certain feelings you had in connection with this scene (or image). Can you think of any situation in your life recently that may have touched off such feelings?"

5. Our dreams often use hyperbole to make a point by exaggeration. Feelings that went unnoticed in waking life may be more vividly experienced in the dream. The intensity of a feeling in a dream provides a clue to the real nature of a feeling that was sensed only dimly or brushed aside while awake. A waking incident that seemed to be only a mild irritant may, when reflected in a dream, result in feelings of rage or images of aggression.

6. In the same way, the dreamer can be helped to explore a particular situation in the dream: "In the dream, you depict a situation in which you find yourself in enemy territory. Can you think of any situation in waking life analogous to the situation in the dream?" This may succeed in eliciting

associations that establish the connection. Not infrequently, further associations occur without the dreamer's seeing any connection at the time. He may see one later, or if not, the possible connection can be offered later in an orchestrating projection.

7. Sometimes, it can be helpful to reverse directions and work backward from waking life to the dream. This might take the following form: "In response to the situation you described earlier, you had certain feelings. Keep these feelings in mind as you go over the imagery and see if any further associations occur to you."

In putting a question like that to the dreamer, we are going a step beyond just eliciting information and are more actively attempting to facilitate connections in the dreamer's mind. We are not actually making the connection for him as we do in the next phase of the dialogue, the orchestration, but we may be selecting certain things the dreamer said, and by inviting further associations, we may seem to be implying a connection. If the question is put as openly as the example just offered, it can be facilitating without being directive. The same holds true when a dreamer, stuck for further associations to a given image, is then reminded of what he has already said about the image. Here, too, the questioner has to be careful to be facilitating without being directive. When the dreamer still fails to make the connection, the questioner should not try to validate her own impression by the way the question is put to the dreamer. There is a fine line between going after further associations and challenging a dreamer, however subtly, to see a connection that seems obvious or possible to the questioner.

> *Right way:* "You have said a number of things about this image (list all that the dreamer has said). Keeping them in mind, do they help you develop any further associations to this image and its appearance in the dream that night?"
>
> *Wrong way:* "You have said a number of things about this image (again list them). Keeping them in mind do you see any connection between what you said and the meaning of the image?"

This last question can be experienced by the dreamer as too direct a challenge. Questions are primarily probes to elicit information, leaving the dreamer free to make the connection himself. Toward this end, if a question is put in a way so as to imply an obvious connection and the dreamer fails to see that connection, it can be frustrating.

8. Has the dreamer's attention been called to certain words in the dream that may suggest puns or double entendres? What about attention to the

possible meaning of any numbers that appear in the dream or to the meta-phorical power of color?

9. Remember, you are the advocates for the dream. You can point up discrepancies between what the dreamer is saying about a scene and what the dream is saying. Intervention is only for the purpose of bringing the dreamer back to what the dream is saying. This also helps to focus the dreamer's attention when his associations appear to be wandering astray. This kind of focusing is especially important when dreamers tend to be too verbose or scattered.

Orchestrating the Dream:
Stage 3B.3

Because this stage has been extensively covered in Chapter 7, there is little to add. Offering orchestrating projections is an exercise in versatility. It involves learned skills and considerable practice. Once I began to encourage the participation of the entire group in orchestration, it soon became apparent that they were picking up the skills involved, learning how to use their sensitivity and imagination within the constraints of the structure, and coming up with ever-more helpful orchestrating comments. It is now a routine feature of the work for all who wish to participate in this phase of the dialogue. My usual practice is to give all group members a chance to say whatever they want to say and then offer what I have to say. In many instances, they leave me with little to add. It may be little more than affirming my agreement with what has already been said or putting it together into a more cohesive whole. On other occasions, I may take a completely different tack. The dreamer remains the ultimate arbiter of what is helpful.

More About Discoveries

We possess two languages—the one we use to communicate with others while awake and the one we use to communicate with ourselves while asleep. The task of dream work is to connect these two languages so that neither sounds strange to the other. To arrive at the meaning of dream imagery is much more a matter of finding the common ground between these two languages than it is a matter of undoing repressions. Certainly, repressed material rises to the surface in dream work, but the emphasis on that aspect has been far too great and at the expense of underestimating how readily much of what was hidden rises to the surface when the natural curiosity of the dreamer is met by a supportive and nonintrusively helpful social context in which the dreamer's authority is respected. Once a group learns how to listen to the dreamer in a way that gives the dreamer's thoughts priority and learns to ask questions in a "data-eliciting" way, it is remarkable how much what is ordinarily thought of as repressed spontaneously becomes visible. To continue with the two-language analogy, the group provides the dreamer with the dictionary by means of which one language can be translated into the other, leaving it up to the dreamer to look up the specific words that resonate with the imagery. It is a very special kind of dictionary, one that provides her with new meanings for words she thought she knew.

The strategies used by group members in the interest of discovery can be summed up as follows:

- They receive the dream with interest and in a nonjudgmental way.
- They proceed in a manner at all times concerned with the safety of the dreamer.
- They stimulate the associations of the dreamer through the feelings and thoughts that they associate to the dream during the game. It is as if they have opened a dictionary in a random way but in so doing made it possible for some words to catch the dreamer's eye.

More on the Question of Safety

The success of the process depends on the development of trust: trust in the intrinsic value of dream imagery, in the group, in the leader, in the reliability of the process, and in oneself to get to where one wants to go with the dream. There are no special therapeutic interventions by a skilled therapist to take you there. You go there by yourself with the others in the group trying to ease your way. Your motivation and curiosity provide the energy and, on occasion, the courage to see it through.

There is always the question raised in connection with this process as to whether the dreamer is at risk by having more exposed about himself than intended. Theoretically, there is this risk and, on rare occasions, it has happened. This risk is minimized by a number of factors—for example, the nonintrusive way in which the group conducts itself, the control the dreamer has over the process, and over time, the reassurance that develops as a result of the way other members of the group entrust their secrets when it is their turn to share a dream. The dreamer is not up against an external authority. There is no one there ready to use a theoretical body of knowledge or technique about which the dreamer is ignorant. He is never put on the spot to reveal his thoughts. He is always in the position of allowing his own healing mechanisms to operate according to their own timetable.

In general, the relief one feels at unloading one's secrets far outweighs any anxieties that go along with it. The lesson that has to be and is learned eventually is that there is a direct relationship between the honesty and openness with which one shares oneself and the degree of insight, relief, and the feeling of deepening contact with other people that one comes to. As one's defenses go down, the clarity of one's emotional vision becomes sharper and deeper. Trust opens the dreamer up to the possibility of discovery. In turn, the act of making discoveries deepens the openness.

Traps to Be Avoided

There is an ancient Scottish game, played on ice, called curling. It has devotees both in Scotland and in North America. A player sends a polished stone straight down a lane on the ice, aiming at a target at the opposite end of the lane. As the stone slides on its way, two members of the same team move down the ice with it, sweeping the ice in front of the stone with brushes, trying to keep the stone on a straight path rather than curving off to one side. This strikes me as an apt metaphor for group members to keep in mind as they put questions to the dreamer. The sweepers in curling never touch the stone, never push it. They clear the path in front of it so that the stone goes along on its own momentum, influenced only by the friction it generates. We never push the dreamer with our questions. Questions are used to keep open the path that the dreamer needs to follow on his own. Questions should minimize the friction (resistance) but never increase it. We respect the importance of the dreamer, staying with the path of the dream rather than deflecting him into a path of our own making.

These principles are more easily set forth than followed. There are many ways for group members to give that stone a nudge in the direction they would like it to go. We have already alluded to two sources of difficulty—the failure to let go of one's own perspective of the dream and, as a corollary, the failure to pay close attention to and take seriously all that the dreamer shares in his response (Stage 3A). Each of these tendencies plays into the other, pushing the group member into trying to validate his own view (pushing the stone) instead of working along directions being hinted at or actually mapped out by the dreamer (sweeping the ice in front of the stone). The problem with pushing is that it evokes a counterpush that becomes apparent in the defensiveness it evokes in the dreamer.

Pushing tactics can take various forms. One of the most common is when someone moves into what I refer to as a "pseudotherapeutic" stance. I say *pseudo* because I don't think it is ever truly therapeutic to approach a dreamer with an a priori conviction about what a dream means, based on a particular theoretical point of view and preconceived ideas about what certain images mean. It is fine to have ideas derived from theory, but it is wrong to assume their a priori validity because some of the images seem to be congruent with a particular theoretical formulation. The place to interject theoretically derived ideas about the imagery is in Stage 2 in which they are offered as personal projections. This leaves the dreamer free to follow up on them or not. Having a priori convictions tends to lead to manipulative questions with the resulting heightening of the dreamer's defensiveness.

Example. In a dream, a young man finds himself in the bedroom of an older woman who is also present. The dreamer has made no reference to his mother. Moving into a pseudotherapeutic stance, the questioner assumes that the older woman is the dreamer's mother and that the situation reflects an oedipal conflict. "Can you tell me something about your relationship with your mother?"

The issue is not whether the questioner is right or wrong in such an assumption. It is simply inappropriate because the dreamer has not connected the older woman with his mother. The following questions might be more appropriate:

"Have you any ideas as to who this older woman might represent?"

"Have you been preoccupied with or concerned with any tension connected with an older woman?"

"Have you had any recent encounter with an older woman that might account for the image's appearing in the dream?"

Another example is the tendency to pursue an area in a way not appropriate in dream appreciation work but that may well be appropriate in formal therapy where one is not obligated to stay just with a dream. Consider the following example: Assuming that the dreamer has made a connection between the woman and his mother and recalls a recent incident between them, a therapist may choose to carry the dreamer back into his past: "Tell me more about your relationship with your mother when you were younger."

In dream appreciation work, we stay close to the dream and do not move into areas not yet opened up by the dreamer, however profitable it might seem from a therapeutic point of view. The dream and what the dreamer has shared about it remain the template that shapes the form and content of our questions. They should always lead back to the dream and not into other areas of the dreamer's life that occur to us but have not occurred to him.

The simplest way of avoiding either of these traps is to abide by the dictum that the question you put to the dreamer has to be *obviously* related to the dream (obvious to the dreamer) or to something the dreamer has shared; its meaning, content, and possible implications then do not come as a surprise. Any situation in which a dreamer is made to feel the object of indirect or manipulative questioning tends to touch off defensiveness and undermine the trust that has been built up. If a dreamer is compliant or intimidated, he can be led where he doesn't wish to go and end up feeling manipulated and resentful. The goal is to lead the dreamer into dialogue with his own dream. Anything other than that is to shift the dreamer's attention from the dream to the motives of the questioner. Any effort to make the dreamer move faster than at his rate will eventually backfire. When a questioner moves into a therapeutic stance, it may appear helpful at times and the dreamer may even wish to go along with it, but in the long run, it will undermine the process. It fosters an interaction between the "therapist" and the dreamer that excludes the other members of the group, draws the dreamer away from his own dream, and orients him to the person acting as therapist and what he or she is pursuing. What sometimes seems like a simple, innocent, and useful question may radically transform the process from an experience in dream appreciation into a clinical interview. In therapy, one can take off from the dream into any area that will be most productive for the client. Our task is to stay with the dream, electing to have the dream itself as the only therapist in the room. The goal is to place this therapeutic instrument in the hands of the dreamer, to help him learn to use it in his own way toward his own ends. There is quite a difference between this goal and assuming therapeutic responsibility.

There are other ways that the dialogue can get off track. For one thing, it is easy for an individual to experience the group as powerful and authoritative. This is especially so with a self-effacing, suggestible, or compliant person who is too timid to exercise his right to control the course of the dialogue and who may feel impelled to respond uncritically to any questions put by the group. When this happens, the leader has to step in to remind the dreamer of his rights and to temper any tendency of a group member to push in the direction she thinks the dreamer should go. It is sometimes so difficult for a group member to divest herself of a point of view about the dream that she continues to try to foist it on the dreamer. This problem is more likely to arise when the dialogue has been going on for some time and the dreamer still seems to be in the dark about what the dream is saying. Tension rises in the group as the members sense their inability to help the dreamer. In desperation, some may try to force fit their ideas onto the dreamer, losing sight of the rule that we follow rather than lead the dreamer. Our role is to uncover clues, not to sell them to the dreamer.

Sometimes, group members are led into making supportive or reassuring statements that have little or no connection to the dream itself. Such efforts fall short of their mark. They are more reassuring to the questioner than to the dreamer. It takes some experience with the process before people begin to realize that the only true reassurance or support lies in the dreamer's ability to feel, see, and appreciate the transparent honesty of his own dream imagery. The message itself may be a disturbing one, even a frightening one, but it is still more reassuring to have the courage to confront oneself with it than to be offered false reassurance that glosses over truths contained in the dream. It is a difficult lesson to learn that our dreams, whatever their content, are our allies, our friends, and can be, if approached properly (and up to a certain point), our therapists.

Concern With One's Own Process

We are all concerned with ourselves. In group dream work, we have to learn how to harness this concern in deference to the dreamer's needs. Putting the dreamer first means managing our own reactions. For the most part, these are readily managed. There are, however, subtle ways in which such reactions may intrude inappropriately into the process. This can happen at any stage. In Stage 1B, when you are trying to clarify the dream, you may put questions to the dreamer more because of what an element means to you than because of the need to clarify the image. In Stage 2, you can get carried away by your response to the dream and develop a lengthy personal biographical exposition. During the first two phases of the dialogue (search for context and playback), this tendency can lead to premature orchestrating comments, as if trying to validate your own felt responses to the dream. However well-intentioned these efforts may be, they tend to get the process off track and are not in the best interest of the dreamer. If unchecked, they will gradually transform the process in the direction of group psychotherapy where attention is given to one's own process and where everyone's process deserves equal attention. Group dream work demands a certain altruism on the part of the participants. It means giving priority to the needs of the dreamer. Being given this special place is something deeply felt by the dreamer and in no small measure plays a facilitating role in the dreamer's freedom to share with the group.

A more serious problem occurred on one occasion when someone with considerable experience in group psychotherapy, heedless of the dream group structure, insistently called attention to his own reactions to the dream, the dreamer, and what others in the group had to say. His experience made it difficult for him to contain his own process in the interest of maintaining the focus on the dreamer. This is quite different from those occasions when a group member is so deeply affected by the dreamer's dream that there is a temporary loss of composure. Here, in the face of a legitimate need for support, the process is temporarily stopped until the person having difficulty is ready to go on.

Minor Misunderstandings

1. The stricture not to look at the dreamer in Stage 2, when offering a projected feeling or metaphor, is often misconstrued to mean one should never look at the dreamer during this stage. This is certainly not the case. Not only the leader but everyone should be aware of the state of the dreamer, and this means being free to keep your eye on the dreamer; the only exception is when you are offering your projection. Having a sense of where the dreamer is will not only alert the group to any difficulties the dreamer may experience but can also provide the group with cues to which projections are having an effect. Often a dreamer cannot help nonverbally registering some of the responses she is having to the work the group is doing with her dream.

2. Members of the group sometimes feel they have to respond at every stage of the process. This is not so. In Stage 2, for example, if one does not have anything to say, there is no need to say anything. In the final stage of the dialogue when group members are invited to offer their orchestrating comments, one should not feel obligated to make one up if it does not arise spontaneously.

3. Working with the dream in the second stage, one sometimes holds back for fear of giving an "interpretation." Whatever that word may mean to the person raising the question, he should be reassured that he can say whatever he likes about the dream, providing he speaks of it in the first person as his dream and works with the given context of the dream.

4. The group should not assume that when a dreamer invites the dialogue she is agreeing automatically to go through all three phases of it. The

leader should check in with her at the end of each successive phase to see if she still wishes to go further.

Other Considerations

What follows are some helpful reminders. First, keep in mind that in Stage 2, group members can work with any context known to all if they feel it could be useful in the formation of their projections. Even though group members have been told that any context that is known to all can be used in their projections, it is often lost sight of until the leader offers an example that proves to be helpful to the dreamer. Such known contexts could include obvious features of the group, such as the number of participants, as, for example, if that number should appear in the dream; recent world events; or the possible meaning of a holiday occurring around the time of the dream. In other words, any current happening known to both the dreamer and the group that can be seen to have a possible connection to the dream can be included in the projections offered to the dreamer. In a group that has been working together for some time and in which a dreamer has shared many previous dreams, material divulged by an earlier dream can, if it is appropriate, be worked into the projections offered in Stage 2. Something the dreamer shared on an earlier occasion might prove relevant to the current dream.

Second, learn to recognize and respect the fact that dreamers have different styles in working with a dream. Two main styles soon become apparent. There are those who readily experience and embrace the feelings that emerge in the course of dream work. They tend to be more trusting, to be less apt to feel defensive, and generally, are more in touch with their feelings. Then there are those who, despite a genuine interest in their dream lives, approach the work with greater caution and who, despite their conscious intent, maintain a certain distance from the dream. There is a general hesitancy about the public display of feelings, a greater defensiveness, and a tendency to disown feelings. These disowning strategies can become manifest in a number of ways:

1. There may be an attitude of helplessness with regard to exploring one's inner processes and an inappropriate dependence on the group to provide all the necessary information and give meaning to the dream. The dreamer acts as if she were unable to see even very obvious connections between an aspect of her life and its portrayal in the dream. The helplessness here takes the form of providing the group with information but being completely dependent on the group to offer a metaphorical projection. This leaves

the dreamer still in the position of disowning a projection coming at her from the outside.

2. Another way of disowning a dream is to seemingly embrace it, say a good deal about it, but remain impervious to the group's effort to help uncover all that a dream has to offer. The dreamer stays with the parts of the dream that feel safe and that validate her way of looking at the dream but does so at the expense of honestly taking into account all that a dream may be saying. The dreamer is unconsciously excluding the group and, by doing it all herself, protects herself from allowing the dream to come up with anything new. Some dreamers go further than this and seem more interested in defying the group than in exploring the dream.

3. The dreamer who tends to be detached from her feelings may rely on intellectualizing to obscure the feeling base of the dream. She might settle for a satisfying intellectual view of the imagery, overlooking any genuine felt connections to her life.

4. Some people have all the potential for dream work but are excessively timid and, as a consequence, are inhibited about doing what they are perfectly capable of doing.

None of these defensive mechanisms needs be tackled head-on as they might be in formal therapy. Instead, they tend to recede if the dreamer stays with the work, learns to trust the process and the people involved, bears witness to the deep-level sharing by others, and gradually allows what is genuine about herself to rise to the surface. Persisting in the work results in a greater awareness of the true nature of inner processes, less fear of self-exposure, and the ability to make a greater investment in the sharing of oneself. As one feels the support, concern, and respect of the group, there is more freedom to share what is deeply personal.

Third, remember that you are charged with the responsibility of bringing every detail in the dream to the attention of the dreamer. When working with the dream as your own, you attempt to focus on every element in the dream in forming your projections. When playing the dream back, you are concerned with whether or not the further associations of the dreamer bring him any closer to what the dream is saying. If not, you are prepared to stay with follow-up questions until either the dreamer can't go further or doesn't wish to. One has to learn where the line is between prematurely breaking off a line of questioning and being intrusive by going beyond the dreamer's capacity or desire to continue working in that direction.

Another thing to keep in mind is that there are two aspects to the dialogue—adequate preparation and engagement with the dreamer. Preparation involves the capacity to listen attentively to all that a dreamer shares and to be able to make that information available (either in your head or in your notes). You are always looking for cues from the dreamer to the recent emotional context that shaped the dream, the issues being developed, the connections that the dreamer is making by himself, and the ease with which the dreamer engages in self-disclosure. Careful listening is your only reliable guide to what areas remain to be explored and how to avoid repetition. Engagement refers to the way you go about trying to help the dreamer enrich the informational base of the dream and facilitate the flow of information. Your goal is to do this without being intrusive.

Also remember that in the first two phases of the dialogue (search for context and playback), it is up to the dreamer to discover the metaphorical meaning of the imagery to the extent that he can. Too often, the group loses sight of this and begins to offer connections of their own either directly or through the way questions are formulated.

Finally, a word about bending some of the rules. A structure is necessary if dream work is to unfold in a safe and effective way. It is important, however, to fully understand its rationale so that a certain degree of flexibility can be introduced should that become necessary. There is a tendency on the part of some people to be too rigid in their handling of the process. They adhere too compulsively to the structure at the expense of a reasonable degree of flexibility. There are times when modifications can be made and rules bent to accommodate particular circumstances. When working with a long dream within the ordinary time constraints of 1.5 to 2 hours, Stage 2 can be shortened by combining Substages 2A and 2B and having the group work freely at the level of feelings and metaphorical possibilities. By setting a limited time for this, say 15 to 20 minutes, most of the session will be left free for the dreamer's response and the dialogue. Something will be lost, of course, but that can't be helped when working on a long dream.

Some rules, when broken, are not harmful to the dreamer, but if they are continuously disregarded, the effectiveness of the process is limited. Consider the following examples:

- In Stage 1, the dreamer gives extended associations either in relating the dream or in responding to questions.
- In Substage 2A, metaphorical projections are offered instead of focusing on feelings.
- Premature connections are offered during the playback.

Other rules, if tampered with, are potentially disturbing to the dreamer:

- Asking leading questions
- Failing to talk of the dream as one's own in Stage 2
- Not checking with the dreamer concerning fall-back strategies in the dialogue
- Projecting personal and extraneous material into the orchestration
- Compromising confidentiality

Also consider these final words of caution:

- Don't read into a dream more than is in it, and don't settle for less than is in it.
- As a helper, view yourself as learning from the dreamer all that you have to know to be of help to the dreamer.
- In listening to a dreamer, train yourself to discern the difference between genuine feelings expressed by a dreamer and pseudofeelings—that is, something may be expressed as a feeling, but it doesn't ring true.

A Word About *Dreamism*

I use this term to denote an adverse evaluation of the potential value of a dream based on a judgment made in the waking state. It occurs in connection with a dream that does not fulfill the expectations of the dreamer as to what a dream should be. The dreamer registers his dissatisfaction or even disdain for the dream by regarding it as too insignificant or too banal to bother with, or he thinks that its message is so obvious that it is hardly worth the effort of the group. What is being invoked here is an irrational prejudice that in no way reflects the potential significance of the dream. Hence the term *dreamism*. A dream is to be appreciated, not judged. It is a grandiose act on the part of our waking ego to take onto itself the right to render a judgment about an event that was the product of a totally different state of being. No dream should be judged before it is worked on, and then once it has been worked through, it soon becomes apparent how irrelevant any judgment is. All our dreams have something to say to us. Dreams may vary in their significance for us at a given moment in our lives, but that remains to be discovered through the work we do with the dream. It doesn't depend on how long, short, exciting, or unexciting it may seem at first glance. Even veteran dream workers, including myself, show signs of this widespread bias. Here is an example.

A dreamer, new to the group, is hesitant to volunteer to share her dream. She does share it but somewhat apologetically introduces it by saying, "It's not very interesting. It seems so sterile."

There was a pink ribbon on the ground. I simply was following the ribbon. It seemed to be endless. There were no people around.

Were you to agree with the dreamer that the dream lacked substance how wrong you would be! The dreamer is a therapist, and the dream was triggered by and shed light on the interaction that took place in a session with a child the day before the dream. The child presented serious problems. The therapist felt very much alone in trying to cope with the situation, because she had not yet had any supervisory help with the case. The fact that the child's favorite color was pink established the link to the dream. What emerged in the course of the dream work were the feelings stirred up in herself by this particular child. In describing the child's behavior, she emphasized the child's sudden unprovoked mood swings. She would be pleasant and delightful one moment and violently out of control the next. As the dreamer related this, she suddenly realized that this was the same kind of behavior she endured at the hands of her own mother, behavior that left her helpless, frustrated, and enraged. In the dream, she had a feeling of frustration and of not reaching a goal. Working on the dream she became aware of the countertransference (the feeling she had toward her own mother invoked by the child). Driven by her own perfectionistic trends, she had lost sight of the fact that this was more than she could handle by herself. She would have to pursue supervisory help more actively to resolve the feeling that she had started a process with this child that seemed endless.

Waking reactions to a dream color one's feelings about the dream. We see in a dream what is easiest for us to see and what fits most readily into our waking emotional set. If we are depressed, we are apt to focus selectively on what seems to validate our current mood. Other elements in the dream simply don't register or are glossed over if they are not congruent with our waking emotions. Only a thoroughgoing look at all that the dream is saying can offset this one-sided response.

A Few Final Comments

The informational and emotional range of dream imagery is greater than our unaided waking resources have access to. The dreamer is the only one who can test the limits of the range, but it is a task that requires emotional and informational support from others. Only the dreamer can venture into this unknown territory, but the contributions from the group serve to make it more accessible.

The dreamer is always in a tension between his waking view of himself and the view now offered by the dream. In relation to himself, his moral integrity, his capacity for honesty, is on the line. In relation to the group, there is the tension between how he envisages the distance between his private and his public self. Dream work seeks to close that gap.

Each stage of the process puts to the test the delicate balance between the dreamer's interest in discovery and his investment in security. There is a palpable sense of tension between the risk to respond spontaneously and honestly and the impulse to keep private what has heretofore been private. As one becomes experienced in dream work, the balance shifts to the former. The dreamer has been witness to the experience of mutual sharing. He soon learns how the honesty of his own effort captures and maintains the interest of the group and frees the group to be of greater help.

If one learns nothing else from dream work, one develops a keener sense of one's capacity for honesty. In a sense, dream work is an effort at rehabilitation—namely, to restore that virginal honesty and innocence we came into the world with. I include innocence here because one of the unfortunate lessons we learn is that innocence makes us vulnerable, and we become enmeshed in dishonesty (defenses) to protect ourselves. These childhood virtues never die in us even though at times their presence becomes known to us only through our dreams. The rehabilitation involved in dream work is to undo what is, in effect, a kind of disuse atrophy. Every dream image we remember can be used as a prosthetic device to enable us to recapture a bit of that open innocence and natural honesty.

It is not a particularly easy task, nor is it free from fear. People have understandable anxiety when they start dream work. What will they find when they dive into uncharted waters—fish to nourish them or monsters to devour them? With the proper lifeline to the surface provided by the safety features of the process and the diving equipment provided by the group, the dreamer is given a clearer vision of the underwater scene, and the necessary balance between security and discovery becomes manifest. The dreamer returns to the surface with a mix of insight, perspective, and emotional clarity. There is also a mix of the new and familiar. One may have fished in these waters before and come up with fish that are quite familiar, or one may encounter unexpected sea life. In either instance, one doesn't go home empty.

The commonality that results from dream sharing makes people feel better. In the words of a younger colleague of mine (Deborah Hillman), perhaps we are put on this earth to heal each other. Dream work moves us toward a more compassionate view of others. It is difficult to dislike anyone who shares a dream and honestly works at it.

13

∎

Forming a Group

Dream groups can be organized by people who know each other, have a common interest in dreams, and feel they know enough about the process to begin working together on their dreams. There are a number of practical considerations.

Size of the Group

The optimal size for an ongoing group is six to eight, including the leader. Above that number, there is too long a wait for a chance to present a dream. When it is less than six and a few are absent, the power of the group input is greatly diminished and there is too much pressure felt by those who are present to come up with a dream. Because I have open groups, there have been times when we have gone along with ten or eleven without too much difficulty. There were also times in some of the smaller groups when only four, including myself, went through with the process.

Makeup of the Group

How homogeneous should the group be with regard to age, sex, education, and common cultural background?

Age

Because I accept anyone who applies to the group, I have had very broad ranges of age distribution, from late teenagers to people in their 80s. The essence of dream work is honesty and depth of self-revelation, and this is appreciated by young and old alike, despite the differences in the issues involved. Generally, I am the oldest, but there is no end to the penetrating insights those much younger have come up with on occasions when I have shared a dream. The visions of the young and old come out in complementary ways in dream work. Each moves into the future from a different perspective—the young with energy, openness, and anxious concern, the old struggling to untangle the various strands of the past. Each needs a little of what the other brings to the work. Also, dream work exposes intergenerational issues in a way that is helpful to both.

A more homogeneous group, one made up of peers, has its own virtues. The mutual support deepens as the commonality of themes emerges. In the young, there are uncertainties about establishing relationships or how they will work out. With those who are older, the concerns focus more on loss or separation.

My experience with homogeneous groups at either extreme is limited. Regarding teenagers, the process works better with older teenagers than younger ones, mainly because of the verbal and conceptual demands it makes. There is also the special problem posed by the degree of self-consciousness a teenager feels in exposing himself or herself to a group of peers. It is hard for a teenager to risk letting go of the social image he or she is trying so hard to maintain.

My limited experience with older people in both an Italian and Jewish senior citizen center has convinced me that here is fertile ground for dream work. People in their 70s and 80s are fairly set in their ways and are apt not to pay too much attention to the rules set down in an effort to maintain the structure. But despite the fact that in most instances this was the first time in their lives they ever took their dreams seriously, they went about it with much interest and enthusiasm. This age group in particular has been neglected with regard to dream work, as has been the case in so many other ways.

Let me describe how a 78-year-old Italian woman went about telling her dream to illustrate how in so touching a way she ignored the dictum to relate only the dream and withhold any comments about the imagery. She presented a dream that had to do with her late husband. As she came to the part where he appeared in the dream, she broke off her account to say, "He died last year. He was a good man. He did everything for me." I thought she would then continue with the dream. Instead, she turned to the woman sitting next to her, obviously her friend, and said, "But I was a good wife, too. I took care of him." Finally, with a few more slight meanderings she got to the rest of the dream. If the leader is prepared to be flexible and to gear the process to the older person's perspective, the returns are very much worthwhile.

Gender

When this issue is left up to fate, the likely outcome is that the group will turn out to be predominantly female. I think the reason comes down to culturally imposed influences that leave women more concerned with their feelings and men more oriented to the world "out there." Be that as it may, the ratio in my weekly groups turns out to be five to six females to zero or one or two males. I prefer a mixed group because of the greater diversity of input that is likely to occur. When a dream is gender specific (e.g., a pregnancy dream), it is a challenge to the role-playing ability of the opposite sex. A little reassurance overcomes any shyness about the need for undergoing a temporary sex reversal. Only on one occasion did I have the opportunity to work with an all-male group. I had the impression in that instance that the men were freer in the absence of females. It is more common for me to work with an all-female group, and here, the addition of a male has a positive impact.

Education and Cultural Background

Some degree of homogeneity with regard to educational level and cultural background has both favorable and unfavorable features. With a more or less homogeneous group, people are able to move into each other's lives in a more fluid fashion, sharing common problems and, in general, feeling more at ease with each other. On the other hand, when there is some disparity along these lines, new and broader horizons are opened up. A blue-collar worker who joins a group of suburban housewives brings a different perspective, testing the empathic potential of everyone concerned.

At this stage in the development of dream work in the community, it is unfortunate that it has attracted a predominantly white educated middle-class segment of the population. There would be much to learn about dreams and dream work if greater effort was made to include ethnic, racial, and other minorities.

Because my groups do not undergo preliminary screening and because they are open to anyone interested, I get an unpredictable mix of therapists, clients of therapists, and ordinary mortals. No difficulties have arisen. On the contrary, the mix has been a salutary one. The process depends on one's capacity for openness and sensitivity and the ability to use one's metaphorical imagination. It is not beholden to any theoretical approach to dream interpretation so that specialized knowledge is relatively unimportant in the equation. Each one's life experience is the resource put to use in the group. There is a pooling of talent and experience oriented toward the benefit of the dreamer. Although the mix may vary, it is not different in a way that defines a role difference, as is the case in therapy.

Does the process work better if people don't know each other? On occasion, someone joining the group will feel more comfortable inducing a friend to join as well. People react differently about opening up before strangers. When the process is fully understood, particularly the emphasis on the degree of control the dreamer has, most people have no difficulty. Some start more slowly than others, testing the waters for a number of sessions before enough trust is built up to share a dream. Sometimes, the anxiety about sharing a dream works in the reverse, and the person who is most anxious may be the first to volunteer, almost as if he or she were eager to get it over with.

Generally, friends who are in a group together experience it in a mutually supportive way and find it helpful in deepening the relationship. As already noted, a dream group is not the place to go to for the purpose of resolving preexisting tensions. When friends join a group because of their mutual interest in dreams, the freeing effect of the work can be helpful in dealing with the occasional rough spots that crop up in any relationship. This holds also when two or more members of the same family are in the same group. It is not the place to resolve family tensions. If the primary motive is mutual interest in dream work, then interesting things may occur that can contribute in a positive way to the relationship. Messages never before verbalized can be conveyed by one spouse to the other that may be difficult to communicate in any other way. Frustration, anger, or even rage can be expressed toward a partner in a way that does not provoke defensiveness in the other. It is not being expressed vindictively. It emerges as part of a difficult and courageous attempt at openness and honesty. The partner's awareness and appreciation of this results in the message's getting across. That appreciation overrides any impulse to defend oneself.

I have had only a few situations in which parents and a sibling participated in the same group. Again, what was noteworthy was the freedom with which parent and child interacted. It is important to feel sure that the central focus of all parties is dreams and not some hidden agenda having to do with preexisting family problems. On only one occasion did difficulties arise when a husband and wife were in the same group. The wife had been in the group for some time. Her enthusiasm for the work resulted in her husband's wanting to join. Thinking he wanted to join because her enthusiasm had been contagious, I was not prepared for what occurred. Whereas she had been a very active member of the group before he came on the scene and had shared her dreams freely, she now became very quiet, hardly participating at all. He, on the other hand, used it as an opportunity to take over and outshine her. Needless to say, their joint participation ended soon after he entered the group, unfortunately aborting her participation as well.

Practical Pointers

Organizing and conducting a group involves a number of other practical considerations.

Frequency. There is a good deal of flexibility, depending on the circumstances of the participants. I prefer weekly sessions. This keeps the interest high, is more productive with regard to follow-up comments (Stage 4), and does not allow too much time to elapse before a dreamer has another opportunity to present a dream. Biweekly sessions can work well. Some groups have continued to meet every third or fourth week despite the disadvantages. Whatever time span is agreed on, it is important to keep to a regular schedule.

Duration of the Sessions. My preference is for 1.5 hours, which is generally enough time to do one dream. Beginners often feel more comfortable with 2-hour sessions, taking more time at the various stages than I do. This is a question of experience and learning how to terminate a particular stage before it gets repetitive or nonproductive. I would discourage going for periods longer than 2 hours because that tends to encourage going beyond the limits of the process.

Time of Day. Mornings are the best time to do dream work. Recall is fresher, and one has not yet faced the stresses and strains of the day. Practically, however, groups most often have to arrange to meet in the evening. This turns out not to be a drawback because the excitement and stimulation of dream work offsets fatigue or outside concerns. If people are ready to give up part of their weekend, Saturday morning is an ideal time.

Number of Dreams. Unless one is working with a time frame longer than 2 hours, it is best to focus on doing one dream leisurely and thoroughly.

Meeting Place. Any living room where comfortable seating can be arranged in a circle is suitable.

Rotating Leadership. When people who know each other get together to form a group and they are all at the same level of experience, the leadership can be on a rotating basis.

Confidentiality. It is important to keep in mind that whatever is revealed in the course of dream work is of a confidential nature. Unless permission is given by the dreamer, nothing concerning the dream should be discussed with anyone outside the group.

14
■

On One's Own or With Another

Up until now, we have been talking about the group arrangement for dream work. Most people do not wake up in the morning fortunate enough to have a group at hand, ready to help them with their dreams. What can you do working on your own? Although the group remains the most powerful medium for dream work, there are many aspects of the group experience that can be carried over into individual work with dreams.

Perhaps the most important is the realization that dream work is *work,* that it takes time, effort, and persistence. Dreams do not yield their secrets easily. The group experience leaves one with a realistic assessment of the ground to be covered, the distance from the dream that has to be overcome. You also become more aware of the various ways in which you may booby-trap your own efforts—for example, by derogating a dream that at first glance does not seem all that interesting or by underestimating your own knowledge and capacity to do the work necessary. A side benefit of the group work is the impetus it gives to dream recall. The group work can be of help in several ways in working with dreams on your own.

The Time Factor. You now understand the importance of placing the dream as close to its temporal setting as possible. The dream has a certain fleeting

208

quality. It has to be captured before it and the relevant emotional context begin to fade. Optimal, of course, is to find time on awakening in the morning. If you do go about it in this way, be sure to leave yourself enough time to do it leisurely. Dream work cannot be rushed. Although insights themselves are sudden, the preparation for those insights proceeds more slowly.

Gathering the Residues. Aware of the importance of recent emotional residues, you are now left to your own devices to recapture them. You can initiate the kind of dialogue that would have taken place were you in the group and ask yourself the same kinds of questions in an effort to recapture the emotional climate of the prior day and evening and the feelings and preoccupations that lingered until bedtime. All you are trying to do is reconstruct in memory a diary of your recent experiences and the feeling tones connected to them.

Associations. You know now how critical to dream work are your own associations to each and every element in the dream. You can go about this in two ways. First, search your mind for whatever feelings or thoughts occur to you as you examine each element in the dream as well as the way they connect with each other as the story unfolds. Then, depending on how imaginative you are, you can distance yourself from the dream, pretending you are someone else who is working with your dream and playing with it the same way the group does in Stage 2. This means calling on your imagination for whatever feelings or ideas may occur to you about the imagery, no matter how far-fetched they may seem at the time. You are asking yourself what possible associations you can bring to the imagery without regard as to whether it makes any immediate sense in relation to the dream. As you do this, keep in mind the ever-implicit question as to why those images were created at that specific time in your life. You are looking not only at the images as distinct entities but also their sequential development. You have chosen the characters and written the script to express the emotional currents in your life at a given moment. Try to see them as indicators calling to your attention something not yet in full view. Sometimes, it can be helpful to see the opening scene as a statement of the interplay between an existing status quo and recent intrusive events. Then follows the development of this interplay in the dream along with reference at times to historical antecedents and finally a resolution, at least to the extent possible at the time.

Orchestration. Because this is a solo performance, there is not much point talking about orchestration in the sense that the term is used in the group. As you struggle with the dream on your own, you are constantly striving for an inner sense of closure, a felt sense of what your sleeping psyche has to say to your waking ego. If you have made a serious attempt to work the dream out without getting to a point of closure and if you have made a written record of the work you have done, then let it go and go back to it after some time has elapsed. You'll find that a second look, what we refer to as a *delayed orchestration,* may help you see things that escaped you earlier. Once you have a record of the information that you can go back to, other reviews may prove helpful. Life events and dreams subsequent to the dream may shed additional light.

Recently, I canvased members of my dream group about what they found most helpful from the group experience in working with dreams on their own. The three features around which there was the most consensus were what they had learned of the importance of retrieving the recent emotional context, the importance of noting and working with any feelings experienced in the dream or suggested by the imagery, and the usefulness of assuming an impersonal stance in ferreting out the range of metaphorical possibilities of a given image when their spontaneous associations failed to shed light.

In a sense, a dream recalled is like a newborn infant, totally dependent on an outside agency to keep it alive. That infant can be nurtured in a way that makes it possible for it to be what it can be, or it can be manipulated and exploited to meet the needs of that outside agency. Working on a dream on our own, that outside agency is the waking ego. Keep in mind how difficult it can be for that ego not to read its own waking agenda into the dream and, instead, afford the dream that degree of respect that allows it to say what it has to say and all that it wants to say. That requires some humility on the part of one's ego and an acceptance of the fact that we all have much to learn about ourselves. Our dreaming consciousness, through the power of our creative imagination, provides us with an unending flow of imagery addressed in a most precise way to fulfill that quest.

A Very Small Group:
Working With One Another

Many people seek out the opportunity to work with their dreams in a mutually shared way with a friend, relative, or spouse. This can be very helpful, providing there is trust and genuine concern for each other. A prior exposure to the group experience can facilitate the task by its emphasis on how to explore the current emotional context of the dream and how to evoke the relevant associative matrix. Prior experience with the process also teaches one how important it is for the dreamer to be the gatekeeper as to what becomes public and to be the final arbiter of how the dream articulates with his waking life. Keeping the guidelines for maintaining the safety of the dreamer in mind, there can be an informal mix of the various strategies we have spoken of with regard to the discovery factor.

Generally, it is best to start with the dreamer's own associations to each and every image in the dream. One might then pursue the search for context and for further associations in much the same way as in the dialogue. When it comes to offering orchestrating projections, the helper has to bear in mind that, as someone close to the dreamer, she is in possession of a good deal more knowledge about the life of the dreamer than is apt to come out in the exploration of this one dream. That knowledge can be brought into play in connection with orchestrating ideas but only if the helper discovers a link to the present associative context that would warrant making such a connection. In other words, knowledge of a dreamer's past must be used with tact and not in the service of substantiating some a priori notion about the dreamer not connected to anything the dreamer has said about the current dream.

Stages 2 and 3 of the process need not be followed as systematically as in the group arrangement. By an informal mix, I mean that any or all of the strategies of these two stages can come into play at the discretion of the helper, as long as there is respect for the limits being set by the dreamer. The success of the undertaking depends more on the skill shown in helping the dreamer discover the information needed to give meaning to the images than on any intellectual adroitness on the part of the helper in reading the metaphorical significance into dream imagery. This is so, notwithstanding that because of the feeling bond with the dreamer, the helper is able to approach the dreamer in a freer and less structured way than in the group. It is still basic to dream work that we respect both the privacy of the dreamer and the authority of the dreamer over the dream.

Dream sharing of this nature can serve a dual purpose. It can be of help to the dreamer and, if pursued over a period of time, can clarify and deepen the relationship between the two people involved.

Hints to the Helper

- Listen carefully to the dreamer's recall of the dream and any spontaneous associations offered in the course of the recall.
- Include clarifying questions that identify characters, feelings, colors, and the age of the dreamer in the dream.

- Draw the dreamer out with regard to recent thoughts and feelings, helping when appropriate with your own recall of recent shared experiences.
- Encourage the dreamer to associate to every element of the dream.
- Engage in the playback much as one does in the group situation.
- If indicated, offer the dreamer your own integrating projections.
- Note whatever aspects of the dream still remain puzzling to the dreamer, continue to explore anything further the dreamer can say about those images, and offer any further integrating ideas that you may have.
- Encourage the dreamer to assess how far she has come to a sense of closure.
- Learn from the dreamer which aspects of your approach were most helpful and whatever other reactions she may have had about the work you did together.
- Keep in mind the possibility that work on subsequent dreams may shed light on the current dream just as work you did together on past dreams proves helpful with each new dream.

15
■

A Note on Repetitive Dreams

Occasionally, a dream is brought in that has occurred with similar images many times in the past. Although it can easily be recognized as a repetitive dream, generally, subtle differences can be noted from one time to another. In working with a repetitive dream, the awareness of such differences is a critical factor in helping the dreamer understand how the persistent underlying issue is affected by current life experience.

In the following instance, a repetitive dream was presented that had occurred three nights before the session. In presenting it, the dreamer indicated that she was well aware of the problem it was portraying. It had to do with the difficulty she'd had all her life in making choices.

Betty's Dream

I was at the hospital in a big room, something like the present one. It was more like a living room. A meeting was going on. There were two men there, both masseurs. They were handsome. They were both there to give me a massage. I wanted both but knew I had to make a choice. Making a choice filled me with such anxiety that I woke up. My fear was

that because of my inability to make a choice, I would get neither and
would be left with nothing.

The dreamer is a therapist who was away from her job at the hospital for
several months because of an accident. Her immediate and spontaneous response to the dream was that it was another example of the difficulty in
making a choice and that it also pointed up her greediness in wanting everything instead of having to make a choice. She felt that wanting both was
almost sinful. Another factor restraining her from making a choice was the
feeling that if she chose one then the other would feel terrible.

The precipitating life context that reintroduced this question of choice was
a call from a new man in her life to whom she felt sexually attracted. The
call made her anxious. She felt this reactivated old feelings of loss and aban-
donment connected with her parents. In the work that followed, Betty
brought out the fact that she was always pitted by one parent against the
other. Neither parent could ever take a stand. She felt frustrated and recalled
wishing as a child that they would divorce. But then she realized she
wouldn't be able to decide who she would live with. None of this was particularly new to her.

The playback elicited a number of pertinent facts that later proved helpful
in shedding a somewhat different light on this basic conflict. The first was
her comment that, on this occasion, in contrast to similar dreams in the past,
the choice was between two men who looked almost identically alike. The
second was that her boss, from whom she felt quite distant, was for the first
time experienced as very nice and quite human when he came to visit her
after the accident.

Throughout her response and during the dialogue, she had emphasized her
greediness in "wanting it all." What came out of the orchestrating comments
was her unawareness of the other side of the coin, her concern for others and
her capacity to give to others. In fact, there was some evidence from what
she said that she had a tendency to be there for others at the expense of
herself. Perhaps there was some connection between this and the greediness
she spoke about. In emptying herself out for the sake of others, she needed
to "have it all" to make up for it. Until she can garner more realistic self-
esteem from her capacity to give, she remains at the mercy of a frightening
self-image of greed and sin when confronted with a choice. It was significant
that, in this dream, the two men were almost identical, in contrast to earlier
versions of the dream where there were clear-cut differences in the choices
she faced. This points up the fact that the problem is not the capacity to make
a real choice but, rather, the resolution of this underlying dynamic. Her

capacity to give was well illustrated by how she shared of herself before strangers[1] as she worked with the dream. She literally emptied herself.

Betty felt that all that was said hit home. This dream was shared in the course of a one-day workshop, so there was no opportunity to see what effect the work might have on the recurrence of this repetitive dream.

In the following dream there is the repetition of a significant image.

John's Dream

John is a social worker in his late 30s who has been pursuing an interest in dreams over the past several years. He has been in other dream groups but has only recently joined my group. The following dream, which occurred the night before the session, is the first he presented. He has had many similar dreams in the past.

> *I'm standing in the woods. Ahead of me there is a rise. At the top of the hill, I see a large wolf silhouetted against the horizon. He looks at me and then starts loping toward me. He comes up next to me and looks at me. He starts to bark and then grabs my right wrist in his mouth. He tries to pull me along with him.*
>
> *I resist. He starts biting me and attacks my arm. I start beating him on the side of his head with a flashlight. He backs off and we are looking at each other. I awaken and then fall asleep again and the dream continues. We are walking. He is following me. It's as if we were together at this point.*

When asked about his feelings in the dream, he said that the apprehension he felt at the beginning changed. At the end, it felt that some sort of resolution had occurred, as if some accommodation had been made. The wooded area was unfamiliar to him.

Group Members Share Their Feelings

"I'm frightened but also intrigued by the wolf. I find myself wondering where he will take me."

"The wolf is related to man's best friend. Maybe he will lead me to something good."

"I feel alone, depressed, and lost in the beginning of the dream."

"There is a feeling in my dream of a stark confrontation, as if I'm being confronted with a moment of truth."

Stage 2B: Metaphors

"I have a very passive attitude at the beginning. I'm just waiting to see what happens."

"Using a flashlight to hit him with suggests to me I am trying to shed light on the problem."

"The presence of a flashlight suggests some kind of an emergency. A flashlight is handy in a sudden blackout."

The group began to explore the metaphorical possibilities of the wolf image:

"Wolf in sheep's clothing."
"Giving a woman a wolf whistle."
"Keeping the wolf away from the door."
"Wolves run in packs."
"The boy who cried wolf."
"Wolves are wild, untrainable."
"The story of the wolf and the three little pigs."
"Ferocity and aggression."
"There is something majestic in that image of the wolf on top of the hill."
"I feel it connects to the film *Dances With Wolves.*"

John's Response

"I've been having many dreams with wolves in them. I've also been reading something about wolves. In this dream, the wolf is up and I'm down below. Usually I'm higher. In an earlier dream, the wolf ripped my throat and killed me. In other dreams, I try to avoid him. In this dream, he comes to me. When I have these dreams, the wolf is usually guarding something, the wolf as the guardian of the underworld.

"In this dream, the time seemed to be predawn. When I hit him with the flashlight, I bloodied his head. He was shocked as if he couldn't believe it. I never had a successful encounter with a wolf before. I thought of the lone wolf up on the hill like a guard. I was perplexed as to where he would take me. I didn't trust him. Maybe some day I will.

"The last part of my dream surprised me tremendously. He was following me like a dog. I recall the Jack London story, *Call of the Wild.* A wolf is pure aggression."

The Context Is Explored

Question Do you recall your feelings just prior to falling asleep?

Response I had been reading on the Middle Ages, the Inquisition, and references to werewolves. I have very negative feelings about orthodoxy carried to the point of burning witches. It could happen today. That's what frightens me about human nature. I had another feeling reading the book. The author was quoting original Latin sources. We do less and less of that now. We're losing touch with that way of being-in-the-world.

Question Any other feelings the day left you with?

Response It was a busy day. I was in three different places. I had a heated discussion with a group who connected the AIDS epidemic with conspiracy and genocide, arguing that it was geopolitical racism. This discussion took place in a jail with very aggressive inmates. Their attitude reminded me of the Inquisition.

Question Can you be any more specific about the feelings you were having at the time?

Response I felt I was in with a bunch of fanatics or terrorists. I was helpless in the situation. There was nothing I could do about it. It made me understand something like Mylai.

Question You had this dream the night before coming to the dream group today. You are new to the situation here. Any anticipatory feelings about this?[2]

Response I'm trying to get more into my dreams. I'm in another study group also working on dreams. This coming weekend, I'll be going to a conference on dreams. I'm looking for all the feedback I can get.

Question Any other feelings connected with this?

Response I have a real wish that something will develop from the dream work. At the same time, I'm aware it's chancy. I went to bed last night hoping to have a dream.

The Playback Begins

The dream was read back to the end of the first paragraph:

Response I've gone out there (into the woods) in a natural way, by walking. This time, the wolf is not hunting me down. He is just approach-
ing. I have the feeling that if I go over that hill with him I'm never
coming back.

Question If you now try to look at the imagery in a more symbolic way
do any associations occur to you?

Response The wolf is an outlaw, a predator. He can't be controlled. If I
were to go along with it, I would be making a commitment to it. My
going with it would mean my identifying with it, with the temptation
within me to be a predator. A predator just helps himself to whatever
is available. I have to fight that in myself. It's difficult at times because of people's weaknesses. People are vulnerable and anxious, and
as a therapist I'm always in situations like that. It is an issue of mine.
I have to avoid being a self-indulgent aggressor. I work in a prison. I
grew up in the same neighborhood as these guys. They live by the
morality of taking whatever they need. I have to make a conscious
decision not to do that. I'm always afraid of being tempted back into
that sort of lifestyle. If I do, I'd go over the hill and never come back.
The wolf's only natural enemy is civilization. The choice is civilization or the wolf.

Question Anything more about the wolf?

Response In the earlier dreams, it was always a very dangerous situation.
In this dream, it's as if I'm trying to get close to that part of me and
to be able to have that power and use it more effectively. I feel that,
through the things I'm pursuing—dream work, meditation, reading—
I'm getting to that point.

The remainder of the dream was read back. John continued the train of
thought he had started:

Response I know it would be of use to me if I could keep that part of me
in the background. I feel positive about that. Maybe the flashlight
means I'm trying to shed more light. I'm hitting it in the head with
something that has to do with light. When the dream first ended, I
was glad I survived. The wolf was stunned. My expectation was that
it was going to lunge at me. I was then surprised when it didn't. I
don't know why I had the flashlight with me, since it was almost
dawn.

Question Consider the feelings you have been describing, at first feeling helplessly endangered, resisting, fighting back with a flashlight, and then surprise at the effect it had on the wolf. Can you take those feelings and then work back to any aspect of your recent experience and see if any further associations are stirred up?

Response Well, I did get angry with my wife last night. She didn't come home after work but hung out with her friends. When she did get home, she was on the telephone until about 10:30. The kids were still up and running around. I finally got to the point where I told her to hang up the phone. It was enough already. I'm usually fairly passive and don't say anything in situations like that, but this time I fought back a little.

Comment: This was a critical question, evoking as it did the memory of an important incident that, up to that point, had escaped his recall. It was obvious from the feelings John displayed in the telling that it played out in miniature his concern with his own aggression, his ever-present need to keep it under wraps, and finally allowing some of it out under justifiable provocation. Here was the source of the confrontation in the dream, his fighting back, and finally, the accommodation.

Despite the fact that all this was quite obvious to John by this time, he seemed eager to hear from the group.

Orchestrating Projections

"You spend a lot of energy and time trying to control this aggressive wolf potential. It pops up in your sleep following the incident with your wife, but it didn't end in either her or you being destroyed. There was more control in the picture."

"This place (referring to the dream group) is where you can bring up any feelings whatever. It's a safe place to deal with aggression and get it out in the open."

"Sometimes, we have to embrace what we most fear. You're aware there is something valuable in the wolf image."

My own orchestration went like this:

I think you're very much in touch with the dream and its connection to your life. Precipitated by a current incident, a lifelong struggle is opened up and played out in a dream with images similar to dreams of the past. I'm going to focus on two details. It was almost dawn. There is still no natural light on your conflict. You are still not able to deal with provocation in a natural, un-self-conscious, self-assertive way. In the dream, you have a flashlight with you. You use it in a way that it isn't intended to be used. You use it as a blunt instrument of aggression instead of as an instrument that can light up a dark area. The important thing is that, by letting out some of the aggression, it had a salutary effect. You successfully transformed the situation. Dawn can now break. You can face the new day in a different relationship to the wolf.

John's Final Comment

"There's a lot of history to this struggle. In working with dreams in the past, I hadn't paid that much attention to the day residue. I can't get over how long it took me to bring the incident with my wife to the surface. I know I've been carrying all this around with me for a long time and that ultimately it's me doing this to myself."

Comment: In dealing with repetitive dreams such as this, it's important to notice changes over time. Here, we see a significant change from one dream to the next. Instead of being killed, there is an accommodation in which the wolf goes to where the dreamer is taking him rather than the other way around. This is an important step in the direction of using that wolf energy for effective self-assertion rather than as a demolition bomb. Here, too, one can see the importance of making every effort to uncover the pertinent feeling residues that shape the dream. The specific concrete life situation exposes our vulnerable areas. If this dream had been worked on after the lapse of several weeks, the specific incident involving John's wife might have vanished from his memory. Without the ability to root the dream concretely we would be working more abstractly and in far less productive a way with the *idea* of aggression rather than with *feelings* arising in a specific life situation.

We were all grateful to John for sharing of himself so openly.

Follow-Up

The following week, John had this to say about the work that had been done with the dream:

"I was amazed at how long it took before I finally got the piece about the beef with my wife. My initial reaction to the dream had been, 'Oh, it's here again, my aggression.' Thinking that way, it's easy to lose sight of where it comes from. Although it's an issue I've dealt with before, in this dream, the aggressive animal was not being all that bad. It was interesting to me that the question 'Why now?' with regard to the dream went over my head. This helped me in a weekend workshop I went to about dreams in the way I approached the dreams that were presented."

A Note on Dream Time

As one's experience grows, a number of unique features of dream work emerge occasionally. One of these has to do with time. Our unconscious thought processes are said to be timeless. In the work I have done in Scandinavia, a year may elapse between sessions there. Under these circumstances, the day residue not infrequently may include a connection with a dream presented the year before. For one woman in the group, images of cars appeared a year apart and in both instances related to the dreamer's being in a dream workshop with me. The first reflected an aspect of our initial encounter, the second a changed feeling about dream work.

In the first dream, there was a scene in which the dreamer and her mother were driving down a narrow street blocked by a big car. Without going into details about the dream, it had to do with feelings of sadness and guilt toward her mother at one level; at another level, there was both interest in dream work and, at the same time, some reticence about self-exposure, particularly in a group that included colleagues. In the same group, she presented a dream a year later in which she is driving "my little old car." At one point, she hesitated about continuing or not as the asphalt road changed to a narrow path. In the end, she decided to continue. She herself drew attention to the possible connection to her earlier dream: "I've been thinking of Ullman's visit last year. It's a kind of an anniversary. Two nights ago, I had a dream that seemed to be a continuation of last year's dream." Recalling the sadness connected to last year's dream she began to cry. She then went on to describe her far more positive feelings about the current dream. "Last year, it was a big American car blocking a narrow road. I couldn't get through. I felt blocked. This time, I dream of my own unpretentious little car. It is small and not so heavy, but it enabled me to continue to where I wanted to get."

In another dream in a Scandinavian workshop, illustrating the carryover from one year to another, the dream image was that of two sections of a neatly folded newspaper. The dreamer was aware that the first section contained awful news and that the second section contained interesting cultural material. She linked the first section to a dream she had presented the year before and the second section to the current workshop. She had been very troubled at the time of the earlier dream because it occurred soon after the death of her father. In the interim, her life had changed for the better, both personally and professionally. She was anxious to bring me the good news.

Notes

1. This is the dreamer's first experience of sharing a dream in a rather large group made up of people she did not know.

2. Despite the "leading" quality to this question I consider it appropriate when a dreamer who is new to the process has a dream the night before the group meets. The thought of presenting a dream for the first time can be a very powerful anticipatory day residue.

16

■

Dreams and Healing

I have alluded to the personal benefits that accrue from dream work. They derive from the greater freedom that results as one gets to know, on a more profoundly honest level, the nature of one's connections to oneself and to others. I don't know of any more effective way to bolster self-esteem than to work through in a supportive social milieu the nighttime vision of oneself that appears in our dreams. There is not only greater regard for oneself but also a deepening respect for others who share of themselves. The real meaning of the word *communion* comes to life. For those of a religious persuasion, it could be characterized as a spiritual experience. Raising one's genuine self-esteem through interaction with others is the essence of emotional healing.

Let us look a bit more closely at the nature of healing. Physical healing goes on naturally and unconsciously, and only occasionally is a medical assist necessary. Evolution has left us with talented bodies that have learned how to cope with toxins, injuries, and infections. Although recent work continues to shed more light on the interplay between feelings and the body's response to noxious elements, the fact is that the healing response is automatically set in motion and operates quite apart from any conscious intent.

When it comes to emotional healing, we are faced with a challenge, but one about which we have a bit more to say. There are natural healing powers at an emotional level, but they take a form quite different from what occurs at a physical level. Aside from possible genetic factors predisposing us toward certain forms of mental illness, the emotional hurdles we face come about because of other people. It takes other people and the social institutions that shape their lives to limit the well-being of the child and channel his or her energies into defensive and ultimately self-defeating maneuvers. Because limitations in our emotional life are largely social in origin, other people play a significant role in removing those limitations. Emotional healing is a social happening. In contrast to physical healing, it takes place in a social field that goes beyond the confines of our own skin. We need the help of others to expose and help dispose of the defensive residues that stand in our way.

In recent years, concern with issues of psychological well-being and self-fulfillment has become ever more visible. The impetus for this goes back to the 1930s when the psychoanalytic movement opened our eyes to the deeper dimensions of the human psyche. As interest in psychoanalysis began to recede by the 1960s, there ensued a search for more rapid-fire approaches to self-healing. In the past decade or so, dream work has come to the fore. What all of these approaches had in common was the creation of a social arena in which people came together to learn about and shed limiting and stereotypic accretions and, in so doing, get closer to the range and power of their own resources. Social intercourse was the necessary ingredient for movement to a higher level of self-awareness.

The Virtues of Group Dream Work

What more can we say about emotional healing? Regardless of where and how it takes place, it has always seemed to me to be composed of three essential attributes and a supportive social milieu in which these three attributes could all become known to the person involved. The first is the awareness of and clarification of a current tension. The second is the awareness of how the past has paved the way for the appearance of that tension. The third is the awareness that there is an agency within us that can attest to the honesty of our new vision of ourselves, based on the information we are bringing together to resolve the tension. This third feature is the most important of the three. Without it, we can easily resort to defensive measures to temporarily rid ourselves of an annoying tension. One of the virtues of pursuing the goal of healing in a group context is the way the others help keep the dreamer honest. Mutual sharing, the support offered, and the distance others have from whatever the person is struggling with all facilitate the degree of honesty needed to take a fresh look at oneself.

Dreaming consciousness provides us with the possibility of realizing all of these attributes. Our dreams amplify present concerns by selectively bringing to bear on them relevant experiences from our past. Most important of all is the honesty with which we confront ourselves with both our weaknesses and our strengths. As we work in full public view with the dream, we are engaging in a healing experience. Others serve the dreamer by helping to locate the current tension and explore its ramifications as more and more threads are uncovered in the matrix of associations. Secrets rise to the surface and in their social visibility no longer serve to hamper personal freedoms.

Group dream work can and does create the conditions for a kind of natural healing process to take place. It is as if the impulse to self-healing is always alive in us, awaiting only a favorable social climate to become manifest. For that climate to be right, there has to be respect for the authority of the dreamer and a readiness to let the dreamer proceed at her own pace. The variables that enter into that state of readiness are too subtle for anyone other than the dreamer to assess.

The healing potential of the dream arises from the different view you have of yourself asleep and dreaming compared to the way you experience yourself awake. You are encountering a familiar self in different surroundings. Put another way, it's as if on awakening you have returned to earth after a satellite view of that earth from an entirely different perspective. What is unique about that perspective is that you not only see the present, but you see the present in its link to your historical past and to the implications this has for the future. Like the astronaut, you have had a privileged view of the system from outside the system. Unlike the astronaut, who views the world from a novel position in space, you, the dreamer, move into a novel temporal domain. At night when we are creating these visions, we seem to step out of the time dimension that frames our waking life. Starting in the present with what may seem like no more than background noise in the waking state, we take soundings from our past and work through our concerns for the future. We do this by bringing that background noise into focus, tracing its origins, and assessing the meaning it has for our future. What is ultimately uncovered is more or less familiar rather than totally unknown. It has made its presence felt in one way or another, but until it emerges and is worked through in a dream, it remains shunted off to one side, never fully appreciated for what it is. This accounts for the frequent reaction, once a dream has been worked through, "In a sense I've known that all along."

Several features of the dream are more readily understood once we keep in mind the altered vision we have of ourselves while asleep and dreaming. We can better appreciate the importance of identifying what I have referred to as the current context—namely, the recent emotional residues that accompany our falling asleep. They constitute the background noise that now comes into its own. We can also better appreciate why it takes work to uncover those residues. The group engages with the dreamer in as thorough an exploration of the recent past as possible. The more carefully this is carried out, the more likely it is that the relevant feelings and concerns will become evident. It takes careful listening to pick up nuances of feeling that come through in the course of this reconstruction, feelings so subtle that even the dreamer is not aware of them. Remember that in this initial stage, we are concerned with any emotional residues that can be recovered, whether or not a connection to the dream is readily apparent.

Because recall of felt experience is so crucial to healing through dream work, let us look more closely at some of the problems involved. One of the main difficulties is that we are trying to help the dreamer recover feelings that were not explicitly recognized at the time of their occurrence and that can be identified only in retrospect in the course of a very careful reconstruction of recent life events. Keeping a diary can help but offers no assurance that doing so will provide the clues to the relevant residues. Furthermore, people vary a good deal in their ability to recall details of their lives. All of us have difficulty getting down to specifics when the dream is not a fairly recent one.

There are two problems with regard to this recall. The first is simply a question of memory. How clearly can a dreamer recall events around the time of the dream? The second has to do with unconscious defensive blocking of recall. For the most part, however, this latter is not the main obstacle to dream work when dream work is pursued with the support of a group and in the manner I have indicated. The challenge that emerges is not one of being up against forces acting to keep memories repressed but knowing where and how to look for them. In dream work, we are for the most part disturbing a kind of blanketing unawareness rather than undoing a defensive maneuver. Awake, our orientation is to get on with the business at hand as best we can. Any annoying background noises may be handled defensively, but when one is pursuing the dream, there is a dramatic reorientation to what has been excluded from awareness. Learning replaces defensiveness. One begins to learn how transitory subtle feeling tones and chance impressions become the starting point for the metaphorical imagery that appears in the dream. Once such residues are identified, their connections to the past are more readily pursued. Long forgotten feeling residues and the incidents that provoked them spring to life.

It takes the active help of others to engage the dreamer in a search that uncovers the felt present in the sense we have been talking about. Without that kind of systematic reconstruction of the recent context, the prey we are after may escape notice because of its subtlety or seeming innocence. As its importance becomes recognized, the images and the story being told in the dream become more transparent. The feelings form a bridge to the past that results in the spontaneous emergence of relevant memories. To a great extent, the art of dream work lies in looking in the right direction. Associations become more focused and more fruitful. The dreams that initially appeared so mysterious soon come to be recognized as direct and straightforward portrayals of what before was only a dimly lit corner of one's existence.

Dreaming, Healing, and Creativity

There is a direct connection between the dream's healing power and what I consider to be an innate creative impulse at work in all of us until the day we die. When we witness a creative event, we experience a bit of reality in a new and uplifting way. Something analogous occurs in dream work.

The emotional residues we have spoken about have the quality of intrusive novelty. They come at us as if in a dim light, their nature and intensity not yet discernible. There is an impending sense that something unknown and alien is threatening to become known. To the extent that these feelings have not yet been clearly recognized or conceptualized adequately, they represent a confrontation with something new coming into being in our lives. When we are awake, they elude our grasp; when we are asleep and dreaming, they occupy center stage. Creativity enters the picture in connection with the three essential features of dreaming:

1. The novelty is recognized as novelty. There is an explicit focus on what seems to be bubbling up in our psyche.
2. We create a unique symbolic system that contains and expresses the tensions in our lives. It is also a highly unusual way of depicting what we are feeling.
3. The symbolic portrayal we resort to takes into account relevant past experiences as well as present needs and resources. We come to a new and more penetrating view of ourselves that goes beyond whatever blocks our vision while we are awake.

This may strike the reader as a somewhat strained usage of the term *creativity*. The fact is that the dream's metaphorical language involves the creative act of inventing and shaping pictorial representations that capture and express in an elegant and specific fashion those features of our subjective existence that are coming into being. In common with other forms of creativity, it is a response to what is happening at a feeling level in a way that succeeds in exposing significant truths. Creativity in the sense that I am using the term is a general and essential property of living tissue, an ability that orients the organism to new features of the outer or inner world that need attending to in new ways. It is an attribute we all possess that, if not blocked, propels us into our future in a freer and more fulfilling way. We ordinarily regard creativity as something that gifted artists and scientists are endowed with, whereas the rest of us live more or less uncreative lives. In contrast, the view I am putting forth is that creativity is central to feeling truly alive and should be intrinsic to every aspect of living. Unfortunately, the civilizing process as it has evolved has not yet made room for the full expression of human creativity in everyday life. Once we say good-bye to childhood, it gets buried under rigid and stereotyped ways of organizing our lives. Life then loses the quality of being a continuous challenge to realize this innate creative potential. Our lives become both limited and distorted. We are no longer open to novelty. We retreat into ordinariness.

The one area in which our creativity flows spontaneously and unhampered is in our dreams. However limited or distorted our lives may be, we retain the ability while dreaming to display in an inventive fashion the interplay between our limitations and distortions and the healthy aspects of our psyches. Dreaming may then be regarded as the way we experience the freely acting creative impulse within us all under the conditions of sleep. In the new sense of self that dreams bring to light, they offer us the possibility of becoming more whole, which is, of course, what healing is all about.

17

Dream Appreciation and Therapy

I refer to the group work I have described as dream *appreciation* to distinguish it from the use of the dream in formal psychotherapy. There is some confusion around the use of the word *therapeutic*. Experiential group work with dreams is therapeutic, but it is not therapy in the formal or technical sense of the term. The latter implies the existence of a therapist-client relationship, the application of a theoretical body of knowledge, and a particular set of techniques to expose and resolve the problems in living presented by the client. The client is subjected to, but not privy to, the workings of this theory and technique. The self-exposure flows in one direction mainly, from client to therapist. To that extent, the process is hierarchical. Its very one-sidedness provokes reactions in the client that in turn are analyzed. The therapist, for example, has a certain authority and is regarded as an authority by the client. This feature elicits earlier entrenched attitudes toward authority—hostility, dependency, self-depreciation, or ingratiation. These attitudes often accompany and color the presentation of the dream to the therapist. These are the client's defenses, his characteristic way of trying to establish a safe relationship with someone in authority.

Differences and Similarities

In a dream appreciation group, we are dealing with a flat process in which everyone, including the leader, engages in the sharing of dreams and in the offering of personal projections; no one assumes the role and responsibility of therapist, and everyone involved clearly understands the rationale for every move that is made. Even in groups led by trained professionals, the sense of leader as an authority is considerably modified once the leader begins to share dreams of her own. Any defenses operating in relation to authority are further dissipated as the group witnesses the way the leader participates as a peer member of the group at each stage of the process. There is a gradual recognition that the true leader of the group is the dreamer. The control of the process lies in his hands. He is under no contract to share all that goes through his mind. If he feels safe, his curiosity will carry him as far as he chooses to go. The freedom to be in charge of his defenses gives him the freedom to test what it feels like to move away from them. Increasing openness is the hallmark of successful dream work. Entrenched dysfunctional behavioral traits do not dissolve magically but begin to be modified in the light of the increasing freedom being experienced. The way we make an end run around defenses in group dream work is like the experience of swimming in the nude in the company of others all doing the same thing. We put our clothes back on when we get out, but we feel refreshed. There is a feeling of being all in it together, a kind of equal partnership in contrast to the expert-client relationship that prevails in therapy.

The group stimulates one's curiosity, offers ideas of what one may find, and provides the support needed to look inside. The key to that inner domain never leaves the dreamer's hands. All the group does is help him appreciate the treasure he will find once he has the courage to use the key. The equilibrium between curiosity and defensiveness becomes modified in favor of the former as the dreamer gets more involved in the process.

The therapist stands in a different relationship to the dreamer than do the helpers in the dream group. She has to bring to bear her special knowledge of psychopathology and psychotherapy in the effort to engage the client actively in the struggle to change. The therapeutic arrangement sets up an *interpersonal* field that is then subject to minute scrutiny. In dream appreciation, we are not examining the field set up by all the participants, including the dreamer, and the leader in their interaction with each other. Such would be the case when a dream is worked on in the context of group therapy. The group therapist works with a complex interpersonal field to effect change.

In the case of the dream group, the focus is exclusively on the *intrapersonal* field of the dreamer. Whatever personal reactions the others experience in the course of the work are not made the business of the group but are managed on their own. The participants come together as a kind of ancillary force at the disposal of the dreamer.

The task that faces the therapist in working on a dream is a good deal more complicated than what we undertake in a dream appreciation group, in which we work only with the dreamer's associations to the dream (or earlier dreams shared in the group) in the effort to close the gap between the view of the dreamer awake and the view being presented in the dream. The therapist works with much more than the associative context of the dream. She is working with the manifest behavior of the client as she observes it, she is working with what she knows of the client's past; she keeps in mind the rational and irrational components of the client's relationship to her, and she is concerned with whatever resistances the client may be manifesting in connection with the dream. In contrast to what goes on in a dream group, which most of the participants join because of their interest in their own dream lives and their eagerness to get more from their dreams, the client's motivation for bringing a dream to the therapist may be anything but a genuine interest in what can be learned from the dream. The client is engaged in a war on two fronts. He is coming to change self-limiting or destructive behavior. At the same time, the whole weight of his characterological conditioning pushes him to avoid change by continuing to operate in the same old way. This is known as *resistance*[1] and becomes manifest in a wide variety of ways in connection with dreams. Without being aware of it, a client may offer a dream as an ingratiating present to the therapist, as a hostile challenge to the therapist's ability, as proof of the client's helplessness to do anything with it himself, or as an exhibitionistic display; it may be associated with any number of other devious or manipulative strategies. It is the task of the therapist to recognize and deal with resistances of this sort, both preliminary to and in the course of actual dream work. Not infrequently, the nature of the resistance is clearly manifest in the content of the dream.

The therapist, having a knowledge base about the dreamer's life, uses that knowledge in a way that places the dream in a broader framework of all that has thus far become known of the dreamer's problems and his struggle to change. The interpretive work she does, therefore, is built on earlier therapeutic work and is then generalized further through theoretical formulations—for example, Freudian concepts, such as oedipus complex; Jungian concepts, such as anima and animus; and so on.

The time factor may present a problem for the therapist when a client presents a dream. A sufficient expanse of time is needed to go as far as one can with the dream. The therapist has to deal with the time limits imposed by the client, depending on at what point in the session the dream is brought in. Other items on the client's agenda may crowd out the dream. Even if a dream is presented at the very beginning of the hour and the entire session is devoted to it, there may still not be enough time to do it justice. Therapists often have to resort to what Walter Bonime (1982) refers to as "headline interpretations." Certain metaphorical features of the dream are selected to illustrate aspects of the ongoing therapeutic work.

Before developing the similarities and differences further, let me stress the congruence between the dream appreciation group and formal therapy. They are not and should never be oppositional. When they are concurrent, they should be mutually reinforcing. A dream touched on in therapy can be worked through at greater leisure in the group. Conversely, a dream worked on in the group can be explored in greater depth and privacy in the one-to-one situation. On occasion, difficulties that arise in therapy (e.g., countertransference[2]) emerge quite clearly when the dream is taken up in the group. Sometimes, the dream group serves the purpose of a transitional support system, easing any concerns about the termination of therapy.

That there are similarities between the two approaches should come as no surprise. The respect extended to the client, the reliance on the associative matrix provided by the client, the sensitivity to the feelings of the dreamer as she struggles with unconscious components of her personality, and the importance of reaching the dreamer at a feeling level are features common to both approaches. Therapists exposed for the first time to the process I use often comment on these similarities. My response to them is to agree and to explain that what I have tried to do is to make explicit all that I learned about dreams in the course of my career as a psychoanalyst and to adapt that to a group setting in which the goal was to teach others how to work with dreams. Formal therapy and the dream appreciation group are both concerned with the liberation of natural healing energies. Both promote growth through the exploration of an unconscious domain. The task I set for myself was to transform the therapist role into an educational role with the goal of teaching others how to engage in group dream work.

There are special features to the group approach that facilitate dream work. First and foremost is the fact that sufficient time is set aside to explore the dream in its entirety. There are no other items on the agenda, as there might be in therapy, that preempt the time. The built-in safety features, the flat structure, and the freedom the dreamer has to maintain her defenses all have the effect of loosening those very defenses and encouraging an ever-deepening sharing of the self. No one in the group functions as a therapist, and so no issue arises concerning whatever level of defensiveness (resistance) the dreamer wishes to maintain. The combination of control by the dreamer and trust in the process by the way the group functions has a powerful effect in lowering the anxiety level associated with dream work. The truth about ourselves is of deep interest to us, if we can face this without the fear of it's being used against us. The concern of others, the support, the atmosphere of imaginative free play, and the way the group in a nonintrusive way provides the dreamer with what she needs to bring the metaphorical imagery to life all encourage the free flow of these natural healing currents. The truth is embraced as it emerges under those circumstances.

Safety and trust should be built-in features of any therapeutic arrangement. This is possible only up to a point, being contingent on the client's capacity to feel trust and on the peculiar nature of the therapeutic enterprise to generate and maintain trust while at the same time exposing and challenging preexisting character traits that the client counts on to provide a sense of security. In therapy, the anxieties and defenses generated are grist for the mill and a major feature of the work. In the dream group, the dreamer's character is not under siege. There occurs an amazing degree of freedom, often resulting in the opening up of deep and painful dimensions of one's psyche that might in the usual course of therapy take a good deal more time.

Professional Responses

The group approach I have been using has met with a mix of resistance and interest on the occasions when I have presented it to my psychoanalytic colleagues. There have been a small number who have been interested and have followed through with leadership training in the process, ultimately conducting groups of their own. For the most part, however, they have viewed it as a way of deprofessionalizing dream work and, as such, lying outside their sphere of interest. They did not share my feeling that dream work should extend beyond the consulting room to the public at large and that psychoanalysts, as the most highly trained members of the therapeutic community, had a responsibility to make dreams more widely accessible. Put more bluntly, it was as if their tacit assumption about dream work was that it should remain a psychoanalytic monopoly. Being trained to use psychoanalytic theory as the template through which the client's associations are filtered, they have felt both uncomfortable with and rejecting of an atheoretical approach. Used to seeing the dream as an elaborate mechanism of concealment, they had little heart (except for the Jungians) for a technique that so insistently focused on the revelatory power of manifest content.[3]

I suspect that more than theoretical and scientific concerns are at work and that issues of economics and social status also play into the resistance. With due regard to the heavy investment of psychoanalysts in their own profession, demystifying dreams and helping the general public gain access to them should not be a cause for concern. It could only broaden the healing base of any formal therapeutic situation. The final common pathway to each undertaking is the search for the truth.

Those "lower" in the status hierarchy—psychologists, social workers, and psychiatric nurses—have taken more of an interest in this approach to dream work. Their perspective changes to one in which they begin to see dreaming as an intrinsic part of the organism's natural healing resources. Equipped with a "hands-on" approach, they enter into the excitement and even playful aspect of dream work. Making maximum use of the client's own dormant resources and capacity for self-healing takes some of the onus of full responsibility off the shoulders of the therapist and makes the whole effort much more of a collaborative venture.

By way of summary, what follows compares the psychotherapeutic use of the dream to the approach taken in a dream appreciation group. The constraints and advantages of each are noted. The term *constraint* is used to refer to anything that limits the fullest or most efficacious exploration of the dream with due regard to the fact that the constraints noted in psychotherapy, although disadvantageous for group dream work, may be both necessary and advantageous for the goal of therapy.

Psychotherapy Constraints

The time factor: Often, too little time available; too many other items on the client's agenda

The hierarchical arrangement: Makes for one-way sharing of dreams; lack of mutual self-disclosure; maintains therapist in an authority role; reinforces dependency role in regard to dream work

The role of theory: Therapist in possession of specialized body of knowledge and technique not privy to the client; plays into the hierarchical arrangement

Dream Appreciation Constraints

The size of the group: May act as a check on the sharing of very private and sensitive material

Knowledge of the dreamer: Limited to what is immediately forthcoming in the work on the dream or has come up in connection with earlier dreams

Psychotherapy Advantages

Dyadic arrangement: Offers a more private domain

Knowledge of the dreamer: Therapist has extensive knowledge of the dreamer

Therapeutic skills: Have been honed to a mastery of the art of listening and to the sensitivity needed in dealing with the unconscious domain

Therapeutic techniques: Geared to recognize and deal with psychopathology

Dream Appreciation Advantages

The time factor: Sufficient time available to pursue the dream work leisurely; no other item on the agenda

The size of the group: A rich source of metaphorical input

Flat rather than hierarchical structure: Dreamer in control of the process; dreamer the authority on how far to go; absence of any external authority; dreamer in the role of expert

Mutual sharing: Leader participates in all aspects of the process, including the sharing of dreams; structure minimizes transferential and countertransferential tensions; sharing of dreams by all participants creates a deep-level sense of communion

Atheoretical approach: No hidden theoretical assumptions and no technical manipulations involved; rationale for each step in the process fully known to all

Generally, the congruence between these two approaches has been recognized by the therapist when they have been ongoing at the same time.

Notes

1. Defensive maneuvers that block insight.
2. Reactions evoked by the client in the therapist that block the therapist's objectivity.
3. A more systematic comparison of my approach with that of Freud and Jung is offered in *Working With Dreams* (Ullman & Zimmerman, 1979).

18
■

The Future of Dream Appreciation

We live in an age when people are beginning to take more responsibility for the maintenance of their own health. Up to now, this has been true mainly with regard to the preservation of physical well-being. What has come more into focus recently is a concern with emotional well-being and the goal of leading a more fulfilling and more humane existence. To move in that direction involves precisely the kind of insights that dreams provide us with. It is no wonder that many have turned to dream work in this quest. Where else would we find a so readily available and spontaneously generated source of information about ourselves that is immediately relevant to our lives, a source so in touch with the deepest dimensions of our being? Through our dreams, we come to know of a self-healing energy analogous to the self-healing capacity we take for granted when it comes to illness or injury.

Were you to engage in dream work consistently, you would soon develop a dreamer's view of the world, one in which human foibles are exposed. We encounter dormant resources, and we become sensitized to values that enhance genuine self-esteem rather than perpetuate spurious self-images. We become more interestingly unique as well as more alike. The quality of our connections to others becomes the measuring rod of this self-esteem. What do we take from others, and what are we capable of giving? Our dreams speak to us of any one-sidedness in this equation—giving too much at the expense of the self or taking too much at the expense of others.

I have offered a detailed presentation of my approach to group dream work, its rationale, the roles played by each of the participants, and the structure within which they operate. Particular emphasis has been placed on the role of the leader and problems that are apt to surface as one engages in dream work. I have tried to balance the seriousness with the fun and joy that can accompany it. Dream work is not to be undertaken lightly. It requires a certain commitment, a respect for the precautions that are necessary, and a realistic assessment of both the limits and the benefits that can accrue.

There is nothing magical about dream work. There is still a good deal of mystery about our dreams and how those images come to be so elegantly expressive of the complex emotional currents that swirl about in each of us. For too long, however, that mystery has been endowed with magical properties, subjected to much ambitious theorizing, and easily misused by too over-zealous a waking ego. I do not place much stock in the idea of controlling our dreams, an idea currently much in vogue. We may seem to be in control when, as if in response to our wishes, our waking and dreaming agenda seem to coincide. That is more apparent than real and should not obscure the fact that the dream is more broadly and more honestly based than is our waking agenda, and for that reason it is more apt not to coincide with that agenda. At any rate, dreams offer one pathway to greater self-knowledge, and that is sufficient basis for encouraging much more attention to them than is now the case.

I have emphasized a group approach that offers the general public guidelines and a structure within which to pursue dream work without compromising in any way the fundamental principles that guide the experienced clinician's work with dreams. It has proven as helpful to therapists as to laymen by clarifying the role that theory plays clinically in contrast to the atheoretic path to dream appreciation.

One aspect of the process I have described is its easy and ready applicability to groups of people in very different circumstances. There are many such groups, and my hope is that at some time in the future, dream work will include target populations of addicts, prisoners, patients in hospices, students in high school and college, workers in factories, and corporate executives and find a larger place in adult education programs generally. The point is that one does not have to have any particular degree of psychological sophistication or be acquainted with various theories about dreams to partake of the process I have described. What has been the case thus far is that the dream group movement has been limited largely to a white, middle-class population with a good deal of prior knowledge about dreams. Growth centers draw mainly from this segment of the population, and their curriculum usually includes a course in dreams rooted in Jungian or Gestalt psychology. In any approach based on a particular theoretical system, some distance is likely to remain between leader and participants. The knowledge involved is not readily transmitted in depth unless one undergoes the same professional training. These groups tend to perpetuate the model of the expert lending his or her knowledge to the dreamer rather than one cultivating the skills of the participants to the point where they are competent to assume leadership. For that to occur, all that is implicit in the way the leader works must be made explicit. When there is an elaborate theoretical coloring, as in the case of the Jungian and Freudian schools in particular, this is not easy without specialized and rigorous training.

The process I use arose from my effort to transform what I learned about dreams in the course of my clinical practice into a procedure that could be mastered by anyone. It involved teasing away what I consider to be the essence of dream work from the specialized techniques of formal therapy. Although over time the principles have stood firm, the process itself has evolved and will continue to evolve as my experience in using it and teaching it grows.

Frequently Asked Questions

The following questions are frequently asked of me concerning the process:

1. *Does growth really take place in the dream groups, or do people simply become habituated to another form of social diversion?* I think there is this danger. From my own experience, however, I am convinced that those who stay with the work over a period of time do so because behavioral change occurs, palpable to them and obvious to others. Most people who come to the group have a healthy curiosity to learn more about themselves, are capable of change, and have the capacity of realistically assessing that change.

2. *Won't people who stay in a dream group keep dreaming of the same thing and come to a point of no return?* The same issues do continue to surface in our lives, and we continue to dream about them. Each time we engage with a particular issue in a dream, we arrive at a different position in relation to that issue. The emotional heritage from our past and the new problems we face as we move into the future provide us with endless challenges. The pursuit of our own identity is a lifelong task.

3. *Is the process as atheoretic as you say it is?* It is, and it isn't. It is atheoretic in the sense that it is not committed to any overall theoretical formulation of the human psyche, such as Freud or Jung proposed. It is based, however, on certain empirically based assumptions about the nature of dreaming itself—for example, the role of the day residue and the self-confrontational nature of imagery. The process I use is an entry into the world of dreams that bypasses the need for a specialized theoretical background. As a training instrument for therapists, it bridges the gap between their theoretical knowledge and the skills and techniques they need in working through a client's dream.

4. *Are you creating a special "hothouse" effect, valid only for the environment in which the dream sharing is occurring?* It is true that dream work takes place in a very special setting, one that should provide for a totally nonviolent atmosphere. Most other social situations in which we find ourselves do from time to time give rise to irritating tensions of one sort or another. When one is involved in dream work in an intense way or over a period of time, one becomes very much aware of the differences between life inside and outside a dream group, and at times there can be an "aftershock." Nevertheless, there is a carryover from what one has gained through the dream work into life outside the dream group.

Criticisms and Objections

Over the years, a number of criticisms have been made of the process—some of a minor nature, some more substantive:

1. *Objections have been raised to my characterizing the second stage, in which group members offer their projections, as a "game."* Some regarded the use of the word *game* at this stage of the process as somewhat demeaning to dream work. Actually, I have referred to this stage both as a game and as an exercise. I prefer to retain the analogy to a game because there is an element of play involved as group members try to make the dream their own and search for the feelings and metaphorical possibilities appropriate to the imagery. The emphasis on the free play of the imagination rather than making light of the dream is the important point.

2. *Another semantic difficulty arose out of the use of the term* dialogue *in the third stage.* Technically, the criticism is correct because it is not a dialogue in the full sense of the word, in that one of the partners to it, the dreamer, is not obliged to respond. It is, however, a verbal interaction appropriate to the special aspects of dream work, and so I prefer to retain the term.

3. *A more important issue has to do with what appears to some to be an undue emphasis on what I have referred to as the recent emotional context, that aspect of the recent life experience of the dreamer that has triggered the dream.* This emphasis is intended only to convey the idea that a dream starts in the present with some feeling, thought, or preoccupation surfacing during the period prior to the dream. When the dreamer is helped to uncover the feeling tones associated with such recent experience, it brings into focus the issue explored in greater historical depth in the dream. The term *recent emotional context* covers ongoing preoccupations and concerns that continue into the present, as well as recent events that triggered certain felt residues.

4. *People who have been in other kinds of groups, notably encounter groups or group therapy, are often uncomfortable with the structure and feel frustrated by the restrictions on spontaneously ventilating all of their feelings and reactions to what is going on.* This is notably the case when a dreamer is so guarded in her response that some degree of disappointment, frustration, or even anger occurs among the members of the group. For the most part, there is the ability to abide by the contract we have made with the dreamer—namely, that she controls the process and is in charge of what she wishes to share. Those used to engaging more actively with their own processes feel the urge to challenge the dreamer and the process itself to work through whatever discomfort they may feel. Their preference is for a looser structure that would allow for that kind of interplay. Were the structure to change in that direction it would lose what, in my opinion, is essential for a nonclinically oriented dream group—namely, the respect we have for the dreamer's right to remain the gatekeeper of her own private domain. That very power results ultimately in the dreamer's ability to trust the process sufficiently to begin to open the gates. The only occasion in which the dream process should justifiably be transformed into a group process is if a tension arises between one or more members of the group to the point that it impinges on the dream work. This doesn't involve a change in the dream process but simply holding it in abeyance until the tension can be resolved. Anyone who cannot accept the degree of orientation to the needs of the dreamer that one has to sustain should seek a means of personal growth other than group dream work.

Looking to the Future

Will we ever become a dream-conscious society? Despite the current upsurge of interest in dreams, an interest greater than at any time since white settlers took over the land from native Americans, it is not likely that this will happen in the foreseeable future. Dream work is very low on the list of priorities in an industrial society geared to technological development and an emphasis almost exclusively on material well-being. This should not, however, detract from the importance of making every effort to promote and expand dream work.

Looking to the future, we face a number of issues aside from enlisting the help of the professional community in launching an educational campaign aimed at the public. There is the problem of training competent group leaders. As things stand now, anyone can go into the business of leading dream groups. This leaves the public at a loss as to how to evaluate a leader's competence or what his particular approach has to offer. There is no easy solution. The public is caught between the present somewhat anarchic situation and the disadvantages of institutionalizing the training of dream group leaders. Although the latter step might go far to ensure some degree of competence, institutional structures, particularly if set up too soon, might have a tendency to congeal around a specific approach and be resistive to further change. At the present time, faced with a largely unsophisticated public, were we to set up an institutional structure, it would probably result in its being too exclusively the domain of the professional. Such an organization, of course, would face not only the general problems common to training programs but also the special problems involved in training people for dream work. The aptitude for this work cannot be measured in terms of credentials, years of training in a mental health field, or any other easily identifiable signpost. It has to do with many intangibles in the personality of the applicant—sensitivity, capacity for empathy, a feeling for metaphor, and a certain humility when confronted by the challenge of a dream. When factors such as these are taken into consideration, the line between professional and nonprofessional becomes blurred, and the former does not automatically have a higher standing than the latter.

The only course I can envisage is to continue over an extended period of time the effort to educate people to the value of dream work and to the responsible role they can play in its further development.[1] People are more health conscious now than formerly. A place can and should be found for the contribution that dream work can make to emotional well-being. This means undertaking the difficult task of demystifying dreams, separating dreams from the cult of the expert, and placing the responsibility for dream work squarely in the hands of the dreamer.

Perhaps a time will come when there are enough well-trained leaders, both lay and professional, to make a significant difference. Ultimately, it will be up to the public to judge which of the many contending approaches it finds most helpful. What gives me hope for the future is that, based on my experience, I'm convinced that dream work is teachable. Those who have had training and who have the personality attributes favorable to leadership not only do manage a group well, but more important, they begin to perfect their skills as they gain more experience. There is, of course, another side to the picture, in which people may have had a good deal of training but will never make good leaders (although they may think they do) or in which they have had but limited exposure to dream work and then take off on their own. In either event, there is the danger of misuse of the process and exploitation of those with whom they work. The only safeguard, again, is the increasing sophistication of the public as to what to expect from a leader and what to gain from dream work.

At any rate, some progress is being made currently on the dream front. New books that guide the public into dream work are appearing with increasing frequency. Although this is a good omen on the whole, it leaves the public somewhat confused by a plethora of choices that offer different approaches. One can find Jungian and Gestalt techniques, a variety of interviewing techniques, dream drama, and if one is so inclined, drawing or painting one's dream.

For me, the critical question is whether a particular approach will be a contribution to the task of extending dream work into the community or whether it will simply remain a variation of the expert-dreamer model, now applied to well people rather than sick people. It is my deep conviction that certain principles relating to the safety of the dreamer should prevail in any approach to dream work and that certain skills need to be learned. The emphasis on safety and on these skills has been the central focus of this book. An awareness of their importance can serve as a guide to helping the reader discriminate between the various choices available. The task remaining before us at the moment is the extension of dream work through the education of the public and the preparation of competent leaders. Ultimately, this will involve a much broader networking among interested people than now exists and the coming into being of arrangements that can develop and enhance the skills of those who are assuming leadership roles. The time seems ripe for our dreams to receive the respectful audience they deserve.

Note

1. It is to be hoped that in the future, dream studies will find a secure place in the educational system at all levels and will reach out to all segments of the population.

Epilogue

Dream work satisfies our curiosity about ourselves. The knowledge we gain sheds light on our psychological makeup. There are, however, other dimensions to our existence that sometimes intrude into our dreams. These include the biological, the social, and for lack of a better term, the *cosmic* (our connection to the mystery of the universe itself).

I have called attention to the fact that subtle bodily changes may first make their presence felt in a dream image. From an evolutionary point of view, there may be another role that our biology plays in connection with our dreams. I think dream work brings us into closer touch with a vital aspect of our natural animal heritage. Animals depend for survival on the accuracy and truthfulness of their sensorially perceived world. That dependency is still with us in our effort to adapt to a still imperfect human environment. The task is a bit more difficult for us because of the pitfalls and falsehoods that our cultural heritage has subjected us to. To the extent that we are victimized by false notions, we are not free to truly fulfill ourselves. Asleep and dreaming, we are in pursuit of freedom in those areas that have eluded us while awake. The relationship between freedom and truth is the driving force of our dreams. They are an ever-available ally in the struggle to get at the truth.

As a colleague of mine, Milton Kramer, has noted, "Liars dream but dreams don't lie."[1] True self-esteem rests on our capacity to be honest with ourselves and with others. To confront dream images with the courage it takes to listen to what they are saying is a remarkable antidote to the day-to-day vicissitudes of our self-esteem.

A sociology of dreaming has yet to be developed. Cultural anthropologists have addressed the significance of dreams in preliterate societies, but very little has appeared until recently on the role of dreams in modern industrial society. Yet to be explored is the way in which social sources of support and constraint are reflected in our dreams. Dreams speak to the unsolved problems of society as well as to those of the individual. An inner and outer world exists for each of us along with the task of integrating the values that prevail in the practical world. Perhaps one reason dream work is not pursued more vigorously is the challenge it might pose to current social values. Social stereotypes appearing in dreams speak to still active racist and sexist attitudes. Power over others, exerted in a one-sided way, is not a nocturnal value. It is, however, a prominent feature of waking life, crowding out collaborative and cooperative solutions to problems. The price we pay for manipulative and exploitative relations with others becomes visible at night. Dream work might make us more aware of the one-sided development of society in its pursuit of material gain and the enormous drain this has been on our emotional resources. By making visible the tears and holes in the social fabric, we would be better able to engage in the process of repair. The inevitable result is both a greater respect and a greater tolerance for ourselves as well as for others. We are not just what our limited waking ego makes us out to be. We develop a deep appreciation for the remarkable ally at work in our own best interest, and in a way that is never at the expense of the real self-interest of others.

Were we as a society to embrace dream work on a large scale, there might be mounting pressure for more humane ways of relating to both our natural and our human environments. Analogous to the way that dream work brings hidden assumptions of the individual to light, we may learn more about the way that hidden ideological assumptions set social priorities. It may be no more than a utopian hope that our dreams could play a significant role in restructuring our society in the near future, but this doesn't stop our dreaming psyche from egging us on in the right direction.

There are times when our dreams seem to go beyond our ordinary lives and open us to vistas that are ineffable in their beauty and depth of feeling.

Jung referred to these as "great dreams." Perhaps they are reminders of our connections to the cosmic, that aspect of our existence that has no agreed-on name but that goes beyond our everyday world to touch in some way the larger mysteries that surround us. It has also been variously referred to as the transpersonal or spiritual dimension. By whatever name, its subject matter addresses the unknowns of our existence. What is our place in the universe? Where have we come from? Where are we going? We are creatures of a universe we have hardly begun to understand.

This dimension of our lives is generally obscured in the course of our day-to-day affairs, except for its formalized presence in one or another religious pursuit. Within a religious perspective, the reference to the spiritual implies a realm over and above the mundane. The closest I have come to the meaning of the word *spiritual* has been through the group dream work I have done. If spiritual implies a sense of communion that links each of us to each other and to the larger order that prevails in the universe, then this is precisely what surfaces in dream work. It kindles a kind of deinstitutionalized spirituality, a quality that is largely lacking in the world. Our underlying connectedness to each other becomes more palpable. We can feel ourselves moving toward a more realistic reconciliation of the two worlds we live in—the world out there and the private world of our own subjectivity. We become more tolerant of ourselves and of others as we move beyond the limitations imposed by our waking egos. The honesty intrinsic to the dream provides us with an opportunity to be in touch with the better side of our nature. A felt sense of brotherhood results. Institutionalized religions have not yet succeeded in nurturing this sense of brotherhood on a broad enough scale to prevent the fragmentation of humankind. Just as the religious impulse is universal, so is the experience of dreaming. Perhaps a closer link between the two may take us further along on the path toward universal brotherhood.

I have presented dream work as one possible avenue that fits into the general trend of people's taking more responsibility for their own state of well-being. Dream work offers not only access to hidden sources of our own tensions and needs but orients us to the resources we have for coping with the limiting aspects of our character structure as well as the externally imposed limitations of a still imperfect social order. Values shift. People are experienced differently, including oneself. People become both more interesting as individuals and more alike one another. As you become more and more involved in dream work, you begin to develop a dreamer's view of the world, one in which people's foibles stand out more sharply and your sensitivity to what is really important is greatly enhanced. There is nothing quite like it.

Note

1. From a mimeographed paper courtesy of the paper's author.

APPENDIX

Theory

It must be evident to the reader who has come this far that in this book there has been a conspicuous absence of theoretical formulations derived from the Freudian, Jungian, or other schools of dream interpretation. In fact, I have eschewed the term *interpretation* in favor of referring to the work I do as dream *appreciation*. In this appendix, I will examine the relevance of theory to dream work and what exactly there is to theorize about.

Theory is useful if, when applied to a body of data, it enables us to discover and explore further possibilities. It becomes dysfunctional when adherence to theory has the effect of limiting the search for new possibilities. Theories are no more than potentially useful generalizations that endure only for the time that they continue to be useful. They are instruments to be used with caution when applied to the complexities of human behavior.

Since the publication of Freud's classic volume on the interpretation of dreams, there has been an almost inextricable interweaving of theory and dreams. The existentialist therapist made a valiant effort to extricate the dream from the theoretical casing that psychoanalysis has provided for it.[1] Dream work as we know it today was born in the psychoanalytic setting that Freud provided for it. To use a somewhat strained metaphor, if the dream was the child emerging from the womb of psychoanalysis, it was born connected to the afterbirth that nurtured it in the womb. That afterbirth was Freud's early theorizing about the nature of hysteria.[2] In the evolution of psychoanalytic thought, that afterbirth was never severed from the baby. Until the experimental scene was initiated in the early 1950s,[3] the dream had no independent existence of its own. It remained a creature tied to its psychoanalytic origins. The afterbirth overshadowed the baby.

Therapists do feel the need for theoretical generalizations in dealing with the complexities of the data that confront them as they explore the vicissitudes of the human psyche. This is where theory is seen to serve a useful function (although existentialist therapists have renounced psychoanalytic formulations in favor of a more phenomenological approach[4]). Dreaming consciousness is still a mysterious event. Our knowledge of both the form and content of our consciousness under the conditions of sleep is still quite fragmentary. We are very much in need of theories that address dreaming in a way that dispels the areas of our ignorance.

The following theoretical views are based on my clinical experience, my knowledge of the experimental literature on sleep and dream research, and what I have learned about dreams from the group experiential work I have done. Although I personally believe the formulations I offer can enrich work with dreams, I want to stress that an acquaintance with or acceptance of those views is in no way a prerequisite for engaging in the dream work I have described.

I should like to start with the premise that there is a basic identity between dreaming consciousness and waking consciousness.[5] In seeking to establish this underlying identity, let me begin with a consideration of the nature of the stimuli impinging on us in both states and how they are handled. One constant feature of the waking state is the way we are bombarded by stimuli from the outside. In fact, were these stimuli to cease altogether, we would find it difficult or even impossible to maintain our ordinary state of consciousness. Fortunately, only a small and selective portion of these stimuli requires our attention. Most are dealt with automatically and unconsciously. That small fraction serves to keep us alert and interested and engages our attention.

Our ordinary perceptual processes are quite complex. To "see" an object we must have had prior experience with that or similar objects before. The form, shape, or other sensory attributes initiate a quick memory scan and, based on models we have available from earlier experience, recognition occurs, and we perceive the object for what it is. It is a process in which we move almost instantaneously from simple sensory stimuli to accurate perception. This is so habitual with most objects we encounter that we are unaware of it as a process. We become aware of it only when we are up against a novel stimulus of some sort. If we come on an unfamiliar object unexpectedly in dim light and when there is no immediate recognition, we automatically scan the environment for more information to see if we can fit it into a model available to us. If we cannot, we remain in the dark about what precisely it is. The crowd that catches a glimpse of Superman in the air cries out, "It's a bird! It's a plane! No, it's Superman!" The interplay of information and interior modeling finally results in a perceptual response.

Waking consciousness has something in common with a radar system. In our concern with what is going to happen in the future, we scan the environment as well as our past to shed as much light as possible on what is happening in the present. When we come up with the resources needed to cope with what is novel in our lives, we succeed in enlarging our behavioral repertoire. When we cannot or, for one reason or another, avoid dealing with what confronts us, there results a lingering tension of greater or lesser intensity,[6] depending on the significance of the issue.

We go to sleep with varying degrees of success in setting to rest the tensions that accompany our forced march into the future. The lingering tensions continue to linger and initiate the search for further information. As in the waking state, we pursue our interest in stimuli arising in our field of consciousness. The difference lies in the nature of the information that is processed and the way it is processed. Nature has seen to it that, even while asleep, we are aroused periodically and, by means of dreaming consciousness, take stock of how things are with us at the moment. Asleep, we are still moving into the future but passively, without (with occasional exceptions[7]) the exposure to the external stimuli that impinge on us while awake. The tensions left over from the previous day surface when our brain becomes sufficiently aroused and form the matrix for the dream that ensues. In contrast with the waking situation, however, the end result of the way we think while dreaming is not an immediate or projected external behavioral response but, rather, an interior change. Dreaming affects the level of arousal of the brain by the intensity and quality of the feelings evoked and causes us either to awaken or allows us to return to dreamless sleep.

Freud referred to the kind of daytime event that is relevant to our nighttime thoughts as the "day residue." He defined it as any event, regardless of how trivial or incidental it might seem at the time, that finds its way into the dream that night because it serves to carry a message from the dreamer's past, dimly sensed but not clearly perceived during the day. For the dreamer, the element of novelty arises insofar as the feelings evoked by the day residue are at first unclear and unfamiliar, an upsurge from the past that makes its presence felt in the dream. This leaves the dreamer with the task of perceiving more accurately the nature and the source of these feelings so as to assess their implications for the future. In contrast to the effort to gather sufficient sensory information to identify the nature of an external object, the dreamer struggles with feeling tones so as to define more accurately an internal subjective state. The dreamer needs more information, and as in the case of an external object, that information has to be "real"; that is, to be perceived, it must reflect accurately the internal reality.[8]

The dreamer, however, has no place to turn to fulfill this task except to her own store of memories and feelings. Both poles of the process that we describe for the dreamer awake—namely, searching the environment for further details and matching the information against memory models—have to be carried out internally in the case of the dreamer asleep. This results in scanning whatever past experiences have left residues of feelings similar to the current residue. It also involves scanning past modes of dealing with such feelings, all with the intent of shedding further light on the situation. If we come up with answers that allow us to remain comfortable with the current tension, we remain asleep. If the result of our search evokes feelings that are too strong to be contained while asleep, we awaken. Only in the waking state can we return to the cushioning effect of our social environment and ultimately gain the additional experience needed to cope with whatever emotional outcropping from our past now faces us.

The nighttime processing of information is unique. We experience dreaming consciousness mostly in the form of visual imagery. In effect, we create our own internal supply of stimuli as we dig into the past and clothe the information we come up with in sensory visual form. The goal remains the same. Only by perceiving current happenings accurately can we prepare for what is apt to happen next. The pursuit of clarity and information while awake orients us more realistically to the present and prepares us more effectively for the future. Asleep and dreaming, the historical exploration of the feeling residue helps to assess its significance for the future. Consciousness in whatever form it occurs is future oriented.

The unique value of dreams for our waking life rests on the fact that we do something asleep and dreaming that we cannot do nearly as well while awake. We look at ourselves with greater honesty and in greater depth. This ability rests on what I consider to be the three cardinal features of dreaming consciousness, all of which I have already noted. The first is the fact that dreaming is connected with current concerns. As we go through the day, feelings and moods evolve that register with greater or lesser clarity. In general, feelings serve as a kind of connective tissue between ourselves and others. When feelings flow freely and appropriately, they do not leave any troublesome residue. When, however, that free flow is impeded by a tension that we fail to resolve, there is a tear or rupture, so to speak, in this connective tissue. The aftereffects persist as a kind of background Greek chorus reminding us that there is some unfinished emotional business from our past that needs attention.

While dreaming, we not only have the opportunity but also face the necessity to look further into the situation. The way we do this is the second unique feature of dreaming consciousness. We take the feeling provoked by this break in the connective tissue and run it through our memory bank to gather more information and clues about its historical source in our particular life story. That is why references to the past so often find their way into the dream. The more available the information, the more accurately we can assess the extent and significance of the break. In addition, our backward search reminds us of the many coping mechanisms we have at our disposal to deal with it.

The third and most significant quality of dreaming consciousness is its utter honesty. It may seem strange to think of the bizarre and confusing pictures we create at night in terms of honesty. To understand it, we must take a closer look at the situation we are in when our sleeping brain gets the signal to be aroused and start dreaming. At that point, the dreamer has been aroused from a state of seeming unconsciousness. He is also very much alone, having temporarily suspended his connections to the outside world and the cushioning support it offers. The consciousness then shaping itself is geared to three implicit questions:

- What is happening to me?
- How has it come to be this way?
- What can I do about it?

In other words, the dreamer is reorienting himself to his life at that moment and to his subjective state in particular. When we orient ourselves to our surroundings while awake, we do so by means of language. That remarkable tool, as we have noted, is a two-edged sword. We can use it to communicate honestly, or we can use it to deceive ourselves and others. Many unconscious strategies of self-deception are resorted to in the waking state when we do not wish to be confronted by what is distasteful or frightening.

We have no such leeway when we dream. This is because we have a most important question to decide, and we are left completely to our own devices to come up with an answer. We cannot look it up in a book or get help from anyone else. The question we are faced with is whether, in the light of the residual tension that now occupies us, Is it safe to remain asleep and alone or is it important enough for us to awaken and return to a more familiar landscape? This is a decision that involves a more radical change of state than we are ever called on to make when we are awake. It also requires a greater degree of honesty.

When I talk about the honesty that underlies the images we create while dreaming, I do not mean to imply that we are transformed into superhonest creatures endowed with halos. Rather, we allow ourselves to catch an honest glimpse of our subjective state, one that displays whatever self-deceptive tendencies may be at work. This truthful encounter with ourselves, warts and all, makes the remembered dream a powerful therapeutic instrument. I will have more to say about the inexorable quality of this honesty later on in my discussion of the connection of dreaming consciousness to the survival of the species.

What we have not yet addressed is why dreaming consciousness takes the form of imagery to carry out its potentially alerting function. Characteristically, dreaming occurs during the rapid eye movement (REM) stage of sleep. This is controlled by subcortical mechanisms, and from a phylogenetic standpoint, it is considered the most archaic stage of sleep. The ability to think in imagery seems to be carried over from our prehistory. That such imagery is so closely linked to the repetitive physiological stages of arousal during sleep, the REM stage, suggests that the imagery serves an alerting function (Snyder, 1966; Tolaas, 1978; Ullman, 1961). The need for this may have come about because from a phylogenetic standpoint, it may not have been safe enough, in the presence of predators, to remain unconscious for too long a period of time. Lower animals have the same periods of arousal during sleep that characterize the dreaming stage in humans. Animals are more immediately dependent on their natural environment than are humans, and their survival is contingent on possible dangers from that environment. As primitive people evolved into social beings, their concerns shifted gradually from the possibility of physical danger from the outside to dangers inherent in maintaining the fabric of social existence. The problem of survival was transformed to what was happening in the social environment. This, in turn, was contingent on the quality and nature of one's connections to others. Social dangers become more manifest through the play of feelings and mood, contingent on the vicissitudes of social intercourse. To display concerns of that kind, the simple literal imaging mode, presumably possible for lower animals, had to be transformed into a more sophisticated use of imagery that ultimately led to the use of the image as a visual metaphor. Vigilance with respect to physical danger has been transformed into social vigilance.

This formulation stresses the underlying identity between waking consciousness and dreaming consciousness. Both are concerned with the effect of impinging stimuli. Both involve the challenge of novelty. Awake, we scan an external environment. Asleep, we scan an internal environment. When we are awake, perception begins with sensitivity to form and motion and is directed outward. When we are asleep and dreaming, perception begins with sensitivity to feelings triggered by recent intrusive events and is directed inward. Awake, we strive toward conceptual clarity as a guide to action in the world. In the case of dreaming, there is a flow of imagery that both expresses and contains feelings. The "action" that results is an internal one affecting the level of arousal. Both forms of consciousness serve a communicative function. Awake and through the power of language, we are able to keep in touch with others. Asleep and dreaming, we use a different language to tell ourselves stories about ourselves that we have not heard before.

In summary, dreaming consciousness serves the same function as waking consciousness with regard to laying the foundation for interconnectedness between members of the human species. It does so under different circumstances, deals with different content, and processes that content in a different way. In each of us, there is an incorruptible core of being, sensitive to the way we hurt ourselves or others and concerned with undoing the fragmentation that has resulted. We have not done too well as yet in preserving our animal heritage of being at one with nature or our human responsibility to be at one with each other. Our dreams are constant reminders of the infinite number of ways we have managed to get derailed and, at the same time, provide us with the opportunity to get back on track.

DREAMING AND SPECIES SURVIVAL

I regard waking consciousness as an evolutionary adaptation that enables us to move into the future as social creatures bent on shaping our own cultural and social destinies. At our disposal in this endeavor are the memories of our past; the free play of our imaginations; the range of our desires; and the energy, hope, and creativity that we bring to this task.

The building tool for conscious social adaptations is language, a somewhat unreliable tool. Lies can be presented as truths, and all kinds of deceptions can ensue. In other words, there is nothing so compelling about the nature of waking consciousness that would ensure its success as an instrument for survival. Not only individuals but whole nations have been deceived into thinking the emperor is parading through town wearing beautiful clothes. Might dreams be the child in us protesting the deception? Rycroft (1979) refers to the "innocence of dreams," an innocence we otherwise seem to have lost. Might dreaming consciousness serve our survival needs as a species by the way it cuts through illusions and, with considerable drama and a good deal of hyperbole, calls attention to both our basest and our loftiest attributes?

There is, of course, a two-way equilibrium between the survival of the species and the survival of the individual. Our biological heritage moves us in the direction of a concern with species survival. Our cultural heritage provides us with a collective setting within which we attempt to fulfill our individual destinies. Dreaming consciousness, rooted in both domains, reflects both the priority of species survival as well as the significance of the role played by the individual. If this view is correct, then dreaming is an unconscious ally in the struggle of the species to survive and an ally in the struggle of the individual to fulfill a role in society that favors species survival. That role goes beyond the purely biological to include cultural and social goals as well. The range of our personal experience is sifted through a "survival filter" when we dream in a way that highlights those aspects of that experience that are either strengthening or hindering our capacity for collaborative ties with others. Seen in this light, dreaming is an even more reliable ally than waking consciousness in that there are no spurious ego needs to pander to. It is more spontaneous, more insistent, more compelling.

Is there any evidence for endowing dreaming consciousness with so transcendent a function? I must admit that the evidence is circumstantial and inferential, and the most I can hope for is that, although it is personally convincing to me, you may find it of some interest. The case rests largely on what I referred to as the third important feature of the dream—namely, its intrinsic honesty. Poets and writers have known all along about this quality of our dream life. Emerson (1947) described it in one of his essays:

> Dreams have a poetic integrity and truth. This limbo and dust-hole of thought is presided over by a certain reason. . . . Their extravagance from nature is yet within a higher nature. They seem to us to suggest an abundance and fluency of thought not familiar to the waking experience. They pique us by independence of us, yet we know ourselves in this mad crowd, and owe to dreams a kind of divination and wisdom. (p. 246)

Jung (1953) referred to this quality of the dream in a very apt way: "so flower like in its candor and veracity that it put us to shame for the deceitfulness of our lives" (p. 46).

This honesty is not expressed in any literal way but makes its presence felt figuratively as imagery, reflecting our existing subjective state. Dreams tell it like it is with regard to the range and depth of our feeling life regardless of whether or not it is disturbing to our waking sensibilities. Our dreams inform us as to the stage of our emotional development, the degree to which we have consolidated our identity, and to what extent freedom and honesty characterize our exchanges with others and with ourselves.

What concerns us here is the facilitating role that dreams can play in fostering greater harmony than now exists among us. Dreams speak not only to the disconnections in the immediate life of the dreamer, but through the social stereotypes that find their way into the dream, they also address issues that confront society as a whole. The honesty of the dream points to what is irrational and prejudicial in society and ourselves. As Bertrand Russell (1961) notes, "The irrational separates us, the rational unites us" (p. 184). None of us grows up perfect, and irrationalities enter into our behavior with others. This is where we are all vulnerable and where the state of our connections to others is at risk. This is precisely the area of interest to our dreaming self. I do not mean to imply that our dreams discriminate in favor of these negative residues. It is only that they, more than positive experiences, give us more to mull over while we sleep.

If we take the trouble to permit those nocturnal reflections to find their place in our waking world, they provide us with a starting point in the continuing struggle to transcend our limitations. The nature of our interdependence is such that, as personal connections evolve more solidly, there are effects that reverberate upward toward ever-larger social units. Dreams can point us in the right direction. They reveal our strengths, acknowledge our weaknesses, expose our deceits, and liberate our creativity. They deserve far greater attention than they now receive.

I think there is a parallel between Jung's intuitive grasp of the dream and the point of view I have been developing. He freed dreams from the stranglehold of instinct, called attention to their compensatory function, and attributed a commonality to dreams in the form of a collective unconscious. He regarded the latter as the repository of our archetypal heritage and, as such, a genetically determined objective form of consciousness. Archetypes had their source in the developmental struggles common to all mankind and made their presence felt in dreams through universal images that arise during periods of tension and transformation.

Although I do not share Jung's conviction about the specifics of the collective unconscious as he defined it, along with its archetypal derivatives, I do see this concept as revealing Jung's sensitivity to what there is in dreams that binds us together, points to a common heritage, and provides us with a common language with which to speak together of common issues. In a manner somewhat analogous to Chomsky's (1976) view of our intrinsic structural preparation for language, I prefer to postulate an inborn structural preparation for a nocturnal language capable of communicating to ourselves any tears in the social fabric of our existence. No one taught us this language, but we all speak it fluently. Our dreaming self has never lost sight of the fact that we are all members of a single species, and it makes use of this intrinsic capacity to keep reminding us of that fact.

An early pioneer of the psychoanalytic movement, Trigant Burrow (1964), wrote extensively on what he referred to as species or phylic consciousness. He spoke of the preconscious stage of development, referring to the sense of total union experienced by the infant with its environment. For him, the preconscious stage of unity between mother and child offered a template for all future relatedness. His emphasis was on how, in our subsequent development, we fail to preserve this common biological heritage and no longer feel linked in a total way to our natural and human environment. Burrow felt that our vulnerability to this kind of split began with our mastery of language and capacity for symbolic expression:

> The word that links us now is a poor makeshift for the bond that unites us organically—the bond initially experienced in its individual aspect in the union of the infant and maternal organism. In our dependence on the flimsy consistency of the word we are really at war with one another while we think that there is only one covenant and understanding. (p. 111)

I have quoted from Burrow because I feel that the breadth of his vision has generally not been appreciated in the current era. Although reared in the psychoanalytic tradition, he transcended it and wrote extensively on what he considered to be an insidiously pervasive form of social pathology[9] that influenced even the practice of psychoanalysis. Our fate has been to overemphasize our existence as discrete creatures and discrete nations at the expense of species unity. He felt that psychoanalysis played into this trend in its failure to take into account that both analyst and patient alike were victims of this larger "social neurosis." His was an attempt to shift attention from individual pathology to social pathology. For this heresy, he was drummed out of the American Psychoanalytic Association, an organization he once headed as president.

We certainly have succeeded in fragmenting ourselves as a species. In our long struggle to become civilized, we have exploited fully every conceivable line of cleavage that can separate human beings from one another. Not only have we failed to overcome geographical boundaries, we continue to throw up barriers on the basis of religion, class, race, sex, and so on. The failure to master the use of a technology capable of destroying each other, as well as life on the planet is both symbolic of this fragmenting process and, unfortunately, an accurate and true picture of where our history as a species has brought us. Our artists and writers reflect and rebel against the fragmentation; our scientists, through their increasing specialization, play into it; our philosophers worry about it; and our politicians seek in vain for solutions. Religion offers an ideal but fails in practice. The rise of interest in Eastern philosophies seems at one and the same time to be a retreat from the problems and an attempt to transcend them.

An individual human being can lead a self-centered and selfish life, live to a ripe old age, and die peacefully in bed. From all indications, that possibility does not exist for humankind considered as a whole. The nations of the world are just beginning to face the reality that, only through cooperation and collaboration, will it be possible for all to inhabit the same planet.

The writings of the distinguished theoretical physicist, David Bohm (1986), have relevance to this point of view. He postulates an underlying order of reality not directly knowable but constituting the ground of all being. He referred to this as the implicate order. Out of this an explicate order arises:

> The external relationships are then displayed in the unfolded or *explicate* order in which each thing is seen as separate and extended and related only externally to other things. The explicate order, which dominates ordinary experience as well as classical physics, is secondary in the sense that ultimately it flows out of the primary reality of the implicate order. (p. 114)

Bohm's (1986) writings on wholeness and the implicate order do not explicitly address the issue of dreams. He does, however, consider the nature of thought as representing movement from the implicate to the explicate. When wholeness is lost sight of, as it tends to be in our current worldview, thought processes, like other objects in reality, are experienced only in their discreteness. Their connections to the implicate are lost or ignored.

How do these considerations tie in with dreaming? Extrapolating, one might assume that the dreaming psyche concerns itself with impediments to the free flow between implicate and explicate. In a general and analogous way, the view presented here is more intrinsically related to notions of interconnectedness and "unbroken wholeness" than are dream theories designating reified psychic entities at war with each other. Awake, we are mired in our own discreteness and, by the language we use, trapped by the seeming discreteness of all else about us. Asleep and dreaming, we forsake linguistic categories as a primary mode of expression. We risk feeling our way back into this underlying unity and set ourselves the task of exploring both internal and external hindrances to its flow.

Waking consciousness is narrowly focused on the immediate reality facing us. Awake and tied to the perceptual order, we tend to see things in their discreteness. The important part played by connectedness, Bohm's (1986) notion of the unbroken wholeness, is a distant voice heard dimly or not attended to at all. The reversal that takes place when dreaming brings aspects of that "unbroken wholeness," at least as it applies to our relationships with others, more closely to our attention.

In Bohm's terms, we might say that metaphor is an instrument that carries us close to the mysteries of the implicate order once some aspect of these mysteries begins to impinge on our lives. Through metaphor, we reach out to what is an unidentified, unconceptualized, and as yet only dimly felt aspect of that order. The ordinary use of language is not up to this task. That language is of use only after metaphor has forced the mystery out of hiding. From this, it is easy to see how metaphor acts as a force that propels us into the future. It represents movement, change, and a tampering with the unknown. Directed at the outside world as in poetry, art, and even science, it brings more into the domain of the known. Directed to the inner world, it eases the passage of material from the domain of the unconscious to consciousness. In either instance, it offers to the creator of the metaphor and to those who benefit from its creation a greater degree of freedom than existed before.

In our dreams, these metaphorical images are spontaneously and involuntarily generated. They seem to be our way of capturing a whiff of and encapsulating information about some mystery (unconscious event) about to unfold. Asleep and dreaming, we don't appreciate its metaphorical meaning. The metaphorical activity is experienced as our immediate, not symbolic, reality, and we respond as if we were captives of that reality.

This point of view emphasizes the way in which dreams zero in on issues of connectedness. While dreaming, we confront ourselves with the state of our connections to significant others in our lives, the strategies we use to undermine or restore these connections, and the social pressures that place obstacles in our path. The essence of the dream's natural healing potential derives from the dreamer's ability to produce imagery that reflects recently exposed areas of disconnection with others or with himself. The dreamer concerns himself with ongoing events or experiences that impinge in significant ways on his felt sense of connectedness to others. Such experiences set off reverberating tremors at different levels and define the issue to be explored in the dream.

The relationship of dreams to connectedness emerges clearly in the course of group dream work. In the presence of a safe atmosphere generated by the nonintrusive nature of the process, social defenses melt away or, at any rate, don't interfere with the deep-level sharing and sense of communion that is generated. Group members respond at a feeling level to someone else's imagery. Although this is understandable in terms of sharing a similar social milieu and facing similar life issues, it may also point to a deeper way that imagery has of linking people together, something more akin to a shared aesthetic response. Group dream work discloses an agency that works against fragmentation. Trust, communion, and a sense of solidarity develop rapidly in a dream-sharing group. There is an interweaving of lives at so profound a level that the feeling of interconnectedness becomes a palpable reality.

These considerations have led me to the speculative notion that while asleep and dreaming, we engage with a much broader aspect of our nature, one that goes beyond the concern of the individual. Our dreaming psyche seems to be aware of the vital significance for species survival of maintaining collaborative ties to each other. Somewhere within us, there is the awareness that, if unchecked, disunity carries within it the seeds of divisiveness and potential destruction. Only through constructive and affectionate bonding can this fragmentation be overcome and the species endure. In this sense, dreams may be seen as arising from a built-in mechanism concerned with the survival of the species. The individual's concern with the maintenance of connectedness is part of this larger concern—namely, the issue of species connectedness, the preservation of the individual being necessary for the preservation of the species. While dreaming, we seem to transcend individual boundaries to move toward our place in a larger whole.

A contemporary writer who explicitly addresses the issue of the relationship of dream content to survival is the late Christopher Evans (1983). Drawing on an analogy with computer programming, he suggests that we sleep in order to dream and we dream in order to review and revamp existing behavioral programs or create new ones in response to the previous day's experience. In this way, old programs are brought up to date or replaced by new ones. A neurophysiologically based view of dreaming and survival has been developed by Winson (1986).

Dreaming may very well serve to keep an animal's behavioral repertoire in a readiness state. At a human level, however, the survival benefit derives not only from the occurrence of dreaming per se but also from the opportunity it presents to put its content to good use in the waking state. Metaphor has come into the picture, and only by explicating and appreciating metaphor as metaphor can we make full use of all that the dream has to offer.

A line has to be drawn between the adaptive significance of dreaming for the organism asleep and the use to which we can put the remembered dream once we are awake. Dreaming is a transitory state of consciousness relating primarily to the needs of the sleeping organism.[10] What we bring back from that state—namely, the dream—can then be transformed into an instrument by means of which we can gain a more accurate perspective on who we really are. That, in turn, can help clear away the debris that has accumulated in the path we have to follow to establish deep, close ties with others. All that constrains us and makes it difficult to pursue that path passes before us nightly.

All these and other similar questions can be subsumed under one general question: To what extent are we being limited by our own emotional heritage, by impinging circumstances, or both in our struggle to realize our full human potential for love and fulfillment? Put another way, what are the spurious and harmful limits to the expression of our freedom, where are they coming from, and what can we do about them? This is a central concern of our dreaming psyche. Our freedom as human beings can be achieved only through and with other people. Our evolutionary path has made us social creatures. There is no backing away from that reality. The only way forward is to create circumstances within ourselves and outside ourselves that will allow for the same natural sense of freedom in a social environment as our fellow creatures enjoy in their natural environment. Ultimately, this will depend on whether or not we can ever heal the devastating fragmentation I have referred to. At the moment, this is a distant goal, but the path there exists and the dreaming part of one's psyche grasps it intuitively. It concerns itself with all that limits or stands in the way of the free flow of affectionate ties to our fellow human beings. This is what concerns us as we sleep and dream. What is coming at us from within or without that is affecting those ties, for better or for worse? Strengthening them or undermining them? Enhancing or destroying?

DREAMING AND THE PARANORMAL

I would like to add additional theoretical considerations dealing with a subject that has long been of interest to me—namely, the occurrence of the so-called paranormal dream. How is it that, while dreaming, we are able to transcend the ordinary spatial and temporal limits of our existence and pick up information telepathically, in a way that transcends space, and precognitively, in a way that transcends time? My own experience, clinically and experimentally, has convinced me of the reality of these phenomena (Ullman & Krippner, with Vaughan, 1988). Such dreams are part of a broader range of phenomena known as *psi*[11] and will be referred to as such. Only future research can shed light on this dimension of our dreaming existence.

Let us go back to our comparison of waking consciousness and dreaming consciousness but extend it to the way that psi effects register in consciousness, awake or asleep. We have noted that both waking and dreaming consciousness start with incomplete data, closely associated with an attempt to make sense of the data by retrieving relevant information from the past. When we are awake, the perceptual process begins with sensory input and ends successfully when, based on past experience, the models we have built around similar input enable us to recognize what is now before us. In most instances, we need relatively few sensory cues for recognition to occur.

Dreaming also begins with ambiguous stimuli in the form of feeling residues of recent experience. Again, we have a situation for which the data are incomplete, and a search for more information has to be implemented. The nature and results of that search, unique to the dreaming state, may provide a clue as to how a psi effect, once it comes into being, is processed. For the dreamer, it is the feeling tone that is important. It is the source and significance of the feeling that is about to be explored. In the course of this exploration, the ordinary time frame is bypassed, and time dimensions are condensed into the present moment. The same is true of spatial relations. Time and space are not disregarded but are rearranged so as to gain sensory metaphorical representation.[12] The point is not an accurate factual perception but a feeling-tinged metaphorical image. There is a spontaneous and compelling quality to the way that imagery is experienced.

All of these aspects are applicable to the way psi effects seem to make their presence felt. Here, too, the data are generally experienced in a somewhat fragmentary way. Here, too, it is the feeling tone that plays the predominant role. Here, too, ordinary temporal and spatial relations do not exert a constraining influence and, in a like manner, seem irrelevant. The end point is reached as the dreamer succeeds in weaving together the psi-derived residue[13] and other residues at hand into some kind of metaphorical unity. Although an ordinary dream has a compelling quality in the sense of our being involuntary spectators to what is going on (despite the fact that we may be participating in the action), that compelling quality may be more in evidence when telepathic or precognitive dreams occur. Feelings associated with an ordinary dream that stay with us may pique our curiosity about our inner world. A psi dream, connected as it is to external events to which we are not privy, may go beyond that and leave us with the urge to take some action in the external world.

From a biological point of view, there is a hint of how psi might fit into the scheme of things. The physiological underpinning of the state of sleep associated with dreaming, the REM stage, is located in the brain stem. Phylogenetically, the REM stage is considered an older and more primitive form of sleep than the non-REM stages of sleep. It would seem natural to connect it with more primitive survival needs. As I have noted, in both waking consciousness and dreaming, a scanning process sensitive to novelty is going on but under very different circumstances. Awake and embedded in a social matrix, we scan a limited horizon. Asleep and dreaming, we are alone and have taken temporary leave of that social cushioning. As a consequence, we are potentially at greater risk. We now have to be open to a much wider scanning process, one capable of registering a range of possible disconnections from the most subtle to the most threatening. If we take psi effects seriously, this is so regardless of whether the source of the disconnection lies close at hand or distant in time and space. In the most characteristic anecdotal reports, a psi effect makes its presence felt under circumstances in which external, unforeseen circumstances either threaten or have brought about a significant loss. Our bonds to others are constantly on the line, at the mercy of our own misguided behavior, the behavior of others, constraining social arrangements, and in the case of psi, unforeseen events at a distance in either space or time.

Notes

1. Existentialism, in its application to therapy, is a difficult notion to pin down. Kovel (1976), attempting to capture its essence, notes that "what existential analysis does is to tap directly into the chaos of modern experience, the runaway world, godless, without any inherent moral authority or belief system, a world that so many take for granted" (p. 100). Existential psychoanalysis eschews theory in the direct, immediate way it structures the therapeutic encounter. For an account of an existentialist approach to dream work see Boss (1958).

2. Hysteria, in the technical sense, is a psychiatric disorder either of the conversion type, in which a physical symptom is an expression of an underlying psychological conflict, or as a more generalized personality disorder characterized by self-centered, dramatic, emotionally charged behavior.

3. This refers to the use of the electroencephalographic and rapid eye movement (REM) monitoring techniques used to determine the onset and termination of the successive stages of dreaming in the course of the sleep cycle.

4. Phenomenology is the philosophical underpinning of the existentialist approach to therapy, the effort to work with the here-and-now aspects of the therapeutic encounter stripped bare of a priori theoretical considerations and subjective biases.

5. Here I am referring to the fact that both forms of consciousness are adaptive in nature. Both involve the central processing of data in a way that involves behavioral change. When we are awake, the behavior relates to the outside world. When we are asleep, the behavior refers to internal change as manifested in the level of arousal.

6. I use the neutral term *tension* to encompass both positively and negatively tinged feelings.

7. External stimuli occurring during the REM state but not intense enough to awaken us may be included in the dream.

8. What it is we are actually feeling, not what we would like to feel or not feel.

9. Those aspects of social arrangements and institutions that foster alienation, aggression, and so on.

10. Much has been written about the need or needs that sleep and dreams fulfill, but little is known for certain. My point is simply that dreaming arose in connection with sleep and presumably serves adaptive functions connected with that state. For a very readable account of the various aspects of the REM state and its functions for the sleeping organism the reader is referred to Shafton (1995).

11. The term *psi* is a generic reference to what was formerly known as psychic phenomena and what is now the subject matter of parapsychological research.

12. For example, using spatial distance to represent emotional distance or rearranging time by combining in a single usage components from different time periods.

13. For example, telepathically or precognitively apprehended.

References

Bohm, D. (1986). A new theory of the relationship of mind and matter. *Journal of the American Society for Psychical Research, 80,* 114-135.

Bonime, W. (1982). *The clinical use of dreams.* New York: Da Capo Press.

Boss, M. (1958). *The analysis of dreams.* New York: Philosophical Library.

Briggs, J., & Monaco, R. (1990). *Metaphor: The logic of poetry* (2nd ed.). New York: Pace University Press.

Burrow, T. (1964). *Preconscious foundations of human experience.* New York: Basic Books.

Chomsky, N. (1976). On the nature of language. In S. R. Harnad, H. D. Steckliss, & J. Lancaster (Eds.), *Origin and evolution of language and speech* (pp. 46-57). New York: New York Academy of Sciences.

Emerson, R. W. (1947). The witchcraft of sleep. In R. L. Woods (Ed.), *The world of dreams: An anthology* (pp. 243-247). New York: Random House.

Evans, C. (1983). *Landscapes of the night: How and why we dream* (P. Evans, Ed.). New York: Viking.

Jung, C. G. (1953). *Psychological reflections: An anthology of the writings of C. G. Jung* (selected and edited by J. Jacobi; Bollingen Series 31). New York: Pantheon.

Korzybski, A. (1941). *Science and sanity.* New York: International Non-Aristotelian Publishing.

Kovel, J. (1976). *A complete guide to therapy.* New York: Pantheon.

Russell, B. (1961). *History of Western philosophy.* London: Allen & Unwin.

Rycroft, C. (1979). *The innocence of dreams.* New York: Pantheon.

Shafton, A. (1995). *Dream reader.* New York: State University of New York Press.

Snyder, F. (1966). Toward an evolutionary theory of dreaming. *American Journal of Psychiatry, 123,* 121-136.

Tolaas, J. (1978). REM sleep and the concept of vigilance. *Biological Psychiatry, 13,* 135-148.

Ullman, M. (1961). Dreaming, altered states of consciousness and the problem of vigilance. *Journal of Nervous and Mental Disorders, 133,* 529-535.

Ullman, M., & Krippner, S., with Vaughan, A. (1988). *Dream telepathy* (2nd ed.). Jefferson, NC: McFarland.

Ullman, M., & Limmer, C. (1988). *The variety of dream experience.* New York: Continuum.

Ullman, M., & Zimmerman, N. (1979). *Working with dreams.* New York: Tarcher-Putnam.

Winson, J. (1986). *Brain and psyche.* New York: Vintage.

Index

About the Author

Dr. Montague Ullman is a New Yorker who attended Townsend Harris Hall, the City College of New York, and New York University School of Medicine where he received his medical degree in 1938. Following his internship and residencies in neurology and psychiatry, he served as a captain in the army medical corps both here and abroad from 1942 to 1945. A graduate of the Comprehensive Course in Psychoanalysis at the New York Medical College, he became a member of the faculty there in 1950. In 1961, he left private practice to head a department of psychiatry at the Maimonides Medical Center in Brooklyn. His interest in preventive psychiatry led to the opening in 1967 of one of the first fully operational community mental health centers in New York City. His research interests led to the establishment of a sleep laboratory devoted to the exploration of the paranormal dream.

Because dreaming is a universal experience, our dreams should be universally accessible. With this goal in mind, Dr. Ullman has devoted the past two decades to the development and application of a group approach to dream work suitable for the general public and as a way of teaching about dreams to those involved in the practice of psychotherapy. During this period, he has conducted training sessions and workshops in the United States and in Scandinavia.

Dr. Ullman is a Charter Fellow of the American Academy of Psychoanalysis and is currently Clinical Professor Emeritus, Department of Psychiatry, Albert Einstein College of Medicine. Dr. Ullman has written numerous papers on the neurophysiological, clinical, and social aspects of dreams and is the author and coauthor of several books, including *Dream Telepathy* (1988) and *Working With Dreams* (1979), and is coeditor of the *Handbook of States of Consciousness* (1986) and *The Variety of Dream Experience* (1988).